Book Collecting

BOOK COLLECTING
A MODERN GUIDE

Edited by Jean Peters

R. R. BOWKER COMPANY
NEW YORK & LONDON · 1977

The excerpt from the letter of Virginia Woolf to Vita Sackville-West is from the forthcoming Volume 3 of *The Letters of Virginia Woolf* to be published by Harcourt Brace Jovanovich, Inc. and is quoted with their permission. For permission to publish the letter from Frederick B. Adams, Jr., to Virginia Woolf, we are indebted to Mr. Adams. Henry W. and Albert A. Berg Collection, The New York Public Library, Astor, Lenox, and Tilden Foundations, has granted permission to quote from the original letters as listed above. Mary A. Benjamin granted permission to reprint passages from her book, *Autographs: A Key to Collecting* (1966). The excerpt from *The Letters of Oscar Wilde*, edited by Rupert Hart-Davis ©1962 by Vyvyan Holland is reprinted by permission of Harcourt Brace Jovanovich, Inc.

Published by R. R. Bowker Company
1180 Avenue of the Americas, New York, N.Y. 10036
Copyright ©1977 by Xerox Corporation
All rights reserved
Printed and bound in the United States of America

Second printing, May 1978

Library of Congress Cataloging in Publication Data
Main entry under title:
Book collecting.

    Includes index.
    1. Book collecting—Addresses, essays, lectures.
I. Peters, Jean, 1935–
Z987.B68   020'.75   77-8785
ISBN 0-8352-0985-7

To the Memory of
JOHN WAYNFLETE CARTER
President and Gold Medallist of the Bibliographical Society
Writer, Editor, Bookseller, Bibliographer, and Collector

Contents

Preface

THERE ARE many people who read and accumulate books, but who can in no way be considered collectors, because their book buying is without direction. Yet, there comes a time when, for one reason or another, some of these people find themselves buying a copy of a book they already own. It may be a finer edition than the one on their shelves, a first edition of one of their favorite books, or a book that is special in some other way. They may never have considered themselves a collector of books, but once this purchase has been made, they have started on the road to becoming a collector. More than likely a second such purchase will follow shortly. Noting this particular moment, A. W. Pollard advised: "Any one who finds himself buying a book, new or old, for any other reason than a desire to read it, will do well to ask himself, as speedily as possible, what aim he has in view. To buy books except for the sake of reading them constitutes the buyer, though by a single instance, a collector, and to collect aimlessly is a mere waste of money, and possibly also of time. Collecting may begin in the humblest and most insidious of ways" (*Books in the House* [London: Arthur L. Humphreys, 1907], p. 78).

This book is intended both for those who have accumulated books haphazardly over the years and who now would like to give some focus to their collecting and for those experienced collectors—for whom the moment A. W. Pollard described has long since passed—who may wish to learn more about certain aspects of collecting. It presents a philosophy of book collecting for contemporary times, a period when creative new ideas are emerging to replace the traditional approaches to collecting that are generally no longer possible for the private collector. It offers the collector practical ways of building, organizing, and caring for a collection of books and manuscripts.

Each chapter has been written by a different author on the theory that no single person is likely to be knowledgeable on all the subjects covered in the book. The contributors are eminently qualified to write on their subjects. They are not only involved with books in their professional careers—either as librarian, professor, editor, publisher, book dealer, or conservator—but they also maintain private book collections as well. Thus, they write not only as professionals in the realm of books but also as private collectors.

During the 1930s and 1940s, the Bowker Company published a number of fine books for the book collector. Among them were: *American First Editions*, by Merle Johnson, continued by Jacob Blanck; *The Care and Repair of Books*, by H. M. Lydenberg and John Archer; *Autographs: A Key to Collecting*, by Mary A. Benjamin; *Invitation to Book Collecting*, by Colton Storm and Howard Peckham; and *Taste and Technique in Book Collecting*, by John Carter, for which the Bowker Company served as American publisher. It is hoped that *Book Collecting: A Modern Guide* will serve as a worthy addition to this impressive list of titles.

The editor wishes to express thanks to Robert Nikirk, Librarian of The Grolier Club, and to Frederick B. Adams, Jr., for advice and assistance; to Richard Colles Johnson of The Newberry Library, for reading and commenting on a portion of the manuscript; to Mary A. Benjamin for generously allowing us to reprint definitions from her *Autographs: A Key to Collecting*; and to Alice Koeth for the design of the book and its jacket. A special debt of gratitude is owed to Terry Belanger, who helped to initiate the idea for the book and who continued to offer help and advice throughout the many stages of its preparation. Finally, deepest appreciation is expressed to the contributors, every one of whom devoted many hours out of busy schedules to the writing of their chapters. Their knowledge, deep interest in books, and spirit of cooperation made this book possible.

July 1977

Jean Peters

Introduction

Frederick B. Adams, Jr.

THE AGE OF LUXURY in American book collecting ended with the spectacular fireworks of the Jerome Kern sale in 1929. Until then, the assembling of rare books was primarily a rich person's pursuit, conducted along well-traveled highways, guided by English signposts some two centuries old. The noblest collections of the period 1880–1930 followed comfortable literary and aesthetic traditions exemplified in the libraries of J. Pierpont Morgan, Henry E. Huntington, and Robert Hoe, with a civilized mixture of incunabula, literary and historical manuscripts and letters, fine bindings, illustrated books, and landmarks in literature.

The stock market crash of 1929, followed by the Great Depression, changed the picture radically. Values fell so heavily that in 1933 it was customary to pay for Kern copies that were still around no more than 10 to 15 percent of what they had fetched at his sale. Collecting by "lists" and collections of "high spots" lost their savor. New conditions produced new collectors with fresh ideas and sophisticated tastes. They still enjoyed reading A. Edward Newton's *Amenities of Book-Collecting* and *This Book-Collecting Game*, but they were not inclined to follow in his happy-go-lucky footsteps.

The new breed found unmapped terrain to explore, but with pocketbooks considerably thinner (at least temporarily) than those of their predecessors, they felt the need of studying the ground carefully before advancing. This need was emphasized by the publication in 1934 of Carter and Pollard's *An Enquiry into the Nature of Certain Nineteenth-Century Pamphlets*, which presented circumstantial evidence as compelling as Thoreau's trout in the milk to show that the creator of the famed Ashley Library, the paragon of collector-bibliographers, Thomas J. Wise, was a fraud and a forger. It remained for D. F. Foxon to show, some years later, that he was a thief as well.

Many of the new collectors seeking guidance found it in the writings and bibliographical studies of John Carter, Percy H. Muir, Michael Sadleir, Geoffrey Keynes, and John Hayward in England, and of John T. Winterich, David A. Randall, Jacob Blanck, and William A. Jackson in America, to name only a few. In 1934, Carter edited *New Paths in Book-Collecting* for Michael Sadleir's publishing firm of Constable, in which authors of diverse backgrounds wrote of relatively unexplored fields of collecting, such as detective fiction, war books, musical first editions, "yellow-backs," and serial fiction. The emphasis was on books of the nineteenth and twentieth centuries, and the compendium as a whole was more important symbolically than textually.

The demarcation between the old style of collecting and the new was revealed to me one July day in 1932 when I dropped in to Elkin Mathews shortly before the firm adjourned business temporarily for four o'clock tea. The senior partner at that time was A. W. Evans, an ordained clergyman with a vast knowledge of eighteenth- and nineteenth-century literature, who specialized in the writings and religious disputes of Bishop William Warburton. On a twentieth-century shelf I found a copy of Virginia Woolf's first book, *The Voyage Out*, considerably revised by her for a subsequent edition, which I bought from Percy Muir for £25. At tea, I must have looked rather pleased with my acquisition, because Evans abruptly asked me what I had found. My answer induced an expression of mingled incredulity and pity that I should waste such money on a little-known woman writer of avant-garde fiction when for the same price I could have had a (rebound) first edition of Jane Austen's *Persuasion*. Where was I going with my book? To Lyme Regis for a few days of reading and swimming. Then as penance I was to let him know exactly how far Louisa fell. Some days later I sent him a postcard of the Cobb with the message, "Miss Musgrove fell about twelve feet." I hope he was appeased.

Virginia Woolf was one of a dozen favorite authors I was beginning to collect in depth, chief among them Thomas Hardy and Robert Frost. In so doing, I was trailing after some very much more experienced elders, such as Carroll A. Wilson, H. Bacon Collamore, and Morris L. Parrish, who early taught me that every collector has his or her idiosyncracies and amiable prejudices, and his or her own methods of obtaining books and revealing their merits. Wilson preferred books that had significant associations or were interesting bibliographically; Parrish preferred a second state or issue in impeccable condition to an association copy of a true first that had lost its freshness. This led to the possibility of fruitful exchanges.

The 1930s also witnessed the rapid development of remarkable collections devoted to a single author or theme: Wilmarth S. Lewis' collection of Horace Walpole's correspondence and his library; Donald and Mary Hyde's of Dr. Johnson and his circle; Edwin J. Beinecke's of Robert Louis Stevenson; John Fulton's and Harvey Cushing's of medical books; Rachel Hunt's of botanical works; and Thomas W. Streeter's of historical Americana. None of these collectors wished to entomb their books, but rather to write about them, publish them in catalogues, display them in exhibitions, give talks about them, and generally share their enthusiasms, at least with kindred spirits. George Parker Winship and Chauncey Brewster Tinker sent forth from Harvard and Yale a number of potential collectors, often with more ambition than money, but a true collector's normal state is to be short of funds.

There have always been collectors concerned with the history of printing, handwriting, bookbinding, and book illustration—what the founders of the Grolier Club in 1884 called "the arts pertaining to the production of books," but it has been the good fortune of our own time to have two such ardent, generous, and scholarly collectors in the field as Lessing J. Rosenwald and Philip Hofer, who have made Jenkintown and Cambridge centers for the study and dissemination of these arts.

The catalogues issued in the 1930s and the selection of books offered by Elkin Mathews, Bertram Rota, the Scribner axis of Carter and Randall, John Kohn of the Collectors' Bookshop, Capt. Louis Henry Cohn of the House of Books Ltd., and David Kirschenbaum of Carnegie were ideal sources for the new collectors. Several of the outstanding collections of our period, such as those of H. Bradley Martin, C. Waller Barrett, J. K. Lilly, DeCoursey Fales, and Robert H. Taylor, got flying head starts from these sources and have been more useful and inspiring as a result.

Since World War II, the collecting scene has once again changed, slowly it is true, but fundamentally. In the halcyon days it was mainly a question of what one could afford to buy; now it is more what one can find to collect, particularly if he or she is scrupulous about condition. One has only two choices, as Gordon Ray points out in his "The World of Rare Books Reexamined" (*Yale University Library Gazette*, July 1974): "he can collect a traditional subject in a marginal manner or he can make a central attack on a non-traditional subject."

The care and feeding of rare book collections in university and college libraries now to some extent overshadow and even absorb the activities of private collectors. This is in part due to the natural generosity and loyalty of Americans, and in part to the income tax laws, which are the envy of impoverished institutions in other countries. Most of the notable private collections that have reached maturity since 1930, whether they broke new ground or followed traditional patterns, are already in public institutions or destined for them. It is a toss-up whether the steadily advancing price levels will accelerate or retard this process.

The scene has changed in another important particular: the development of new or improved "tools" for buyer and seller. The physical tools range from photocopiers, microprinters, Hinman collators, and Lindstrand comparators, to binocular microscopes and Erastov's beta-radiographic method of watermark reproduction. Among the intellectual tools are William A. Jackson and F. S. Ferguson's revision of the *Short-Title Catalogue of English Books 1475–1640*, being completed by Katharine F. Pantzer; Donald G. Wing's *Short-Title Catalogue* for 1641–1700; Jacob Blanck's *Bibliography of American Literature*, with two volumes still to come; Charles Evans' chronological *American Bibliography* completed and supplemented by Clifford K. Shipton and Roger P. Bristol; Frederick R. Goff's Third Census of *Incunabula in American Libraries*; Fredson Bowers' *Principles of Bibliographical Description*, and his subsequent studies in textual transmission; and a large number of bibliographies of individual British and American authors—the majority of the British ones at least seeming to be compiled by Sir Geoffrey Keynes. For a remarkable summary of the tools that are available today, see the final chapter of this book by Professor Tanselle.

The time is overripe for a modern guide to book collecting suited to a fresh clientele and new conditions and written by the current generation of authorities. It is appropriate that this should be produced by the R. R. Bowker Company, which, during the long reign of Frederic G. Melcher, enlisted the talents of a group of exceptional bookmen and produced a variety of useful and sensible books and periodicals for the world of books. As every good book about books should do, the chapters of this book have stimulated my thinking and recalled some of my own experiences.

It is easier to give advice than to accept it, and it would be a paragon among collectors who would follow verbatim all the sound principles set forth in the following chapters or would read all the literature recommended. Fortunately there is some willfulness in the makeup of every collector.

If one is buying purely to preserve books and manuscripts for posterity, or only for the sake of possible capital appreciation as a hedge against inflation—then the best thing to do is to shut the books up in a fireproof, air-conditioned vault, and never to handle them. This will ensure that no pages will crumble from wear, no handwriting will fade, no bindings will crack, and no texts will be devoured by worms. But books cannot be treated as absolutely dead things. They must live, and speak, and be seen among their fellows. They deserve to be examined and exhibited with proper precautions, but they must not be locked away in anticipation of some better destiny. One thing to be avoided, however, is the traveling exhibition, unless the installation is personally supervised by the owner or curator at each stop.

It is sensible for collectors to specialize, to choose an area of interest that they can make their own. They may get to know more than the dealers and as much as the scholars in their fields. But I know of no addicted collector who has not been guilty of digression. A collector in depth of specific nineteenth-century authors had great sport in putting together a collection of first appearances in print of famous quotations. The Walpole specialist and his wife developed on the side (in an old squash court) a collection of eighteenth-century political caricatures that, by the addition of thousands of photocopies to thousands of originals, has now become almost as significant as the main collection. The pair of collectors devoted to Dr. Johnson and his circle took pleasure in assembling a small but choice collection of Japanese literary and historical manuscripts. When, after the death of its collector, the Mary Flagler Cary Music Collection was being organized for transfer to the Morgan Library, I discovered to my delight that she had acquired Robert Lawson's illustrations for *Ferdinand the Bull*, and I made a special plea that these drawings should accompany her superb musical manuscripts. An extreme case of digression perhaps, but a happy one for all concerned.

I, too, have been guilty of digression, leaving literature aside from time to time to form a library of socialist and communist literature, including utopias and American communities; this was ultimately purchased for the Karl Marx Haus in Trier, where selections from it are always on display.

Unlike private collectors, institutional collectors cannot afford the sin of digression. As their operating expenses devour their income to a point where they have little money to buy anything but reference books, the danger is that they will, in their hunger for acquisitions, accept as gifts material that is both irrelevant to their institution's ongoing academic program and expensive to maintain in terms of both architecture and staff. Gifts have hidden costs.

No printed manual can be a substitute for experience, in collecting as in almost every occupation. It is educative, and pleasurable also, to exercise the eye and the memory by looking at dealers' stocks, at collectors' libraries (preferably with the owner's running commentary), and at books in exhibitions. The recent proliferation of antiquarian book fairs as a medium of exchange offers the collector a new type of browsing area. Reading catalogues is second in importance only to reading the books they describe. An outstanding means of self-education is the assembling of an exhibition, composing the labels, and producing the catalogue. The numerous exhibitions organized by members of the Grolier Club, for instance, have contributed substantially to their education, quite apart from what they have meant to the public.

In the mid-1930s, the *New York Times* undertook to organize a book fair on their premises, with H. G. Wells on hand to outline future history, and a small committee organizing a display of rare books and fine printing. I chose for my contribution "Ten Books That Shook the World," stealing my title from John Reed's eyewitness account of the Bolsheviks' seizure of power in St. Petersburg in 1917. I had only three of the books myself:

the first printing of the 1848 Communist Manifesto, a copy of Freud's *Traumdeutung* that I had bought from a Scribner catalogue for $45, and Charles Eliot Norton's copy of Darwin's *Origin of Species*, with a note in his hand stating that it was the first copy to reach America. Choosing the remaining seven, locating copies of them, and describing their world-shaking qualities on labels, gave me tense moments but increased my sum of knowledge.

Booksellers' catalogues and auction sale catalogues are not infallible; they are often compiled against time, and frequently copy earlier descriptions, so that errors are sometimes repeated. "First state, with the misprint 'happpened' on page 392" may recur *ad nauseam*, when the truth may be that the misprint is found in all copies of the first impression. Exhibition labels are not infallible either. An unusual example of fallibility is to be found in a public institution in Paris with hundreds of thousands of visitors a year. Here the visitor may view a selection of choice manuscripts and printed books in fine bindings accompanied by labels based on the knowledge of the 1890s.

Forgeries, counterfeits, and facsimiles occasionally brazen their way into exhibitions and catalogues. I once bought the manuscript of a mediocre poem by a mediocre American poet for $4 from an exceedingly reputable New York dealer. When I reached home and looked at it carefully, I decided to apply the wet-finger test in an inconspicuous place. Not the faintest smudge appeared. Returning with it to the shop several days later, I asked the dealer what she thought of it. "Not much," she replied without hesitation, "it's a facsimile. Where did you get it?" "It was in your catalogue." "Dear me! Well, I'll be glad to take it back." "Not on your life. I've already had more than four dollars worth of fun with it."

Such misadventures are usually more serious. One that occurred during my term as Director of The Pierpont Morgan Library involved one of the great rarities among early Americana, a rhymed version of Columbus' announcement of his discovery, published not long after the first two Latin issues of the "Columbus letter" were printed at Rome in 1493. The poem was illustrated with a woodcut showing the explorer landing among the Indians—the first of a long line of such imaginings. Because the Morgan Library owned the two Latin "letters," I jumped at the possibility of buying the poem for the library when a *marchand amateur* told me of a copy that was for sale in Venice. In due course the pamphlet reached the Morgan Library, passed inspection, and was approved for purchase by the trustees. The Morgan bank arranged for its correspondent in Venice to pay over to the dealer a large sum in lire. Meanwhile, on the advice of Dr. Lawrence C. Wroth of the John Carter Brown Library, I had asked the Huntington Library to send me photostats of their copy. They sent the photostats accompanied by a warning that a counterfeit pamphlet was supposed to exist. When I compared their photostats with the library's new acquisition, there could be no doubt that the Huntington copy itself had been used to make the plates from which ours had been printed, probably in the nineteenth century. I spent a practically sleepless night, because this was the first time I had been caught, and badly caught. In the mail the following morning was a letter from the dealer in Venice saying that he had refused the payment in lire as he preferred to receive it in dollars. I saw to it that all he received was his pamphlet, and I wonder who has it now.

One of the most beautiful handwritings of all time is that of the artist Raphael. Imagine my joy when the Morgan Library was offered a long letter from Raphael describing what needed to be done to restore the foundations of St. Peter's in Rome. I sent it over to Jensen Yow in the library's laboratory for a routine check, and a few hours later he phoned in great excitement to say I must come to look at the letter through the binocular microscope. The old paper had several small wormholes in it, and where the stroke of the pen went through the area of a wormhole, high magnification revealed that the ink had spread along the edge of the wormhole. Obviously the worms had preceded the handwriting. I tried to get this lovely specimen off the market and into the Morgan collection, but the owner refused to negotiate. Some years later it was offered elsewhere, but fortunately the prospective purchaser consulted me.

Much has been written and doubtless will be written about the significance of, and values created by, editions and impressions, states and issues. Good working definitions of the latter two have been formulated by Professor Tanselle in his "Bibliographical Concepts of *Issue* and *State*," *PBSA* 69, no. 1 (1975). More will be written than John Carter's chapter in *Taste and Technique* about the distinction between absolute rarity and relative rarity and their effect upon prices, and it is well to remember Pierpont Morgan's axiom that the most expensive phrase ever concocted, whether true or not, is *"unique au monde."* I find it salutary to reflect on occasion that if Poe had never written anything but *Tamerlane* its value would be negligible, and nobody would bother to look for it in the proverbial attic. Similarly, if the Bay Psalm Book had been the umpteenth book printed in English America in the seventeenth century, it would be regarded simply as a theological and literary curiosity, despite frequent reprintings.

Let there be no end to the making of books about books. The indifferent ones will soon lapse into decent obscurity; the good will survive and be cherished by succeeding generations.

1

What Book Collecting
Is All About

William Matheson

W RITERS ABOUT BOOK COLLECTING frequently assume that the collector's proper quarry is rare books, and rare books only. Michael S. Batts has gone as far as to say that "there is general agreement among all writers on the topic that rarity is the prime consideration in book collecting."[1]

In my view this is one of the misconceptions about the nature of book collecting. It is true that during the nineteenth century wealthy collectors sought books that could fairly be categorized as rare: first editions of the classic authors, early printers (Caxton, Gutenberg, Fust and Schoeffer), early illustrated books, and early English literature. Thomas Frognall Dibdin and other bibliographers had identified the important and desirable books. The supply was sufficiently great to make the chances good of obtaining a substantial proportion of the desiderata, given time and sufficient funds. This is no longer true in these fields and has not been for years. The diminishing supply, the awareness of categories of books once scorned, and increasing sophistication on the part of collectors have changed the whole nature of collecting.[2]

I would like to begin by addressing some of the misconceptions about book collecting that many people must have if the letters, phone calls, and personal visits that I receive in my position as Chief of the Rare Book and Special Collections Division at the Library of Congress can be taken as a fair indication; and then I would like to turn to the question of "rare" book collecting.

Perhaps the greatest number of inquiries comes from people who are trying to find out whether certain books in their possession have value. I fully sympathize with my inquirers, recalling my own puzzlement in my high school days. For reasons that are obscure to me now I wanted even then to own books and not to check them out from the local public library. Perhaps I was permanently scarred by the experience of reading hundreds of pages into Ayn Rand's very fat book *The Fountainhead*, only to discover that the leaves containing the sensational passages (which were the real reason for my reading the book) had been ripped out. There were no used bookshops in the town, and I turned to the thrift shops—Goodwill, Salvation Army, Volunteers of America, and St. Vincent de Paul—as my sources. At the Goodwill, books were 45 cents the first week, then 35 cents, 25 cents, and finally they hit a plateau of 10 cents. Before long I had a "collection" made up of books by authors I had heard of and that I had bought because a prospective English major "ought" to read them. My curiosity about the value of my finds, and whether they were indeed "first editions," led me to the public library, where I found myself in the position of people who are writing letters to me now.

It seemed to me that in a reasonable world there had to be a single source—comparable to the Scott catalogues of postage stamps—that would list the prices of all books of more than trifling value. In my imagination the number of books suitable for inclusion in this compilation was quite limited, certainly easily to be compassed in a single volume (my experiences in discovering "treasures" among the thousands of volumes I looked at in the thrift shops undoubtedly helped form that opinion). Certainly I thought an individual broadly familiar with the world of books—with my as yet unseen compilation at hand—could field all questions about book values.

It took me some time to understand that the number of books printed from the "introduction" of printing in the mid-1450s to the present is staggering. The student of early printing knows that between the mid-1450s, when printing with movable metal types was successfully developed in the Western world, and the end of the year 1500 approximately 40,000 different editions were published. Specialists have speculated that the average size of these editions was between 300 and 500. In less than half a century in the *incunabula*, or "cradle days," of printing 12–20 million books came from the hand press. If you consider the staggering expansion in each succeeding century, the number of books available to be collected can be seen in better perspective.

It took me a long time to comprehend the significance of these totals. Certainly in the thrift shops I saw few books more than fifty years old and undoubtedly would have thought I had found a treasure if one had turned up printed much more than a hundred years before. Had I been in England or on the continent browsing through secondhand bookshops in the same years, my conception of age and value would have been markedly different. There is a lesson here: For certain kinds of books there are natural places to look. Of course there is a possibility of finding almost anything in a place where numbers of books have accumulated. This is the challenge that keeps people searching. Still the odds were against my finding a book of substantial age in the territory in which I was looking—thrift shops in a city of 30,000 people in the state of Washington.

When I moved to Seattle to attend the University of Washington, still somewhat scarred by my Ayn Rand experience, I avoided libraries and tried to buy the books I needed to write my thesis on William Faulkner's *Light in August*. In retrospect, in light of the high prices Faulkner is bringing today, this was a brilliant idea, because this was a period before many collectors had much interest in Faulkner. But again I chose the wrong territory in which to try out my idea. This was in 1951, and I recall the looks of incomprehension when I asked the local secondhand book dealers (I had broadened my territory by this time) for books by Faulkner. Most of them had not heard of him, and I had very little luck in finding his books. In other cities, even by 1951, Faulkner's reputation had spread in the antiquarian book trade. Dealers specializing in twentieth-century first editions could have given me leads, could have advertised for the books I wanted, and could have given me useful advice of many kinds. I found no such dealers and never did form a Faulkner collection—to my regret today. To save you from missing a similar opportunity I urge you to be sure that you are looking in the right place for the material you need.

I really comprehended the range open to collectors only

when I began to use rare book libraries, to look at exhibits, to talk to other collectors, to visit a wide range of bookstores, and to read the enormous literature that bears on the topic. With this broadening of experience I learned that there are far too many books extant for any grubby finds to have monetary value merely because they are old. This kind of exposure had other useful consequences. In time I became a beginning rare book librarian and found it very hard to judge what might reasonably be expected of me when interrogated on a long-distance phone call or faced by someone who had a book on which he or she wanted my opinion. A broader experience gave me a perspective on what it is reasonable to be expected to know and, most important, where to turn to get information. These are crucial points for any collector. I have had people who should know better tell me that a book they were showing me was "unique" on no better evidence than that they in their limited experience had not seen it before. Few books are "unique," as rare book librarians who announce a "unicum" to the world quickly discover to their embarrassment.

The world of books is full of paradoxes, and this would be a good point to comment on one of them. Again I will need to consider a common misconception. More people than you might think—and in theory informed people—write to ask me to tell them how many copies of a given book survive. This question—particularly as applied to very ordinary books—perplexes me because I never, even when I first started out, believed that this kind of information would be available. There are books for which quite accurate statistics on the number of surviving copies have been compiled—the first edition of John Bunyan's *Pilgrim's Progress*, the Bay Psalm Book, the rare suppressed 1865 edition of *Alice in Wonderland*, the Gutenberg Bible. These books have been in great demand for many years and censuses have been taken by bibliographers, collectors, and dealers. Obtaining such information entails printing notices in bibliographical journals, writing letters to collectors, institutions and dealers, and consulting relevant literature. Even after all this checking, these totals are subject to revision, and the excitement at the discovery of an addition to the list can be tremendous. As evidence of this I refer you to the newspaper accounts of the identification of a forty-seventh copy of the Gutenberg Bible in Immenhausen, West Germany in August 1975.

The collector finds himself in the odd situation (the paradox referred to earlier) of having precise information on the titles he or she is least likely to find and cannot afford to collect and little or no information on the titles he or she has in hand. Experienced dealers can help assess how frequently a particular book comes on the market. Auction records are helpful. The National Union Catalog contains information on the number of copies reported by North American libraries. The absence of a book from one of the great national libraries can be suggestive. Finally, though, it is the collector's deepening knowledge and broadening experience that enable him or her to decide whether he or she can afford to wait for a better copy, whether a price is reasonable, and whether the copy offered has unusual features that make it particularly desirable.

The same letters that ask about the number of copies extant frequently request information on the number of copies printed. There are two misconceptions here—that figures of this kind are commonly available and they have a bearing on the present value of my inquirer's book. It is true that for some books, publisher's records survive, and sometimes these records indicate the size of the press run. Bibliographers write to modern publishers in search of such information (frequently in vain), but such records become more fragmentary as we move back in time. Correspondence may survive between author and publisher, and there are other contemporary records that can be useful. Searching out these possibilities takes time-consuming research and rarely can be completed in a single library, however large its resources. Some books, of course, carry a statement indicating the size of the edition. Though printed information of this kind has the ring of authority, it is inaccurate more frequently than you might think. The colophon in William Everson's *Triptych for the Living* (Oakland, Calif: Seraphim Press, 1951) indicates that 200 copies were printed. Mr. Everson has said elsewhere in print that fewer than 100 copies were actually bound up for distribution. Examples of this kind are endless.

Implicit in at least some of the inquiries about edition size is the conviction that this figure will help establish a book's rarity. Though books have been called "rare" because only a few copies were printed or are known to survive, this is a meaningless and confusing use of the term. In a superb statement on book collecting in the Eleventh Edition of the *Encyclopaedia Britannica*, A. W. Pollard makes the following observation with which I concur wholeheartedly:

> This qualification of rarity, which figures much too largely in the popular view of book-collecting, is entirely subordinate to that of interest, for the rarity of a book devoid of interest is a matter of no concern.[3]

This is just the first of our encounters with the slipperiness of the term "rare." If a book was printed in an edition of only one copy (there are such examples), and no one wanted it, it could not be called rare in a meaningful sense of the term. We can equally be misled by our knowledge that the original printing was of enormous size. Noting that the generalization is a little sweeping but not far from the truth, Pollard observes that the survival rate of books "varies in the inverse ratio of the number of copies originally printed."[4]

From the questions that come to me I feel many people are interested in collecting "rare" books because they have heard there is considerable profit in buying and selling them. These questions suggest that my correspondents are looking for a secret formula to enable them to choose the "right" books with which to gain that profit. The closest I can come to a magic formula is "study and specialize." The emphasis on profit is the attitude of a budding dealer, not a collector. Because I have learned more from, and enjoyed myself more with, antiquarian book dealers than any other group I can think of, I am not offended by that attitude. I simply think it is misguided. If the only connecting theme in a group of books is their long-term investment potential, they can hardly be judged to form a collection. A collection, by definition, has a unifying theme. We all have friends with books—perhaps by the roomful—who are in no sense collectors. Their books have been accumulated aimlessly and can some day be dispersed as casually as they have been formed with no fear that our knowledge or our culture will suffer. Chances are good that this will be equally true of the assemblage that an investor keeps in his or her bank vault waiting for its value to rise.

In writing this chapter I have in mind a collector of relatively modest means who wants to have the pleasure of collecting, of learning, and of possibly increasing the world's store of knowledge. In choosing an unhackneyed subject (A. W. Pollard speaks of the "wearisome frequency" with which some books are found in certain kinds of collections), the collector opens the possibility of finding material in virtually any used bookshop. I am surely not mistaken in thinking that one of the joys of book collecting is the opportunity it provides for discoveries. To the extent that collectors commit themselves to a fashionable and (almost axiomatically) expensive subject, they reduce the range of opportunities. Certain books (for example, those printed by particularly highly regarded printers, first editions of the landmark books in the history of science, original editions of Elizabethan drama) gravitate inexorably to the leading antiquarian book dealers. If you are wealthy enough to collect traditional rarities, by all means seek the advice of major antiquarian book dealers and work closely with the ones with whom you establish rapport.

But what of the beginning collector of only modest means? If my experiences with visitors to the Library of Congress can be taken as in any way representative, the word "rare" has overtones of treasure rooms, ivory towers, superfluity, expense, elaborate bindings, and infrequent use. When visitors are actually in the stacks of the Rare Book and Special Collections Division, they quite frequently let out a startled gasp: "Why I have that book. It isn't rare." That is quite true. In coming to the division they bring their preconceptions about "rare" books and overlook the second half of the division's name: Special Collections Division. One of the collections they see is the Alfred Whital Stern Collection of Lincolniana. In assembling his collection Mr. Stern looked for everything that shed light on Lincoln, the Civil War, and Lincoln's time. To this end he sought not only printed books, pamphlets, broadsides, and ephemera, but also photographs, prints, postage stamps, campaign bandanas, memorabilia (a life mask of Lincoln, a cast of Lincoln's hands), and so forth. He bought biographies of Lincoln right up to the most current, reminiscences of his generals, newspaper accounts of the assassination, and anything else that would extend the usefulness of the collection to a Lincoln scholar. A portion of this assemblage is rare by any definition (a unique broadside printing of the Gettysburg Address, a wide range of the earliest printings of the Emancipation Proclamation, a famous letter Lincoln wrote to Joseph Hooker appointing him commander of the Union Army), whereas some of it could—as our visitors rightly observe—be acquired inexpensively at second-hand bookshops today. Taken as a whole, the collection enables a researcher to do virtually all work on Lincoln in one place and, through the juxtaposition of so much material, to perceive relationships that might otherwise have been missed. The interest and value of the collection is greater than the sum of its parts.

The collectors I admire most are those pursuing a similar approach. They are not seeking conventional (read "fashionable") rarities but rather are building focused collections that shed light on an author, a subject, a period, a genre, or a format. This approach to collecting is actually not a phenomenon of the twentieth century. The English publisher/bookseller George Thomason gathered 23,000 tracts, broadsides, pamphlets, and documents of every kind issued during or relating to the Civil War and Commonwealth period in seventeenth-century England. Virtually all the material was fugitive, and in preserving and organizing it over the 21-year period between 1640 and 1661, Thomason created a resource of tremendous value to later historians. The collection ultimately made its way to the British Library, where it is now one of that institution's major holdings. Though the material was not rare at the time Thomason assembled it, in the ensuing years it has become rare indeed.

A tremendous number of the "rare book" collections housed in libraries were formed by collectors. The collector can focus attention on a single theme and can pursue it with all his or her energy, knowledge, and enthusiasm. This is rarely true of libraries. There the tremendously wide collecting responsibilities and the need to respond to the demands of a specific clientele impose other priorities. The Rare Book and Special Collections Division of the Library of Congress has some 60 special collections, the bulk of them formed by private collectors: the Katherine Golden Bitting Collection of Gastronomica; Jean Hersholt's Hans Christian Andersen Collection; Harry Houdini's library of magic and the occult; John Boyd Thacher's three collections—the spread of printing in the fifteenth century, Columbus and his voyages, and the French Revolution; the George Fabyan collection on cryptography and on the Bacon-Shakespeare controversy. Rarely a week passes that I do not become aware of a collector gathering in books on what strikes me as an imaginative topic. Miniature advertising booklets distributed by commercial firms, Little Orphan Annie, and velocipedes are three that have come to my attention while writing this chapter.

Though he is speaking of library collecting, S. C. Roberts, in his article in the April 1967 issue of *Library Association Record*, provides a model that applies equally well to today's collector. By substituting the word "collector" for "librarian" in a passage from this fine article we come up with the following excellent prescription:

> If a [collector] decides to form a special collection of books which aims to deal exhaustively with a particular topic or field of study, especially of a historical character, then he will inevitably find that, while some of the books are relatively easy to get, others are relatively difficult and some may well be extremely difficult and extremely expensive. . . . [Collectors] do not really buy books because they are rare or because they are expensive but in spite of their rarity and cost because they need them to fit into a preconceived design and without them the design would not be complete.[5]

The concept of forming collections around a central concept has received less attention in the literature of book collecting than anecdotes about uncovering individual rarities. The latter have a fascination I share, but there is nothing to prevent collectors working within an organizing principle from making finds just as exciting to them. A scholar and a scholar-librarian have provided their rationales for "nonrare" book collecting. In "Collecting Modern Imprints," G. Thomas Tanselle describes his collections of imprints of a selected group of the imaginative, smaller, American literary publishers of the 1890s and early years of this century.[6] In forming this record of a publisher's oeuvre, Professor Tanselle seeks all the impressions of the books the respective houses published, their catalogues, and their ephemera. Edwin Wolf, 2nd, librarian of the Library Company of Philadelphia, has deliberately sought less fashionable areas in his collection-building efforts at his institution. Before blacks and women's rights had become the fashionable subjects for collecting that they are today, he was determinedly assembling the relevant literature on both topics. Though he worked for the renowned antiquarian book dealer A. S. W. Rosenbach for a number of years, Mr. Wolf is not one of the writers who thinks that rarity is a prime consideration in book collecting.

Four brief quotations from his "Value & Worth of Rare Books" make that clear:

> It is sound agricultural practice to rotate crops; perhaps, book crops might be better if we sedulously tried to rotate fashions.[7]

> All and any books of a certain period or place or kind are the potential elements of valuable research studies of that period, place or kind.[8]

> Today's trifles are tomorrow's treasures.[9]

> . . . fashions in book collecting—in economic terms, demand—and hence prices, and finally an aura of distinction follow closely on the heels of published bibliographies.[10]

Collecting books in already defined areas can be comfortable, as that final quote makes clear. A statement by A. W. Pollard can serve as the last word on the contribution that collectors who eschew fashion can make. Though written almost 70 years ago, the words are just as relevant today as when he first set them down: ". . . if they can be grouped round some central idea, cheap books may yield just as good sport to the collector as expensive ones, and the collector of quite modern works may render admirable service to posterity."[11]

There is a good deal of fun made of collector's fetishes about first editions and about condition. Though they may be carried to extremes and though collectors may only dimly perceive the underlying principles, both are logical preferences and have a sound bibliographical foundation. The first edition is the one the author is most likely to have personally seen through the press and the one to which he or she is likely to have paid the greatest attention. A dust wrapper is part of the bibliographical evidence. It may provide information on the printing history of the book it covers or biographical information about the author; it may have typographic interest (the first use of a certain type), calligraphic interest, or aesthetic interest (designed by Berthold Wolpe or Stanley Morison). We are not surprised when collectors of books from earlier periods prefer a book in its first binding. When copies have been rebound, the possibility of sophistication (for example, doctoring or faking) arises. The dust wrapper is an extension of the concept of original condition. Though collectors will have to decide whether a perfect dust jacket is worth significantly more to them than one with creases, they will want to have one, whenever possible.

Although there is nothing irrational about wanting the first edition, collectors frequently fail to perceive that later impressions and editions published during an author's lifetime (and in certain instances after his or her death) have equal textual and bibliographical importance. I know from my own work that the editors of the Center for the Editions of American Authors sought every contemporary edition of books published by their respective authors. They had little or no trouble assembling multiple copies of the first editions, but in some instances they failed to turn up even one copy of later editions they knew to have existed by such authors as James Fenimore Cooper and Herman Melville. These editions, neglected by collectors and libraries, have simply disappeared. Though every collector of a given author need not assemble every edition, a collector who is forming a comprehensive author collection and is cognizant of the needs of scholarship will gather the widest range of editions and impressions for the evidence they may provide of textual changes. Substantial collections of this kind are highly useful for studies of printing and publishing history, book design, bindings, and a whole range of other purposes. Randolph G. Adams, another scholar-librarian, put the matter in this light in "Who Uses a Library of Rare Books?":

> Not only does [the] bibliographer want a book—he wants all possible variant editions of that book. He wants to describe them bibliographically, with little reference to their subject, text, or content. He wants to collate them by pages and by signatures; he wants to count the plates and the maps; he wants to examine and describe the binding; he wants to trace the provenance of the particular copy of the book with which he is dealing; he wants to trace the transmission of the text of that book from the time when the author first committed it to writing through its various editions, revisions, and reprints; he wants the stories and legends associated with the writing and the printing of the book; and he may want to see one particular copy of the book, although in fact he has already seen many copies of the same edition of the book.[12]

There are many excellent studies that develop the bibliographical rationale for book collecting. I particularly recommend Professor Tanselle's "Bibliographers and the Library."[13]

Although my remarks have been particularly devoted to literary study, the bibliographical rationale for collecting applies equally well to a collector of Sigmund Freud, of Art Nouveau binding styles, of an illustrator, of books on wine, and of the endless variety of authors, subjects, periods, formats, and genres that make up the universe of collecting. In far too many instances libraries have failed to fulfill their responsibilities, and it is only thanks to the enterprise of private collectors that certain printed sources exist at all.

You may by now be willing to concede that a collector need not collect "rare" books as such, but you may still be curious about what a rare book is. The inquiries I receive suggest that my correspondents think that some distinctive feature sets a rare book apart from other books. If that were true, dealers with years of experience would not slip and provide the opportunities for coups that fill the pages of collectors' reminiscences. Let us take a few instances of books that would require specialized knowledge to recognize: the first book printed on paper manufactured in North America, the first use of the italic typeface, the actual author of a pseudonymously published book such as *The Fiend's Revenge* by Dod Grile, the first book published in St. Louis, California, or Mexico. All of these books could deservedly be called rare, but they are not going to advertise their interest in the text itself. When my correspondents seek the magic formula to which I referred earlier, one that will enable them to identify a rare book, they are seeking something that does not exist. Over a period of time dealers will have seen so many books that they will look twice at one they have never seen before. They will also have a good idea of the kinds of books collectors seek, whether nineteeth-century color-plate books, Baskerville imprints, nineteenth-century books illustrated with original photographs, late fifteenth- and early sixteenth-century books illustrated by Albrecht Dürer—pick your century and your topic. All books in the categories just named will not be equally sought, equally difficult to locate, or equally priced. The literature that bears in one way or another on the value of books is vast. A great antiquarian book firm might well have a reference collection of 20,000 volumes or more, using "reference" in the widest sense of that term. Rare books need not be beautiful. Poe's *Tamerlane* and the Bay Psalm Book are hardly that, though few books would more unanimously be judged excessively rare. Rare books need not in any ultimate terms even be important. An author's rare first book may well be one he or she despises and tries to destroy. H. L. Mencken exercised his vengeance on more than one copy of *Ventures into Verse*, if the story commonly told is true. The reasons why collectors seek books are as varied as the collectors themselves.

If a rare book does not advertise itself, need have no physical beauty, and need have no unusual importance in the conventional sense, what can be said about it? S. C. Roberts, in the article to which I referred earlier, makes the point I am building up to: ". . . there is no real distinction between a book and a rare book. . . . A rare book is just a book like any other, important or unimportant according to the value of its contents. It only differs from other books in that it is more difficult to find, more expensive when we do find it and therefore we naturally tend to look after it more carefully."[14]

Here we have the matter in a nutshell: A book has some quality of rarity when the demand for it is significantly greater than the supply. The reasons why people want the book may be trivial or serious. They may have to do with the text, the binding, the printer, the printing process, the paper, the illustrator, the place it was published, the printer's mark or its absence, the title page or its absence, a state of a particular page, the presence or absence of advertisements, and on and on. Increasingly we recognize that any book has something to tell us in its proper context. Because more and more collectors are adopting a bibliographical approach in their collecting, the universe of collectible books is constantly expanding. Few people would today agree with an opinion expressed by Henry de Halsalle in *The Romance of Modern First Editions*: "Of foreign printed books of the sixteenth century nine out of ten are worth nothing at all."[15] Today the ideas that are shaping the thinking of collectors take quite another point of view:

In such fields [nontraditional areas] it is almost impossible to draw a line between antiquarian books of research interest and rare books proper.[16]

There is no conceivable subject upon which a truly enlightening collection cannot be made.[17]

The whole history of book-collecting consists in attention being drawn to a book or books, or to some feature of them, that had previously been overlooked.[18]

The wise librarian [here I would also say collector] knows that all old books are rare in some sense, that each has a place in the intellectual history of its time, and that none can be neglected.[19]

The bibliographer . . . approaches all books in a library as if they were "rare books."[20]

If we agree that launching into uncharted areas will inevitably be more difficult than following traditional paths, how does a collector assess relative rarity in fields not yet bibliographically cultivated? He or she could follow the course adopted by Matthew J. Bruccoli, who obtains a copy and then looks into the possibility of finding a better copy of the book later. Assessing price, condition, bibliographical variants, and chances of obtaining another copy takes a nose, a sixth sense, and a responsiveness. The nose to tell a rare book from a common one is a feature "denied to many very conscientious and deserving book collectors."[21] It also takes a knowledge of the factors that affect the survival of rare books. John Carter gave a classic definition of these factors in *Taste & Technique in Book Collecting*.[22] This is a book I recommend to the serious beginning book collector above all others for the elegance of its style, its wit, and its solid content. I would like to consider some of the factors that Carter and other writers on the topic have identified. Books that collectors have sought from the time they were printed survive in greater numbers than do neglected books, all things being equal. The longer and more complete the neglect, the greater the scarcity. Recently Edmund Wilson and other literary critics rediscovered the poetry of Frederick Goddard Tuckerman, 1821–1873, an American poet largely ignored by his contemporaries and several generations of later critics. On the evidence of my own searching, Tuckerman's books are far harder to find than are those of such well-known names of the period as Longfellow and Emerson.

Large books tend to be more common than small ones, all things being equal. Think how many hundreds of copies of the 1493 Latin edition of the Nuremberg Chronicle are recorded. Practical books intended for constant use (manuals, handbooks, directories) will ordinarily be worn out and survive in fewer copies than the finely printed books intended for the gentleman's library. A copy of Charles Hutton's *A Course of Book-Keeping According to the Method of Single Entry* (Philadelphia: Joseph James, 1788) recently acquired by the Library of Congress is apparently the only known complete copy of an eighteenth-century edition of a text by Hutton. Ephemeral literature is particularly subject to destruction. Even Archibald MacLeish does not have a copy of his first "book," *Class Poem*, a four-page leaflet containing the text of the poem he read at his 1915 graduation exercises. MacLeish has reported that at the close of the ceremony the ground was littered with copies that people tossed away as they left for home.

Anonymous books are more likely to be discarded than are books by known authors. Unrecognized pseudonyms are a fine passport to oblivion. The Library of Congress's copy of *The Disagreeable Woman*, written by Horatio Alger under the pseudonym Julian Starr, is thought to be unique. Books issued by out-of-the-way publishers are less likely to survive than are those issued from established book centers. As a collector of the contemporary American poet James Merrill, I shake my head about the possibilities of acquiring several titles he had privately printed in Greece.

Books published by their authors before their reputations are established are less likely to survive than are books written at the height of their popularity. At least four factors affecting survival converge in Edith Wharton's first book, *Verses*, privately printed in fragile wrappers in Newport, Rhode Island, in 1878, 19 years before her second book and issued under her maiden name, Edith Newbold Jones. Not surprisingly, *Verses* is one of the rarest books in American literature. Certain books have traditionally been assigned a degree of rarity, which on examination proves fallacious. Many a dealer's catalogue has said that the first edition of Algernon Swinburne's *Atalanta in Calydon* was printed in an edition of only 100 copies. Swinburne collector John Mayfield doubted this early in his collecting career and set out determinedly to prove the Swinburne bibliographers wrong. After "thirty-three years of blood, sweat, and dollars" Mayfield acquired his hundredth copy of the book in March 1976. Even after he publishes his bibliography of Swinburne, the traditional story of the book's rarity will continue to circulate for years.

The destruction of war has reduced supplies of particular books. Collectors of such diverse contemporary authors as Malcolm Lowry, Ivy Compton-Burnett, and Vladimir Nabokov can attest to the difficulty of locating one or more books of each of these authors published in London in the 1930s. The publisher's stocks almost certainly were burned in the blitz. Libraries absorb large quantities of books. Others are censored and suppressed. Excess stocks are pulped. The wear and tear to which books are subject is apparent to anyone who has handled them on a constant basis. It is appropriate that John Carter should have the next to the last word on the subject of survival:

> It is . . . probably safe to say that by comparison with its original printing almost any book of moderate antiquity is likely to survive today in tenuous numbers. It is only by collectors' standards and in relation to a perhaps apathetic demand that it can properly be called common.[23]

In their *Primer of Book Collecting*, John Winterich and David Randall provide an extended and useful discussion of the vicissitudes of an imaginary book, *Thoughts*, printed in an edition of 500 hypothetical copies. Their discussion, too lengthy to summarize here, provides a useful perspective on the survival question.[24]

I would like to conclude this discussion by considering a final paradox. Some of the "rarest" books—that is to say those that the collision of demand and supply have forced to the highest price levels—are among the most accessible. The more a book comes into demand and the more prices rise, the less likely it is to languish unnoticed on a collector's or dealer's shelf. Copies suddenly come on the market. This is a point Nicolas Barker makes in the Autumn 1975 *Book Collector*.[25] Value makes rare books more common. Certainly today I would have less trouble finding Faulkner first editions than in 1951, though they might cost up to 100 times as much. Recognition of a book's importance makes its text more widely disseminated through reprints, facsimile editions, and other reproduction techniques. At a certain point books become part of our heritage and the need to use the originals is reduced accordingly. I do not want to oversimplify the matter in making a point, and I fully perceive that these books have an important role in exhibits, can—in common with all other books—be used for multiple purposes, and afford opportunities for discoveries by each new generation of scholars. Nevertheless it is true that the Library of Congress' copies of the Shakespeare first folio are among the books least frequently used for scholarly purposes. Perhaps you can see why the collector I most admire—and whose long-term contribution I judge will be the greatest—is the one who puts aside fashion and breaks new ground.

In my job I have come to realize that many people have very little idea of the meaning of "collector's condition." Quite early in my career a woman made an appointment for me to look at a "very rare" book that had come down to her through an aunt. She brought it in heavily wrapped in layers of paper and made quite a production of removing it from the protective coverings. Certainly the volume looked large enough to be a fine bird book, an incunable, an important Bible. When she finally unwrapped it, this was probably the most unsightly object I had ever seen. What had once been paper had thickened and become a solid mass; the paper boards on the cover had lost all shape and character. I could barely bring myself to handle the volume. My visitor explained that the book had been dug up in her aunt's yard and must be of great age and value. Very gingerly I ascertained that it was a picture book about the Civil War that was of relatively little value in fine condition and absolutely worthless in this shape. When I gave her the facts she didn't argue with me, as others have done on receipt of bad news of this kind, but—perhaps worse—burst into tears. All this was an eye-opener to me: How could anyone as sensible as this woman appeared to be believe that a book in this condition could be valuable. By now I know that people unfamiliar with books have very little sense of reasonable condition. Quite recently I had a long-distance phone call from a woman who wanted information on a book in her possession. After quoting some prices from the auction records, I explained that the value of the book would be much less if its condition were poor. You, too, would do this automatically if your mail described books that are "in fine condition, except that the title page and two pages [that is, leaves] at the back are missing." Or that the binding is "in excellent shape; all that it would take is a little glue to put the covers back on." In this case my caller did not like what I was saying and grew quite impatient with the information I was imparting. Finally she snapped, "You can't expect a book that old to look good." This is the crux of the matter. For the kind of book she and I were talking about you can very well demand fine condition.

Already in some fields it is becoming difficult in the average antiquarian book shop to see enough examples of some collected fields to get a proper perspective on reasonable collector's condition. If one were to think of condition abstractly, one would say that in ordinary circumstances a book to be judged in fine condition must be complete in all details, must have no tears or other signs of overuse, and must be in an appropriate and intact binding. "Appropriate" can be a slippery word in this connection. Fairly frequently I am startled when people who I feel should know better speak of the beauty of a leather binding that I judge to be an eyesore. There is a great deal of shoddy work done in this field, and it behooves a collector to be able both to recognize good work and to know something about binding styles of the period he or she collects. This is a complicated subject, the ramifications of which I can only touch on here. I have indicated that there are sound bibliographical reasons for seeking books in original condition. To the extent that a book has been rebound or doctored, we have lost some of the evidence. For the early period there is virtually no such thing as an "edition" binding; the printer expected the purchaser to bind the book to his tastes. In the nineteenth century collectors following fashions of that time did not find early bindings to their tastes and rebound some of the rarest and most important books in uniforms of full morocco and gilt. In so doing, ill-informed binders reduced page sizes significantly, trimmed annotations, inscriptions, illustrations, and so on. These tight uniforms make it difficult to examine how the gatherings were put together and to determine whether the copy was "made up" by inserting leaves from another copy. In that period many examples of early binding structure were destroyed and no records retained. Today's knowledgeable collectors are increasingly aware of the importance of surviving early bindings and do not carelessly or routinely remove them. Restoration binders understand the importance of describing the work they have done on a particular volume and of preserving the covers when the original binding is too far gone to be saved. It is in the light of connoisseurship such as this that I am surprised when collectors exclaim over a shiny, inappropriate, badly made binding, executed with poor materials, in no sympathy with the text. A collector would do well to do some reading on bindings and to realize that beneath the outer covers there are various layers of paper, board, leather, tapes, and cord, all serving important functions of support and reinforcement. To the extent that this work is well done, using high quality materials, the binding will protect the text block and, if suitably cared for, have the possibility of long life. If the work is shoddily done with inferior materials, this shiny—and perhaps relatively inexpensive—binding will not be a source of pride to a collector for long. Careful handwork is expensive but fully justified for valuable books. If financial value makes a book an inappropriate candidate for such treatment, it can be placed in a slip-case and left as it is.

I am very much a believer in fine condition. This follows more from my views on the underlying bibliographical rationale of collecting than from the common argument that it is a good investment to buy books in fine condition. Having said that, I would add that there is a good deal of blind following of fashion in this matter. Although ordinarily it would be foolish to purchase a copy of a twentieth-century private press book in poor condition (most of the copies of such books still survive and have been protected by their various owners), we would gladly enough make an exception for a copy that William Morris had inscribed to a fellow writer, to a printing colleague, or to his wife. Having balanced the condition, the importance of the inscription, and the price, the collector would come to a decision, based on a knowledge of the relevant factors.

Perhaps my work as a rare book librarian has given me a jaundiced view, but I am not very enthusiastic about books that are merely signed or are part of a signed, limited edition. Undoubtedly I have seen too many instances of collectors taking stacks of books to a reading and asking the author to autograph them. It may be that some authors are gratified by this evidence of interest, but others I know have expressed doubt about the genuineness of the enthusiasm for their work. Could it be that the stack of carefully protected, pristine copies, showing so little evidence of having been read, leaves a bad taste in the signer's mouth. In my own collecting I willingly buy a book in less than pristine condition if it has another kind of interest. There are too many possibilities to characterize them all, but here are a few. I have already said that a book signed on request, without any personal association, is not a very significant item to me. In a rough ascending order of importance from the book with only a signature or an inscription that has no personal interest or significant content, kinds of desirable "association" copies might be ranked as follows: a book inscribed to a personal friend (to the extent that this inscription provides information on the nature of that relationship it would be judged to be more important), a book whose inscription gives additional details about the author's view of the work, a book whose inscription provides important new biographical or bibliographical information, a book whose text is annotated in a significant way (this could range from the corrections Marianne

Moore made in many copies of a given title to a copy whose text had been revised throughout in preparation for a new edition).

I can think of instances in which I have been able to purchase a copy of a book that is inscribed by an author in what I have taken to be a meaningful way for much less than I would have expected, simply because the dust wrapper was lacking. Mrs. Louis Henry Cohn, owner of House of Books Ltd. and one of the country's veteran dealers in twentieth-century books, has shaken her head about this attitude of collectors. She knows its extent from her day-to-day transactions and has told me that she doesn't understand why collectors pass up desirable books, just because they lack a dust wrapper. In many cases the collector has the option of acquiring multiple copies. This can be a highly desirable approach. By putting multiple copies of the same edition or impression next to one another, the collector can distinguish variants not otherwise apparent: different states of the dust wrappers, variations in the imprint, previously unrecognized changes in binding cloth, lettering, stamping, and so on. For many classes of books, editions other than the first are priced low, and the collector is in a favorable position to uncover variants unrecognized by the dealer. In the case of heavily collected authors, dealers can lose perspective about variants. I recall seeing what I would have taken to be an incorrectly bound copy of Katherine Anne Porter's first book, *My Chinese Marriage* (a book Miss Porter is said to have ghost-written), described as a unique first issue at a price many times the going rate. States, issues, and bibliographical variants deserve the same cold scrutiny I have proposed be directed toward inscriptions.

It is possible that an author may be inspired to provide significant information for a trivial purpose. More than one "collector" has elicited a response from an author by giving him or her a sob story. In my personal collection I have an inscribed copy of a book by Eudora Welty, with a laid-in letter in her hand, written to someone who became known to dealers for his adeptness at eliciting responses from authors. The dealer who sold the book to me pointed out the ruse employed, indicated that the ruse did not diminish the charm of the letter Miss Welty had written to her unworthy correspondent, and priced the book and letter at a rate that seemed fair to him, taking all the factors into account. The letter is charming, and the whole story tells us something about collectors and collecting.

Collectors are constantly faced with decisions, and their ability to deal with them successfully is evidence of their connoisseurship. Winterich and Randall reported that the "majority [of collectors] are opposed to paying a premium for a book merely because the jacket is present."[26] This point of view has surely changed since their book was published, perhaps in recognition of the fact that dust wrappers are fragile and must be preserved and cared for by collectors if they are to survive at all. Justin G. Schiller's account of the sale at auction of the Katherine de B. Parson's library in the *AB Bookman's Weekly*, November 8, 1976, indicates that collectors are willing to pay tremendous premiums in certain cases. In reporting the $3,500 paid for the first printing of Kenneth Grahame's *The Wind in the Willows* in "its rare pictorial dust-jacket," he notes that "at least $3,250 is for the dj."[27]

Winterich and Randall also question the aversion of collectors of modern first editions toward names (other than the author's) on endpapers.[28] Collectors are surely inconsistent on that point. In the case of an early book we regard such evidence of former ownership as part of the provenance and include it in our descriptions of the copy. It would be an unusual collector who thought that a name reduced the value of a book of this period. In the case of a twentieth-century book, a name written in the book—particularly on the title page—is viewed with real aversion. I have been guilty in this respect and increasingly wonder whether this makes sense. It is quite possible that the unknown inscriber may in time emerge as an important figure, either in his or her own right or for his or her connection to the author. Of course it is hard to see how a banal comment sprawled over the entire endpaper will ever be raised up in quite the way I hypothesize. If we know why we are acting as we do, fine; if we are unthinkingly following the herd, it's time to pause and think.

In my position I am often asked for my opinion on "first editions" published in large quantities and talked up for their long-term investment value. Naturally I am suspicious of pre-packaged rarities. To the extent that collectors accept someone else's judgment about what should be housed on their shelves, they have lost not only much of the fun of collecting but also the chance of being a pioneer. The attrition that will be required to make expensive books published in thousands of copies "rare" is staggering. Indeed, books that are published in collector's editions and that are expensive on publication are particularly likely to be preserved. All these factors—and more—work against such books increasing in value. There is nothing magical about first editions per se. Every book is published as a first edition, and a good many never achieve a second. By definition tenth editions are "rarer" than first editions.

Hearty skepticism is an appropriate attitude toward limited editions. They were in great vogue in the 1920s, took a tumble in the Depression years, and are making a strong comeback. In the Rare Book and Special Collections Division at the Library of Congress we have set up procedures to examine all incoming books printed in editions of fewer than 500 copies for possible addition to our collection. You might be startled to see the number that come our way and to hear that we accept perhaps 10 percent of the books submitted to us, which include books in many languages other than English, private press books, poetry, expensive reprints, genealogies, and so forth. Some have said that limited editions are books in which there is so little interest or demand that the printer or publisher knows better than to produce more than a set number of copies. This is a half-truth, but worth recalling. In handpress work the printer may suffer financially if too many copies are produced, and in the case of certain illustrative processes the plates will suffer damage in repeated impressions.

You might point out to me that interest in certain collected authors is so great that a limited edition will go out of print almost immediately, and prices in the out-of-print market will rise. That this may follow from collectors and dealers purchasing extra copies in anticipation of such a rise is a point worth being aware of. For the sake of argument let us say that all the books in an edition are bought because the purchaser is interested in the author, not in a quick turnover. While the collector has the book in his or her possession—let us say for a generation—it will be removed from the market. The interesting question is what happens when a significant number of copies comes back on the market, in the cycle of generations that Winterich and Randall discuss. For Faulkner we have the answer: His reputation continues to rise, collectors and institutions seek his work, and the demand significantly outdistances the supply. For other authors published in limited editions in approximately the same period—the Sitwells, John O'Hara, Willa Cather—the prices are not necessarily outdistancing the cost of living.

A limited edition may be printed on different paper from other copies or have special features such as additional plates, a superior binding, signatures of the author, illustrator, designer, and/or printer. It may, on the other hand, be from the same sheets as the trade edition, bound with a limitation notice, and numbered and/or signed. The limited edition, far from being the "first edition," may be published after the regular edition. In *Dukedom Large Enough*, David Randall tells an amusing story about Ernest Hemingway's *Across the River and Into the Trees*. The publisher, Scribner's, regularly produced 25 specially bound copies of Hemingway's books for the personal use of the author and a few others. On receiving the special copies of *Across the River and Into the Trees*, Randall wrote a penciled note on the flyleaf of each indicating that it was one of the 25 copies before corrections were made, identifying the textual variants, and stating that the blue cloth binding (differing from the black on the 75,000 copies of the first edition) was experimental. Some years later the press manager told Randall that he had nodded that evening and had forgotten the 25 copies that were to be the first off the press. He quickly located some discarded plates and ran off the 25 special copies and bound them up in cloth of a different color. Randall summarizes the evidence, all of it apparently incontrovertible—and all of it quite erroneous:

> (1) The book is bound in a different cloth than any other edition or reprint. (2) It does have errors corrected in all other editions and reprints. (3) It has a signed statement to this effect by an employee of the firm publishing it, signed and dated a month before the book was issued. (4) The proof sheets contain the errors. (5) It is, therefore, exactly what it purports to be.[29]

Randall uses the story to warn us not to take uncritically any statement any publisher, printer, or author makes about any book. I would reiterate that skepticism, whether about limited, signed editions or any other aspect of collecting, is a healthy attitude.

In all these matters knowledge is the essential factor. What might be an appropriate rationale for collecting twentieth-century first editions could well be completely out of touch with reality for a collector of fifteenth-century books. Though few readers of this book are likely to become collectors of books printed by William Caxton, England's first printer, even the greatest collectors recognized much more than a century ago that the books he printed rarely survive in complete copies and that an incomplete Caxton is a worthy object for even the most discriminating and exacting collector. In the last analysis, what book collecting is all about is knowledge, connoisseurship, and a conscious rationale for shaping a collection.

Notes

1. Michael S. Batts, "The 18th-Century Concept of the Rare Book," *The Book Collector* 24 (Autumn 1975): 381.
2. For very useful discussions of these changes see Gordon N. Ray's articles, "The Changing World of Rare Books," *Papers of the Bibliographical Society of America* 59 (Second Quarter 1965): 103–141, and "The World of Rare Books Re-examined," *Yale University Library Gazette* 49 (July 1974): 77–146.
3. *Encyclopaedia Britannica*, 11th ed., s.v. "Book-Collecting," p. 221.
4. Ibid.
5. S. C. Roberts, "The Relevance of Rare Book Collections to a University Library," *Library Association Record* 69 (April 1967): 109–110.
6. G. Thomas Tanselle, "Collecting Modern Imprints," *The Book Collector* 19 (Summer 1970): 203–213.
7. Edwin Wolf, 2nd, "Value & Worth of Rare Books," *Antiquarian Bookman* 27 (February 20, 1961): 636.
8. Ibid.
9. Ibid., p. 640.
10. Ibid., p. 636.
11. "Book-Collecting," p. 223.
12. Randolph G. Adams, "Who Uses a Library of Rare Books?" in *English Institute Annual 1940* (New York: Columbia University Press, 1941), pp. 149–150.
13. G. Thomas Tanselle, "Bibliographers and the Library," *Library Trends* 25 (April 1977): 745–762.
14. Roberts, "The Relevance of Rare Book Collections to a University Library," p. 109.
15. Henry de Halsalle, *The Romance of Modern First Editions* (Philadelphia: Lippincott, 1931), p. 50.
16. Ray, "The Changing World of Rare Books," p. 112.
17. John Carter, *Taste & Technique in Book Collecting* (London, Private Libraries Association, 1970), p. 84. Quoted from Seymour de Ricci, "Book-Collecting for All Purses," *The Colophon*, pt. 2 (1930).

18. Percy H. Muir, "The Nature and Scope of Book-collecting," in *Talks on Book-collecting*, ed. by Percy H. Muir (London: Cassell, Ltd., 1952), p. 8.
19. Nicolas Barker, "Rare Books," *The Book Collector* 24 (Autumn 1975): 366.
20. Tanselle, "Bibliographers and the Library," p. 748.
21. Carter, *Taste & Technique in Book Collecting*, p. 121.
22. Ibid.
23. Ibid., p. 153.
24. John T. Winterich and David A. Randall, *A Primer of Book Collecting*, 3rd rev. ed. (New York: Crown Publishers, 1966), pp. 85–89.
25. Barker, "Rare Books," p. 366.
26. Winterich and Randall, *A Primer of Book Collecting*, p. 117.
27. Justin G. Schiller, "Collecting Historical Children's Books," *AB Bookman's Weekly* 58 (November 8, 1976): 2524.
28. Winterich and Randall, *A Primer of Book Collecting*, p. 101.
29. David A. Randall, *Dukedom Large Enough* (New York: Random House, 1969), p. 240.

2

Buying Books from Dealers

Robin G. Halwas

THIS CHAPTER IS DESIGNED for collectors who have discovered an area in which they would like to collect and who now need advice on identifying and making contact with those dealers who sell books appropriate to their collections.

To find the books you want, you must learn where to look for them. Most book collectors will have visited local bookstores and purchased a miscellany of books long before they discover the subject focus of their collections. At this stage in the development of their collections, collectors can be satisfied by almost any bookseller with a general stock. But as their taste develops, all collectors extend their search to specialist booksellers.

No one can hope to form a significant collection by frequenting small-town secondhand bookstores; collectors of these books will find West Coast and New York City dealers primary sources of supply. The stock of leading antiquarian booksellers, however, will contain few items of interest to a collector of turn-of-the-century decorated trade bindings, who will find it advantageous to extend the search to thrift shops and rummage sales. Common sense will suggest to collectors of, say, French Canadiana, English fine bindings, or Victorian literature, that they must conduct an international search. But how does a beginning collector learn which of the hundreds of dealers at home and abroad are likely to have the right books?

Antiquarian bookselling has undergone great change in the past 25 years. The disappearance of most secondhand bookstores whose entire shelf space was filled with general stock is only one aspect of this change. The chief characteristic of the trade today is its division according to specialties. Those booksellers with a specialty in Americana, for example, often further classify themselves by regional focus, historical period, or into even more precise subclassifications. Another characteristic of the present-day trade is its wide geographical distribution. Faced by increasing rents and taxes and largely supported by institutional customers who order by mail or telephone, many dealers have migrated from metropolitan locations to the country. Here they conduct business primarily by appointment, phone, and mail. Still another development is the emergence of the amateur or part-time bookseller, probably the result of the rise in prices that has brought attention as well as prosperity to the trade.

One result of the antiquarian trade's expansion, specialization, and diffusion across the country is the growing complication for the collector in searching for booksellers in particular fields of interest. Because of competition for practically every kind of book, collectors must actively search for the books they require, and they cannot afford to neglect any possible sources of supply. Some ways for collectors to build up a list of specialist dealers are by consulting book-trade directories and by reading book-trade and book collector's periodicals.

Book-Trade Directories

For beginning collectors, the most useful listing of dealers in old and rare, used and out-of-print books is the membership list of the Antiquarian Booksellers' Association of America (ABAA). Founded in 1949, with the stated objectives of encouraging book collecting and ensuring professional standards, the ABAA is now composed of more than 350 member firms in 32 states and is organized in six regional chapters. Membership in the ABAA implies agreement with an international code of fair practices governing commercial transactions between member booksellers, and between members and private individuals. To be considered for membership in the ABAA, a bookseller must have been engaged full time in the buying and selling of rare books or manuscripts for at least three years. The list of the

ABAA is therefore a directory only of the more established firms in the United States and Canada, and the collector will want to use the ABAA list in conjunction with other directories.

The ABAA membership list is an alphabetical catalogue of members providing full name and address, telephone number, the names of members when they differ from the firm's name, the names of any individuals affiliated with a member firm who have been elected to associate membership, and a description of the member's subject specialties. Over 190 different specialties are listed. Collectors may obtain copies of the membership list by writing the ABAA (Shop No. 2, Concourse, 630 Fifth Avenue, New York, N.Y. 10020) and enclosing a business-sized, stamped, self-addressed envelope. Two chapters, the Middle Atlantic Chapter and the Southern California Chapter, have issued regional directories, and these may be obtained from chapter members.

Another useful guide to out-of-print books is the "O. P. Market—Reference Directory of Antiquarian and Specialist Booksellers," which is a feature of the *AB Bookman's Yearbook*. Now in its twenty-ninth edition, the *Bookman's Yearbook* and the periodical *AB Bookman's Weekly* (formerly called *Antiquarian Bookman*) are among the chief vehicles of communication within the American antiquarian book trade. Book dealers may list their specialties in the *Yearbook's* annual "O. P. Market" after payment of a nominal fee. The advantage, therefore, of this trade directory is that it includes the addresses of many small dealers about whom it is often difficult to obtain information elsewhere. Over a thousand different specialties are indexed in the "O. P. Market," ranging from Bees and Beekeeping through Gold Mining and Theology to Whaling. Collectors can purchase copies of the *AB Bookman's Yearbook* from the *AB Bookman's Weekly*, whose address is listed in an appendix (along with other useful addresses) at the end of this book.

The English publisher Sheppard Press produces a directory of *Bookdealers in North America* (7th ed., 1976), which is basically a catalogue of major American and Canadian dealers. A problem with this list, as well as with B. Donald Grose's *Antiquarian Booktrade, an International Directory of Subject Specialists* (Metuchen, N.J.: Scarecrow, 1972), is that some of its information is already out of date. Some important American firms, moreover, have been curiously omitted from both publications. Nevertheless, a collector would do well to examine the subject indexes of these volumes when compiling a list of dealers, for each directory adopts different subject headings to describe the same specialties; it may well be that you will discover a previously unknown bookseller in your particular field of interest. Because of the vagaries of subject indexing, it is helpful to supplement the trade directories with other sources. For example, a good deal of information about a firm's range of interests often can be gathered by examining its advertisements in bibliographical and trade journals.

Book-Trade Periodicals

Of the several journals that carry the advertisements of American booksellers, *AB Bookman's Yearbook* and *AB Bookman's Weekly* contain the largest number. In a recent edition of the *Bookman's Yearbook*, more than 550 booksellers placed display advertisements specifying such information as hours of business, whether or not catalogues are issued, and fields of specialization. Some dealers list in addition a number of books designated as "Permanent Wants." Besides reporting news and carrying announcements of interest to the trade, *AB Bookman's Weekly* has an extensive classified section where dealers offer books for sale and list books that they are seeking to purchase. From such advertisements a collector can often quite accurately gauge the character and quality of a dealer's stock.

Dealers in expensive books, particularly those who carry on an international trade, tend to advertise in such journals as the *Papers of the Bibliographical Society of America* and *The Book Collector* (London). Some of these dealers use their advertisements to announce recently issued catalogues; other firms find it unnecessary to advertise anything beyond their names and addresses. Some specialist booksellers advertise in the *American Book Collector*, which includes a list of catalogues received, arranged by subject. From time to time an individual firm is featured in an article in the magazine *Book Collector's Market*, which also has a subject index of catalogues received. It is sometimes possible to identify booksellers who deal in particular authors by examining the annual volumes of *Bookman's Price Index* and *American Book Prices Current*. In both of these compilations, the name of the dealer involved with the transaction is part of the typical entry.

Between the various trade directories and periodicals, collectors should be able to prepare a list of probable sources of supply. They will visit as many of them as possible in person.

Other places where the collector can make personal contact with dealers are at book fairs and at the Antiquarian Booksellers Center in New York City.

Book Fairs

The book fair offers collectors an opportunity to view a representative selection from the stock of a large number of booksellers, to refine their list of dealers specializing in their own areas of interest, and to make personal contacts, which are usually more satisfactory than relationships conducted entirely by mail. The book fair is also a prime opportunity for collectors to discuss their collections and desiderata with foreign dealers. They have, besides, a chance to collect catalogues and to compare prices.

Most of the important fairs are conducted under ABAA auspices, and a collector can depend upon several major fairs being held somewhere in North America each year. The Middle Atlantic, Northern California, and Southern California chapters of the ABAA take turns organizing an annual international fair either in New York City or in California. Fairs are also held regularly in Washington, D.C., and in Toronto, and they have recently been held in Boston and Chicago as well. Nonprofit organizations and institutions occasionally hold book fairs as part of fund-raising programs. Announcements of these fairs, and of antique shows where books will be exhibited, usually appear in local newspapers; ABAA-sponsored fairs are always given extensive coverage in *AB Bookman's Weekly*.

The Antiquarian Booksellers Center, New York City

The Antiquarian Booksellers Center is a cooperative bookstore where collectors can examine books, autographs, maps, and catalogues consigned for sale by the Center's 70 member dealers. Though the stock changes regularly, it always reflects the different specialties and the geographical diversity of the Center's members, and it includes items in a variety of price ranges. The Center is not, however, only a bookstore; it is also a referral center where collectors may deposit cards describing their collecting interests. This information is then passed along to specialist member dealers.

The Antiquarian Booksellers Center is a place where a collector can meet booksellers. Since it opened in 1963, one of the Center's objectives has been to stimulate interest in book collecting. Lately, this has taken the form of sponsorship of an annual lecture series, where dealers discuss their specialties, occasionally in conjunction with exhibitions from their stock. Information about upcoming lectures, as well as a brochure that describes the Center and lists the names, addresses, and specialties of its members, can be obtained by sending a business-sized, stamped, self-addressed envelope to the Secretary, Antiquarian Booksellers Center, Shop No. 2, Concourse, 630 Fifth Avenue, New York, N.Y. 10020.

Meeting the Dealer

It is important for a beginning collector to make personal contact with the dealers in his or her field of collecting for several reasons. A close relationship between dealer and collector generally has practical benefits. Booksellers differ from many other merchants in that they have a special attitude toward their commodity. Most dealers are reluctant to sell books to persons they don't like; they prefer to send their books, like favorite puppies, to good homes. A regular customer will often be offered a book before it is catalogued or receive a catalogue in advance of a general mailing. When several orders are received for the same book, a dealer may sell the book to the collector whose order is postmarked the earliest; but it is equally likely that the dealer will favor the customer with whom he or she has a personal friendship. More important, the customer who develops a personal relationship with a dealer benefits most fully from that dealer's expertise and taste. Booksellers historically have played an important role in the development of collectors. As long as the relationship between the book collector and the book dealer is merely one of buyer-seller, it is difficult for the bookseller to influence the collector's taste and technique in book collecting. When their relationship, through trust and understanding, becomes one of collaboration, the bookseller is able to guide the collector toward the achievement of a distinctive library.

Booksellers' Catalogues

Few collectors develop a close personal relationship with more than one or two booksellers. With most of the dealers with whom they do business, a collector's principal means of communication is the bookseller's catalogue. Dealers' catalogues vary in every possible way: in size, in method of printing, in length and importance of annotations and comments. Beginning collectors sometimes make the mistake of neglecting well-made and well-printed catalogues, because they assume the contents to be beyond their financial reach. Similarly, some collectors consider themselves too grand to read mimeographed lists. Both groups need to remember that it is only by experience that they will learn which dealers' catalogues they can afford to avoid: surface appearances are frequently deceptive. This principle also applies when visiting bookstores. A collector should never be intimidated by a prestigious shop. All dealers have books in a broad price range, and every good bookseller will welcome a true collector, whether a purchase is made or not.

Sometimes booksellers acquire stock and issue catalogues well in advance of the taste of the times. These catalogues then become highly prized collector's items in their own right. Other catalogues are notable for the originality of their notes and scholarly sophistication. Occasionally these catalogues constitute the only guide to their subject. They are a bibliographical resource like auction catalogues, and they should be preserved for future use. Still other catalogues are remarkable for the eccentricity of their arrangement and lack of adequate indexing, which can make them as much of a delight as a chore to read. Many book collectors can tell stories of finding exactly the book they were looking for entered under an unexpected subject heading rather than under its author.

When the collector has determined that his or her field of collecting falls within the specialization of a particular dealer, the next step is to write to the bookseller and to be placed on a mailing list for catalogues. It is always advisable to describe to the dealer the range of one's collecting interests in this initial letter. The earlier the collector demonstrates his or her seriousness, the more assistance the bookseller will be likely to offer. When the dealer's catalogues arrive, the collector will notice that although booksellers as a rule use words that are in common usage, they confer on them special connotations, and employ a number of abbreviations. Checklists and other mimeographed productions have a tendency to employ more abbreviations than do the glossy catalogues, which (on the other hand) generally use many specialist bibliographical terms; the frequency of their use, however, depends entirely on the cataloguer's style and the type and value of the books being described.

Although many collectors consider reading catalogues to be the most delightful of recreations, it is not something that always comes easily to the beginning collector. Fortunately, there are a number of guides to assist the collector in interpreting the language of the trade. Many abbreviations and bibliographical terms are defined with wit and style by John Carter in his superb *ABC for Book Collectors* (5th ed., London: Rupert Hart-Davis, 1972), a dictionary of such sustained interest that it can be read straight through. Hertzberger's polyglot *Dictionary of the Antiquarian Book Trade*, on the other hand, is purely a reference book. A publication of the International League of Antiquarian Booksellers, it is available in North America through members of the ABAA. Jean Peters' *Bookman's Glossary* (5th ed., New York: Bowker, 1975) falls somewhere between Carter and Hertzberger in readability; it is also valuable for its definitions of terms in the related fields of printing, publishing, librarianship, and bibliography. After a collector is familiar with these guides, he or she may enjoy a humorous "ABC for Booksellers," which appeared in the Summer 1967 issue of *The Private Library* and contains definitions along the lines of "Columbus: Patron saint of British booksellers."

Booksellers and librarians invariably read important catalogues in their special fields of interest as soon as they arrive, for they know that any delay in ordering will sharply reduce their chances of obtaining the books they want. Collectors should recognize that there is intense competition for many kinds of books, and they must be prepared to pay a bookseller to have his catalogues sent to them by airmail or to use the telephone or cable when submitting an order. A telephoned order will almost always reserve a book pending receipt of remittance.

When ordering from a bookseller by mail for the first time, it is useful to include the name of other booksellers who can vouch for your good character. This will give the bookseller confidence and almost always expedite shipment. As a personal relationship develops, the dealer may permit the collector the option of deferred billing or payment on an installment plan, if such a program is arranged at the time of the order. In most transactions, however, booksellers expect their customers to send a remittance immediately following a confirmed telephone order or promptly after a notice of shipment or upon receipt of the book. Postage and insurance are sometimes included in the price of an item, but sometimes they are extra; the collector will need to refer to the statement of conditions of sale that is printed in every catalogue.

Unless a book is catalogued as "Sold not subject to return," nearly all dealers will accept a book returned because it was improperly or inadequately described; and some dealers will accept a book sent back for other reasons. In both cases the risks of transport are the responsibility of the sender. Each dealer will specify the time period during which returns must be made and state it prominently in his or her catalogues. This period may range from as little as one day to as long as several weeks. If a collector has established a personal relationship with a dealer, however, or if the volume of his or her purchases has been significant, and if the condition or value of a book is untypical, a dealer may permit the collector to receive a book before payment, or on approval.

Approvals

Buying on approval is a special privilege that a bookseller extends to certain customers, and it must not be abused. During the period when a book is out of his or her shop, a dealer may receive several inquiries about it, particularly if it is an item from a recent catalogue. The collector must therefore take pains to return the book within the specified period; and if he or she does not, the dealer is quite justified in assuming the sale to be concluded. Responsibility for the book as long as it is out of the dealer's shop belongs to the collector, who should expect to pay the expense of postage and insurance both ways.

A book dealer is a professional who operates a bookstore, not a bazaar. The wise collector never attempts to haggle over prices. By seeking to do so, you are likely to lose a bookseller's friendship, and if the dealer sells you a good book again, it will be with a sour heart, and only because no one else seems to want it. If you do not respect a dealer's knowledge, judgment, and honesty, you should not frequent his or her store; and if you believe that a dealer's price is inflated, you should keep that opinion to yourself and leave the book on the shelf.

When collectors discuss prices with a dealer, it is often because they have checked various price indexes and discovered that a book has sold for such and such a price in the past. Knowledge of a book's price history is an excellent thing to have—but today's price is the one that you will be asked to pay.

In some cases a bookseller may later lower the price of a book on his or her shelf, but usually you may expect it to be sold at the price marked. When experienced collectors exchange their reminiscences, they speak as frequently of the books they let get away because they believed them too expensive as they do of books that they did in fact purchase for their collections. The collector will want to weigh carefully factors such as the importance of a book to the collection, and the frequency of its appearance on the market, before dismissing it as overpriced. It may be a long time before you have the opportunity to buy a copy again.

Want Lists

When beginning collectors do not see the books they want to purchase either in catalogues or in dealers' shops, they sometimes become impatient and make the mistake of duplicating want lists and distributing them throughout the trade. Some dealers are irritated by such lists, especially if they are extensive, or when they appear to have been sent out unselectively. The main objection to the practice, however, is that it often increases the price that the collector must pay for a book. Responding to the want list, several dealers may advertise for the same book and create the illusion that it is in wide demand, thereby driving up the price; or they may compete more aggressively for it at auction, because they are confident that they have a sure sale. By sending out a list of desiderata, the collector is in effect entering into a contract with a bookseller to purchase whatever books he or she can supply, as long as their condition is acceptable and the price quoted is in keeping with their market value. For this reason alone, collectors should not submit a list to more than a single dealer at a time, for otherwise they may receive quotes on many more books than they can immediately afford to purchase.

Search Services

When a collector asks a dealer for help in developing a collection, the dealer will usually keep a special lookout for relevant books. One way for a collector to broaden the search is by writing to one of the many book-search services listed in the *AB Bookman's Yearbook* directory "O. P. Market" mentioned earlier. These services will advertise the collector's desiderata in the classified "Books Wanted" section of *AB Bookman's Weekly*, which has a circulation of more than 7,000. *AB's* advertising policy does not permit private individuals to advertise their wants (though it does allow anyone to offer books for sale). Some dealers are reluctant to go to the trouble of placing advertisements for collectors in *AB*, and for this reason the search services have an important role in the trade. Some of the well-established services have organized extensive information networks and without advertising can often conjure up a desired book effortlessly. These firms, some of whom are members of the ABAA, particularly merit the collector's attention.

Buying Books from Foreign Dealers

Whether or not collectors buy from abroad depends in large part on the subject of their collections and on the seriousness of their collecting. Some collectors will always discover the books they want in the stock of North American dealers; others will rely on foreign sources from the beginning. A collector's regular bookseller will be able to provide a list of the names of foreign dealers who specialize in the collector's particular field of interest. The *International Directory of Antiquarian Booksellers*, published by the International League of Antiquarian Booksellers (ILAB), will be particularly helpful to the collector if he or she needs additional sources of supply.

The ILAB *Directory* is a bilingual (French/English) guide to booksellers, classified geographically by firm and by subject specialty. It is compiled primarily from information submitted by the various national antiquarian booksellers' associations, and it is distributed in North America by members of the ABAA. A new edition of the *Directory* was published in 1977. Another guide is *European Book Dealers; A Directory of Dealers in Secondhand and Antiquarian Books on the Continent of Europe* (London: Sheppard, 1977). Sheppard Press also publishes a directory of British dealers, the most recent edition of which was published in 1975. The English book trade periodical *The Clique* publishes an *Annual Directory of Booksellers in the British Isles*.

European booksellers advertise in the ILAB *Directory* and in the many national and bibliographical publications, some of the more important of which are *The Book Collector*, *The Library* (published by the Bibliographical Society of London), *Biblos*, *Quaerendo*, and *Philobiblon*. The collector will also find news of the trade and announcements of book fairs in the English journal *Antiquarian Book Monthly Review*.

Collectors may find it useful to solicit the advice and assistance of their regular booksellers when ordering from an unfamiliar dealer, and such advice is particularly valuable when ordering from abroad. It is quite common, in fact, to have an American bookseller with whom one has a personal relationship handle the sale entirely. The collector then benefits from the advantage of his or her bookseller's bibliographical expertise and is also relieved of such troubles as establishing credit and transferring currency. An American dealer will frequently perform this service as a courtesy. A collector is unlikely to receive a book from abroad on approval unless he or she submits a check with the order, but it is a common practice for books to be exchanged on approval between booksellers. The convenience of being able to order from foreign dealers in this way is one more reason for searching out a professional bookseller early in one's collecting career, a person in whom one can place complete confidence, and who can be a guide in the selection of worthy books and the achievement of a distinguished collection.

3

Buying at Auction

Robert A. Wilson

J OHN CARTER ONCE OBSERVED that an auction is primarily a "mechanical convenience" for the bibliophile community that provides important and valuable secondary services: a "continuous barometer of prices"; "color, romance and excitement; surprises, upsets, and disappointments; landmarks, records and historical occasions" (*Library Trends*, April 1961).

It is in the latter terms that the neophyte book collector may think of auctions; yet for all of its aura of excitement, the auction itself, reflecting Carter's primary observation, is a business transaction between the owner of a book who wishes to sell it (the consignor) and the person who wishes to buy it (the bidder), with the auction house acting as agent for the consignor.

The concept seems almost ridiculously simple: A book is offered for sale and people bid on it, with the highest bidder taking possession of the book. So it seems on the surface. But the fact is that buying books at auction is more complicated than it seems, making it the most misunderstood aspect of book collecting. This is due in part to a lack of accurate knowledge as to what happens in a book auction and, in part, to the persistence of popular fallacies, chief of which is the belief that prices will be cheaper at auction.

Perhaps the best way to dispel incorrect, though seemingly cherished beliefs, is to get down to hard facts and trace the progress of a collection of books through the auction course, which has as many hurdles and pitfalls as a point-to-point horse race, both for the consignor and bidder.

Operation of an Auction

Things start long before the books actually appear at auction and, in fact, long before the general public even has any idea that a collection will be coming onto the market. It starts when the owner of the collection decides that the time has come to sell it. In most cases, this comes about at the death of the collector. For some reason, the passion for book collecting is rarely an inherited one. And even when a second generation does collect books, there is little interest in merely owning the books acquired by one's forebears. As in all fields of collecting, the chase is half the fun, and the acquisition, *en bloc*, of a collection, however noteworthy or valuable it may be, seldom has any appeal to one's heirs.

For these reasons notable collections are frequently sent to auction. The first step is to get in touch with the gallery. If it is a matter of a single highly valuable book or a relatively small number of books, the gallery will request that they be brought in for examination. If the collection is a sizable one, the gallery will send its expert in that field to assess the potential of the collection. (It should be noted that a fee is charged for such a visit.) Some galleries have a relatively small staff, which must have a smattering of knowledge in all fields, whereas larger galleries such as Sotheby Parke Bernet or Christie's have large staffs, so that the expertise runs deeper in certain areas.

Auction galleries maintain extensive reference collections of bibliographies and past auction records and can usually come to an immediate decision as to whether a particular collection is suited to the auction process and, if so, whether the gallery is interested in handling the dispersal of it. They are also in a position to advise as to the state of the market for the given property.

There are fashions and trends in book collecting as much as there are in *haute couture* or painting and sculpture. Twenty years ago the books of F. Scott Fitzgerald went totally unregarded. They are now among the most prized items in current collecting. Conversely, in the 1930s Galsworthy was fetching staggering prices but now brings only a fraction of those amounts.

Galleries know from experience what is selling well during any given season and can advise the owners (or estates) when to place materials on the market, or when to withhold them to await a revival of interest in an author or a given field. Also, the gallery can—and must—advise when a situation is hopeless, as, for instance, in the case of the family's "old Bible" or of *The Complete Works of Martin Farquhar Tupper*, an English versifer of the early nineteenth century, who achieved international vogue in his day, but is now virtually unknown.

Assuming the collection is of interest to the gallery, it is then transferred to the gallery's office. Here a crucial phase of the ultimate dispersal takes place—the dividing of the collection into lots. How this is done affects both the sum ultimately realized by the owners and, in many cases, whether dealers and collectors will be induced to bid at all. There is no problem with well-known high spot titles, because each book is offered individually. Every gallery has its own minimum limit as to what a lot must fetch in order to be worth a separate catalogue entry. In the case of two of the principal New York galleries, Sotheby Parke Bernet has a minimum of $150, and the Swann Galleries, a minimum of $50.

The minor items in a collection are generally lotted—that is to say, lumped together in bundles of varying sizes, so that the salesroom need not waste inordinate amounts of time and effort disposing of run-of-the-mill books that would fetch relatively small prices. But lotting is a very imprecise science, and it is in this area that the galleries often commit gigantic blunders, which, if spotted by a keen-witted dealer or collector, can make the acquisition of a valuable item both exciting and inexpensive.

I could recount numerous examples of such finds from my own experience, but one will suffice to show what often happens in lotting. A few years ago an auction catalogue listed several Oscar Wilde titles as separate lots, along with one lot of five Wilde titles bundled together. A dealer bid on the five just to obtain one of them—a long out-of-print Wilde bibliography. After acquiring the lot, he found that, as expected, two of the books were cheap reprints. But there were also two first editions of Wilde: a worn copy of *Lord Arthur Savile's Crime*—a somewhat uncommon Wilde title—and, amazingly, a very fine copy of *The Importance of Being Earnest*, certainly a book well worth a single entry on its own, worth many times what the whole lot had fetched. Apparently no one had checked the lot, assuming that the *Earnest* was a reprint. Finally, incredibly enough, laid into *Earnest* was the first page only (alas) of a letter in Oscar's hand describing the London premiere of Ibsen's *Ghosts*!

The reason for this book having been lotted can only be guessed at. Perhaps, being at the end of the alphabet, space in the catalogue was running out and, thus, *Earnest* was lumped with other less distinguished titles. It is inconceivable that the auctioneers would not have realized its true value had they seen it. However, not discovering the presence of the letter is another matter entirely. It is simply not possible to leaf through every book looking for items inserted by collectors.

Once the books have been arranged by lots, the next step is to prepare the catalogue. Here many factors come into play. The descriptions should be as accurate as possible and also, unfortunately, as brief as possible to allow for more items and also to hold down the cost of the catalogue. The amount of space that can be devoted to any single entry is extremely limited. Only the most exceptional items are given more than three or four lines at best, and in these few scant lines must appear the author's name, the book's title, and place and date of publication, leaving only perhaps a half a dozen words for anything else.

One area in which the auction catalogues of many a gallery are notoriously deficient is the description of condition. Seldom is more than the slightest reference made to condition, and most of the time no reference is made to it at all, even in cases where a book is literally falling to pieces. Condition apart, most collectible books are fairly standard in their physical appearance, and the catalogues assume that interested collectors and dealers will know fairly well what the book looks like and, therefore, do not spend valuable space on elaborate descriptions. With such unique items as important presentation inscriptions, or interesting letters, it is common practice to quote inscriptions in full, and to quote extensively from letters (especially the letters where content will determine the price), because catalogues must be used as the basis for bidding by out-of-town bidders, who may have no other means of determining content.

The catalogues issued by the three main New York galleries differ considerably in makeup. Swann Galleries' catalogues are straightforward, no-nonsense listings without illustrations, whereas those issued by Sotheby Parke Bernet and Christie's almost always are lavishly illustrated, showing title pages, illustrations, bindings, or significant inscriptions. Consequently, catalogues of the latter two galleries are usually more expensive (though not necessarily more useful). Dealers find that the wisest policy is to subscribe to the season's catalogues. Collectors usually find it of value to purchase singly only those catalogues that contain important items pertinent to their own collections. Such catalogues, annotated with prices fetched at the auction, make a valuable reference tool for future use and might themselves be added to a collector's library.

Both dealers and collectors must learn how to read auction catalogues, as much for what is not said as for what is actually printed on the page. As already noted, very little space is given in a catalogue entry to physical description of an item. This includes an indication of the presence or absence of a dust jacket, of missing plates or illustrations, or of other such important factors of condition. It cannot be assumed that a book is perfect or in fine condition just because there is no statement to the contrary in the catalogue. Any book on which a collector wishes to place a bid should first be personally examined. Viewing books prior to the auction will be discussed more fully later in the chapter.

It is absolutely imperative to read the fine print at the beginning of every catalogue in a section called "Conditions of Sale." These terms, most of which have a legal basis, are fairly standard throughout the trade, and a knowledge of them can save you from possible disputes or unexpected expenses. It is especially important to know that all auction galleries sell each lot "as is." This includes damage that may occur while the lots are on display prior to the sale. Many a purchaser has viewed a book on the opening day of the sale, found the item in perfect condition, and then, when picking up the lot after the sale, is horrified to find that the book has suffered damage during the exhibition.

Try, if at all possible, to have a last look immediately before the sale to see if the lot is still as it was when you first viewed it. This is easy to do in some auction galleries such as at Swann Galleries, New York, where the books remain on the shelves in the salesroom. Sotheby Parke Bernet and Christie's, both of New York and London, however, close the viewing the day before the sale, although it is sometimes possible to arrange in advance to have a last quick look at one specific lot.

The listing of lots in the catalogue is usually done alphabetically in most American galleries, although the main British firms have an irritating way of cataloguing in the order in which the lots reach them from the consignors. Thus, it is necessary to read the entire catalogue from page one right through to the end in order not to miss a possible entry for the author or authors in which you are particularly interested. There seems to be no reason for this other than laziness or unwillingness to go to the trouble of alphabetizing on the part of the galleries. But whether the entries are alphabetized or not, you should read every entry. Of course, it is human nature to dive immediately to possible entries for your own pet enthusiasm, but as soon as you have done this, go back to the beginning and read slowly and carefully. The economic factors forcing auction houses to group minor items into lots may result in books you are particularly interested in being buried in a lot under an unusual or unlikely heading.

Do not forget that *you* are the expert on your author or subject, and although the auction cataloguers know a great deal about books, and usually have extensive reference libraries, they have a limited amount of time at their disposal for research when writing catalogue copy, and also an extremely limited amount of space to devote to detail. Thus it happens with astonishing frequency that extraordinarily desirable titles or copies somehow find their way into a lot of otherwise insignificant or virtually valueless titles.

Once the catalogues have been mailed, the books usually go on public view for three or four days prior to the sale. This is a dangerous time for the books themselves. During the public viewing important books have sometimes either been stolen, or have had laid-in items removed, or simply have been handled carelessly and have been badly damaged. Tender spines have been ripped, dust wrappers have been torn and snagged, and, in general, the books have been subjected to much wear and tear. The auction galleries have been slow to take action in this area, but there has been a heartening trend in the past couple of years to have restricted viewing when the condition of the books is of such a caliber as to warrant exceptional care. All of the major New York galleries have stipulated on more than one occasion that the books are not on open shelves for everyone to handle and can be inspected by appointment only—and then only one book at a time while under the watchful eye of a gallery official. This may seem unfortunate to the potential buyer and sometimes is a time-consuming procedure, but there seems to be no other alternative.

Then, as far as the public knows, the next step is the actual sale in the gallery. However, before the sale takes place, the auction gallery receives mail-order bids from out-of-town clients. These bids are generally recorded in a large book that is then used at the sale for the calling out of the mail-order bids by a gallery assistant in competition with bids from the floor. It is in this area that the possibility of irregularity can arise. Most auctioneers are honest and will try to obtain the lot for the out-of-town client at a figure as low as possible. But it is not unknown for an auctioneer to open the bidding at one notch below the mail-order bid, or even sometimes precisely at the mail-order bid.

The Role of the Book Dealer

In the long run, the employment of a dealer's services in doing your bidding will probably save you a great deal of frustration, lost time, and, quite often, money. Many novices feel that they are paying a dealer his 10 percent fee—the standard fee in the trade—merely for waving his pencil in the air, thereby gaining a fee for little or no effort. This may be true of a fairly standard item that is not open to much variation, especially in the case of many twentieth-century books (as, for instance, a proper first edition of *Lady Chatterley's Lover*, of which the only question is its condition). What most people fail to take into account is the fact that the fee is paid only if the bid is successful. The dealer may spend a great deal of time on your behalf, and if the bids are unsuccessful, you owe him or her nothing, despite the fact that he or she may have spent the better part of two or possibly three days in your service.

First of all, the dealer has probably gone to the trouble of notifying you of the items of interest in your field, often times obtaining photocopies of the pertinent portions of the catalogue. Then, if you give the dealer a bid, he or she will assuredly have to go to the gallery to check the condition and authenticity of the lot or lots in question. Then the dealer will have to attend the auction, during which there may be long stretches between bids that are of no interest to him or her or to you, especially if your particular lots are by an author such as Thomas Wolfe or William Butler Yeats. Then, if successful, the dealer will have to return a third day to pick up the lots and, finally, will have to pack and ship them. So the dealer's 10 percent fee quite often is not even recompense for time spent in your behalf.

The employment of a dealer for bidding will also eliminate to a great degree the possibility that your mail-order bid will be opened at your top figure. And if you have developed a relationship with a dealer, he or she will also know when to exercise judgment in exceeding the limit you have set. He or she can quite often sense when one or more increases over your top figure will secure the book. There is also the factor, not to be overlooked, that when you employ a dealer, particularly in the case of a specialist, you have the advantage of eliminating a possible competitor who would very likely be bidding on an item or group of items for his or her own stock.

There is one veteran New York dealer who quite frankly approaches customers, when an important sale is in the offing, with the question: "Well, am I going to bid *for* you or *against* you?" when soliciting their bids. Dealers also generally have a much broader and deeper knowledge of trade trends and prices than does an individual collector, because they generally attend all important auctions and, as a rule, receive and read carefully the catalogues of their colleagues as well as having the day-to-day experience in their own shops. They thus have a finger on the pulse of the book-collecting field, usually six days a week for their entire lifetime. (Rare book dealers practically never retire. I can think of only one such dealer retiring, and that was for reasons of ill health. Every notable rare book dealer of the twentieth century has literally gone on until his last day—which, I am glad to say, is usually at a very advanced age.) Dealers can thus advise you as to how much you will probably have to pay, as opposed to what a book is actually worth—they are quite often not the same thing at all.

Finally, dealers will know, more often than not, who your competitors are likely to be and, therefore, what the probable chances of getting the lot will be. Every so often a new donor will come into the market anxious to form a collection of a certain kind as a gift to an institution, or, perhaps, the institution itself will have been given a fund to acquire certain types of materials. And while these funds or the particular interest lasts, there is sometimes an unusually inflated demand for certain books or certain authors, and a dealer can advise you when to lay low, so to speak, or when really to go after a certain item. Some items appear so seldom that it may be wise to "go for broke" if you are really convinced of the necessity of owning the title. Or conversely, a title may be common enough and appear with sufficient frequency to warrant biding your time until prices resume a more stable level.

There was an excellent example of this in 1975 when for three succeeding sales, Faulkner prices began doubling and tripling for no apparent reason other than that some fresh and apparently unlimited money came into the market. After a couple of seasons, during which the two avid new collectors had obtained most of the desired titles, prices returned to their former levels.

Finally there is the factor of information. Auction houses are generally willing to answer as many questions as possible. But most auction galleries have a sale of some sort or other every day and book sales with some degree of regularity, and there is an enormous amount of work necessary to prepare the catalogues and the physical aspects of each sale. Therefore, even with the best of will, answers will be brief. The galleries' personnel are not specialists, and although their fund of information may be wide, it is not often very deep, despite their access to a wide variety of reference material. A collector or specialist dealer generally has a much greater knowledge of a given area or author than does the gallery. Your dealer will usually know what specifically to look for and will know, for example, the difference between two somewhat similar weaves of cloth that may determine first or second issues of a particular book; the auction gallery, even if willing, might not be able to make such an identification.

If, after having taken all these factors into consideration, you still feel that you want to do your own bidding, you can of course do so and save yourself the dealer's commission. However, when doing so, you must exercise extreme care and pay attention so that you do not fall into any one of many traps. First of all, you must be sure that you are bidding on the correct lot number. Next, you should determine in advance exactly how much you are willing to pay, with a second figure in mind that you will go to if necessary. Most lots are sold so quickly that you will have no time to hesitate while making up your mind. Another factor that most neophytes fail to realize is that bids are rarely, if ever, called out by the bidder. Each house has its own scale of progression, which is sometimes printed in the catalogue, and sometimes not. Beginners must absolutely acquaint themselves with these figures, because the bidding is usually done by the auctioneer calling the figure and the bidders assenting by a nod or flick of the pencil that they are willing to go to the next higher figure. At certain points, the increments increase, and neophytes may find themselves committed to a bid that has jumped more than they are prepared for.

Although a beginning collector can learn a lot by attending an auction simply as a silent witness, it is inadvisable for the beginner to start acquiring a collection at auction, because auction prices tend to be higher than those at which similar or even identical copies can be had from specialist dealers. The beginning collector is wise to rely on a dealer for advice, especially as to the comparative rarity of an item, and buy at auction only those items that may seldom, or perhaps even never, be seen again.

Bidding

It is sometimes difficult to know who is bidding or, in fact, if anyone is actually bidding. The auctioneer's style of rapid-fire delivery makes it difficult to find out where the bidder is seated, for sometimes a lot can be opened and knocked down within 30 seconds or a minute or two at the longest. A good auctioneer will run through perhaps a hundred lots in an hour, and so there is no time for soul-searching or to see who is bidding against you. Many dealers and experienced bidders do not like it to be known that they are bidding and adopt unusual signals that are prearranged with the auctioneer. One book dealer, the late Lew Feldman, of the House of El Dieff, who always sat in the last row of the gallery, seemingly was not bidding, despite repeated lots being knocked down to him. After many years of careful observation, his technique was discovered to be the simple one of placing his glasses not on his nose, but at the top of his head, as many people do who use them only for reading. Then, when he wanted to raise a bid, he knitted his eyebrows, causing a very slight upward motion of the glasses.

The rapid-fire bidding slows down when the bidding reaches a high level and the contest has narrowed down to two bidders. Then the auctioneer is patient, and often cajoling, and at the last, will sometimes offer the underbidder an increase of half the usual escalation in order to extract another increment.

Of course, it is possible for bidding to be artificial in order to create a new price level. This probably happens more often in the art world than in the book world, but it is not unknown for a dealer to bid up items which he himself has placed for auction. Of course, this is improper, but it is easy to have a friend do the actual bidding. It is also, of course, somewhat risky for the dealer, since he may end up buying back his own merchandise. It is also possible for an unscrupulous dealer who has a bid from a client to have a confederate in the room to bid against him until the bidding level has nearly reached the customer's limit, in order to increase the amount of the commission gained thereby. However such practices are rare indeed, and certainly not indulged in by dealers who value their reputations.

Once the hammer has fallen, the lot becomes your property in a legal sense, and anything that happens to it is not the gallery's responsibility. You will be required to pay for it within three days if you have not established credit with the gallery. Especially in the case of books, it is advisable to remove them as soon as possible, because in the hurly-burly of a large gallery, books can be easily lost or mixed into the wrong lot. Many larger galleries, such as Sotheby Parke Bernet, Christie's, and others, have the delivery rooms separate from the gallery itself, and you can pay for and receive the books while the sale is still in progress. In smaller galleries you must either wait until the conclusion of the sale or, in some cases, the next day.

Some Great Sales of the Past

Notable auctions do not happen very often, due primarily to the relative scarcity of large blocks of prime material being disposed of at any one time.

One of the most spectacular American auctions was the Robert Hoe sale in New York, beginning in April 1911. The Hoe library was one of the finest and most diversified private libraries in the world, containing more than 250 illuminated manuscripts and over 150 incunabula, including the first printed editions of Homer and Euclid, the first book ever printed in Greek, two copies of the Gutenberg Bible, and four works from the press of England's first printer, William Caxton. And as if these treasures were not enough for one library, the Hoe collection also contained the four folios of Shakespeare and the first book printed in the Western Hemisphere, a theological treatise printed in Mexico City fully 100 years before the Bay Psalm Book. All together, 14,588 rare items were sold at auction, bringing in a record total of $1,932,000. It was not only the American price record of all time up to that point, but it exceeded the combined receipts of the four most valuable libraries ever sold in England until then and was not surpassed by any American book auction until the Thomas Winthrop Streeter sale, which brought in a total of $3,104,982.50 in 22 sessions held between October 1966 and October 1969.

Usually, if there is a high concentration in a particular field or a particular author, the auction frequently sets new price levels, although this has not always been the case. A notable sale of the 1920s was the Quinn sale, which broke up the famous collection of John Quinn, a New York lawyer and friend and patron of a great number of artists and writers of the early part of the century. His taste and foresight were impeccable. His collections, both of paintings and twentieth-century literature, were sold at auction in several sessions from November 1923 through March 1924. Despite the fact that his collection contained a superb run of authors now in the forefront of collectibility, the time was not ripe. The sale was a financial disaster for Quinn, but a boon for knowledgeable buyers. In addition to superb copies of books, Quinn, who had generously supported struggling writers (particularly Joyce and Eliot), had been given, as tokens of their appreciation for his support, the original manuscripts of *The Waste Land* and *Ulysses*, certainly two of the major landmarks of English literature in the twentieth century. The *Ulysses* manuscript was included in the sale, but fetched only $1,975, a figure so low that an outraged Joyce tried to buy it back from the purchaser, Dr. A. S. W. Rosenbach, who cannily refused.

Another landmark sale occurred early in 1929 when Jerome Kern sold at auction his collection of British literature, primarily sixteenth-, seventeenth-, and eighteenth-century high spots. The prices fetched set record highs, some of which have still not been surpassed. The timing of this sale was the important factor in the high prices. Certainly neither the auction gallery nor Kern could have foreseen how razor sharp their timing was to be, for the sale was held in January 1929, less than a year before the stock market crash. The sale is still referred to both for the quality of most of the books and for the record prices fetched.

It was a long, long time, however, before the economy revived sufficiently for other landmark sales to be held. By the time the world had recovered from the Depression, it was plunged into World War II, during which it was not propitious to dispose of important libraries.

However, things began to turn upward in the late 1950s. One of the important sales that created a lasting effect on the rare book market was the Guffey sale of October 1958, when the extensive and important Hemingway collection of Dr. Don Carlos Guffey was sold. Dr. Guffey, who had been Hemingway's personal physician for many years, owned what was perhaps the finest Hemingway collection ever formed, with extensive presentation inscriptions of every book as well as important letters and at least one major manuscript, *Death in the Afternoon*. Until this point, prices for Hemingway's books had been nominal, including even the scarce first two titles. However, this sale, with its wealth of material, attracted heavy competition. Overnight, Hemingway prices catapulted and he became a top figure to collect. Strangely enough, it took Faulkner several more years to reach the Hemingway price levels, and only after two or three auctions in rapid succession with sizable groups of Faulkner titles to peg their prices at their present high levels.

In the 1960s, the Thomas Winthrop Streeter sale dispersed the largest private collection of Americana ever formed. Prices once again soared and, in fact, made twentieth-century literary first editions look like pretty small potatoes. Even today, over a decade later, this is the sale by which prices are still gauged. And complete sets of the Streeter sale catalogue now change hands at several hundred dollars.

In 1975 another fine collection was dispersed in two successive sales when the William Stockhausen collection was offered. This was a collection of high spots of English and American literature, plus a major collection of Robert Frost. The prices once again set new levels, and many items were offered that will probably never again see the open market—items such as Poe's *Tamerlane*, a superb run of Melville firsts, and all of Jane

Austen in the original boards (early nineteenth-century novels virtually do not exist in original bindings—it was the custom to have books rebound in one's own library style).

Anyone interested in the history of American book auctions is referred to Clarence S. Brigham's "History of Book Auctions in America," in *American Book Auction Catalogues, 1713–1934*, by George L. McKay (New York Public Library, 1937; Detroit: Gale, 1967), as well as to Wesley Towner's *The Elegant Auctioneers* (New York: Hill and Wang, 1970). Lively accounts of the New York auction scene can be found in Edwin Wolf, 2nd, and John F. Fleming's *Rosenbach, A Biography* (New York: World, 1960).

Another major collection has just begun to be dispersed in what will probably be five sessions, spread over nearly two years, so strong is the collection in important items. This is the Goodwin sale, breaking up the collection of Jonathan Goodwin, whose prime interest has been in American literature of the 1920s and 1930s and in a few English authors. His holdings of important first books and complete runs of periodicals is probably unmatched in any other private collection. His is probably the only collection ever to have in it both the first books of Ezra Pound and William Carlos Williams. Pound's first, *A Lume Spento* (Venice, 1908), has survived in only 26 located copies, of which this was one of seven still in private hands. Williams' *Poems* (Rutherford, N.J., 1909) is even rarer. Only 12 copies are known, of which just two are in private collections. At the first session of the Goodwin sale, held on March 29, 1977, *A Lume Spento* brought $18,000, the highest price ever recorded for a modern American book, and Williams's *Poems* provided a close second at $16,000.

The catalogue was in itself an important literary item, printing in full a great many early letters of Hemingway to his family. Dealers and university librarians girded their loins for what proved to be some of the most fiercely contested sales of the generation. New prices were set. In fact, dealers were so sure of this that prior to the first session, several of them delayed their own catalogues until after the sale in order to know just where to set prices. Several universities held off decisions on major manuscript or archive acquisitions until after the sale in order to see whether they had spent all their money at the Goodwin sale or whether they were going to be disappointed underbidders with sums of money unspent, which they could then use elsewhere. In other words, auctions not only set prices, they can also sometimes control elements of the economy of the rare book world.

Prices

There is a widespread misconception among a great many collectors and some part-time dealers as regards prices at auctions. Every dealer in rare books repeatedly has the experience of making a legitimate and fair offer on a book, only to have the would-be vendor say: "But it brought ten times that at auction." Now it may very well be true that a certain copy fetched ten times the price offered by the dealer for the copy in hand. But what is usually not recorded in *American Book Prices Current*, the source of most such information, is any detail regarding unusually fine condition or even possible variants that may have accounted for the high price. These recorded prices must be carefully interpreted to distinguish between ultrasuperior copies as against copies that are cripples, and the like. There is even the possibility that a particular book happened to be wanted at that particular time by two ardent collectors who bid each other up to unusual heights and that a second copy, even if offered at the very next sale, would not fetch anywhere near the record price of the first one.

There is also the possibility that there was some important point that the bidders had spotted but that was not recorded in the catalogue. The time at which the price was obtained must also be noted. There are cycles of fashion in books that can also cause unusually high prices that may not pertain even a year or so later. It is also not uncommon that there are quite often "grudge fights" even within the dignified arena of the posh auction galleries, where one bidder or one dealer will mutter under his breath, "I'll be damned if I'll let him get it at that price," and will run the price up out of spite, with little or no reference to the actual value of the lot. It is a risky game, but one indulged in with some frequency.

And sometimes a dealer will exceed the maximum amount given to him by a customer. Dealers who are clever and know their customers can usually judge whether or not they are taking an unwarranted risk, for, legally, clients do not have to accept the lot if their authorization has been exceeded. There was a famous example of this in 1947, when a Bay

Psalm Book, the earliest work printed in the United States known to be extant, came up for auction and Dr. A. S. W. Rosenbach exceeded his authorization considerably when acquiring this gem, of which only a handful of copies exist, for his client, Yale University. Dr. Rosenbach himself made up the difference, but it caused a considerable speculation as to the proper price range for this book.

From a seller's point of view, the disposal of books by auction usually represents the only means of obtaining the highest possible price for the books at any given moment. Or so it would seem on the surface. It is, unfortunately, not always true, and there is practically no way of being sure. A combination of unpredictable circumstances can alter the course or the volume of the bidding at an entire sale, and the seller is many times left, in the final accounting, with less than he or she might have got from a reputable specialist dealer.

Auctioneers, dealers, and book collectors alike rely heavily on annual compilations of book auction records. Of these, the best is *American Book Prices Current (ABPC)*, begun in 1895 and now edited by Katharine Leab. *ABPC* lists prices fetched for books and manuscripts at major auctions in the United States and abroad (the *American* in the title is a misnomer). Both the annual volumes and the five-year cumulations of *ABPC* are necessarily expensive—they are large books. But all major dealers and a great many public and academic libraries own long runs of *ABPC*, and usually it is not difficult to get access to a set.

Selling Books at Auction

Let us now consider the facts that govern matters from the seller's point of view. First of all, once the gallery's representatives have decided that the collection of books is interesting and/or valuable enough for them to want to handle, a long, slow process begins. It usually takes anywhere from eight to ten months, and sometimes longer, to dispose of books by auction. No matter when your collection is taken by the auction gallery, it can seldom be scheduled for a sale for at least six months. The galleries are quite literally "booked" well in advance, sometimes as far into the future as the scheduling of the major opera houses. If you give your books to a major gallery at the beginning of the year, in January or February, the earliest sale date you can hope for is perhaps October or November. And if it is a sizable collection, necessitating more than one day, it will probably be spread over a period of several months, or even a year or more.

This spread of dates is due in part to the gallery's need to accommodate other clients as well as for the obvious financial reason of the inadvisability of putting too much material of a similar caliber or nature onto the market in too short a time for the potential buyers to be able to absorb it all at once. Thus, sales of major collections, such as the Streeter sale of Americana or the Goodwin sale of twentieth-century literature, have to be spread over a long period of time. And once the sale has been held, payment to you by the gallery will generally be 60 to 90 days later, because the clients usually have 30 days in which to pay the gallery, and their settlement is not made to you in turn until all items have been paid for by the bidders. Thus, it is usually *at least a year* after books are consigned to a gallery before any monies are realized from an auction. This time lag is a factor that must be taken into account by any prospective vendor or estate. If financial necessity is the reason for selling a collection, the auction method may be too slow.

The auction house is, of course, just as interested as the vendor in obtaining the highest bids, because its fees are based on a percentage of the prices realized. Most galleries have a sliding scale, taking a proportionately smaller percentage as the dollar volume increases. Standard commissions range from a minimum of 25 percent of the first $1,000 to 12½ percent in excess of $15,000. This is on each lot, not on the cumulative total of the sale. However, in the case of an exceptional item or even an exceptional collection, special terms are often arranged between the auctioneer and the seller.

There are also other charges, notably insurance during the collection's stay at the gallery until the hammer falls. A second charge that will often be made against the vendor's account will be for photographs in the catalogue. The actual cost of the printing and preparation of the catalogue is borne by the gallery, but illustrations may have to be paid for out of the vendor's receipts, and, ironically, it is the gallery that decides which items to illustrate. However, because only the major, high-yield items are illustrated, the photo charge is usually only a few dollars at most and generally is on an item that should fetch at least $1,000 or more.

In recent years English and American catalogues have followed European leads by providing estimates for the guidance of bidders. The estimates are always in a range. If (for example) the signed limited edition of Hemingway's *A Farewell to Arms* is being offered, the house estimate will probably be $500/700. At the sale, the auctioneer would generally open the bidding on an item at 40 percent of the low figure of the estimate. Thus in the Hemingway example, bidding would probably be started at $200. Then it would go up in increments of $25. Most galleries have standard increments. At Swann Galleries, for instance, where there are more medium-priced lots than at Sotheby Parke Bernet, prices move at $1 increments up to $20, then by $2.50 increments to $50. At Sotheby Parke Bernet the range goes by $5 or $10 (depending on the individual auctioneer) until $200 is reached; thereafter it jumps by $25 until $500; and then by $50 until $1,000, after which it jumps by $100 increments.

One factor about which there is much confusion and misinformation is the business of reserves. A reserve is simply a minimum price below which the lot will not be sold. A reserve is placed, not to force bidding up to unusual levels, but (as Sotheby Parke Bernet puts it) "to provide a safety net to prevent a valuable property from going at a ridiculously low level." This reserve is generally placed at 75 percent of the house's low estimate.

For example, if a book that the gallery thinks should bring $500 is being offered, the owner may wish to place a reserve on it to prevent a fluke whereby it might attract only one bid with no competition, say $50 or $100. It would be patently foolish to let a book that valuable go for a pittance merely because for some unaccountable reason nobody was bidding. This happened one time at Sotheby Parke Bernet a few years ago when a complete collection of the modern poet Charles Bukowski was offered in one lot, worth somewhere between $1,000 and $1,200. Only a handful of dealers are interested in ultramoderns, and of the five present in the gallery, one had fallen asleep and was snoring quietly; a second one had lost track of what lot number was being offered and was one lot number behind; a third had actually consigned the lot for sale and, therefore, could not legally bid on it; and a fourth dealer was running a fever and didn't want to be bothered with the problem of removal. So the lot went to the lucky fifth dealer, who opened the bidding at $100, and obtained it without competition at that price, because no reserve had been put on it. The consignor could, and should, have put a reserve on it, below which it could not have been sold. Such buy-backs on the owner's behalf are not announced as such in the gallery, but are concealed from public knowledge by the auctioneers declaring, "sold to order," which is the phrase that covers all mail-order bids or out-of-town bids executed on the customer's behalf by the gallery itself.

In the event that the bidding does not reach the reserve, the vendor is charged a nominal 5 percent of the reserve as the gallery's fee, rather than the full fee had the item sold on the floor. In the book world very few lots fail to reach the reserve, in contrast to sales in recent years of modern paintings in which on occasion, one-third to one-half of the consigned items go back to the owners.

Book auctions have been held continuously in the United States since the latter part of the seventeenth century, only a few decades after the landing of the Pilgrims, being one of the institutions imported from England at a very early date. Despite perils and pitfalls, they continue with unabated popularity and seem to be drawing a larger and more widespread amount of bidding then ever before. A good sale is not only a chance to acquire rarities, but it has become, at least in New York and London, an important social event. Every dealer of any importance attends, if only to record prices, meet with colleagues and, not least of all, to let himself or herself be seen participating in the tribal ritual. The auction seems likely to be with us as long as book collecting lasts, being woven so deeply into the fabric of the field that it is difficult to imagine collecting books without the periodic thrill that a really good sale will give.

Auction Houses

The following list contains the names and addresses of the major auctioneers handling books of interest to collectors.

California Book Auction Co., 224 McAllister St., San Francisco, Calif. 94102

Christie, Manson & Woods International, Inc. ("Christie's"), 8 King St., St. James's, London SW1, England

Christie, Manson & Woods International, Inc. ("Christie's"), 502 Park Ave., New York, N.Y. 10022

Samuel T. Freeman & Co., 1080 Chestnut St., Philadelphia, Pa. 19103

Charles Hamilton Autographs, Inc., 25 East 77 St., New York, N.Y. 10021

Hanzel Galleries, Inc., 1120 South Michigan Ave., Chicago, Ill. 60605

Harris Auction Galleries, Inc., 873/75 North Howard St., Baltimore, Md. 21201

Huntington-Mann Book Auction Gallery, 467 Alvarado St., Suite 35, Monterey, Calif. 93940

Montreal Book Auctions, 750 Sherbrooke St. West, Montreal, PQ, Canada

Phillips Son & Neale, Blenstock House, 7 Blenheim St., New Bond St., London, W1, England

Plandome Book Auctions, 113 Glen Head Rd., Glen Head, N.Y. 11545

Sotheby Parke Bernet & Co., 34 & 35 New Bond St., London, W1A 2AA, England

Sotheby Parke Bernet, Inc., 980 Madison Ave., New York, N.Y. 10021

Sotheby Parke Bernet—Los Angeles, 7660 Beverly Blvd., Los Angeles, Calif. 90036

Swann Galleries, Inc., 104 East 25 St., New York, N.Y. 10010

4

The Antiquarian Book Market

Robert Rosenthal

THE ANTIQUARIAN BOOKSELLER and the auctioneer are engaged in selling, the collector in buying: Together they form the antiquarian book market. This simple statement belies a rich and complex process that is at once as much cultural as it is economic. Such a mixture is not without contradictions. It allows for great industry as well as for consummate connoisseurship, and for as many gradations in between as could be wished. In fact, antiquarian bookselling thrives on the idiosyncratic and personal character of its participants. The central position of the book imposes intellectual, aesthetic, and emotional values that somehow must be balanced with economic interests. But whatever generalizations can be made about the antiquarian trade, one can be sure that they will be quickly contradicted by the experience of the individual bookseller.

Some Characteristics of the Antiquarian Book

The antiquarian book market would not exist unless old books had some desirable quality. Such quality is usually associated with the desirability of the book's text, binding, illustrations, decorative elements, and its prior history. Desirability is the key stimulus within the market as the seller attempts to identify and locate books having such qualities that will gratify the desires of potential buyers. The collector of antiquarian books will usually define his or her desires as one of the above elements, or a combination of them. Each element has its own rich history as it has its vogues.

Although content of the physical object is the prime characteristic of the antiquarian book, there are other factors that influence its desirability and economic life. As a historical object, an antiquarian book carries with it an aura of age, a reminder of something worthy in the past be it a classic or famous text, an account of a momentous event, the reflections of a great mind, or the description of some unique activity or milestone. In this sense, the antiquarian book assumes an evocative, symbolic value that transcends its content. When an aura exists, it makes no difference whether the book is read or not (though the potential is always there). This attitude toward the book can be dismissed by the more practical or content-oriented person, but such a view belies the traditional view of the book as a "sacred" and precious object. The idea of possessing a transcendent, emotionally charged book can be a compelling one.

An antiquarian book can also be ubiquitous because copies of it can be found in different places and under a great variety of circumstances. It can be moved from place to place with relative ease. Books tend to spread across literate societies, accumulating in cosmopolitan centers; such centers have become the principal sources for antiquarian books although they may also be "fortuitously" found in unlikely contexts and circumstances.

The one sure thing that can be said about any old book is that there will be no more of it. Although books tend to be produced in relatively large numbers, that number is finite. Although reproductions may be adequate for many needs, such copies are not genuine. Because the number of "genuine" copies is absolutely limited, antiquarian books inevitably become scarce as they succumb to destruction or are removed from the market. The probing and, to some extent, the projecting of scarcity is a function of the market and one of the joys of collecting. The degree of known scarcity (or rarity), however, is inexact except in a few possible cases where the original production is known and the subsequent history of each copy is documented. Scarcity is inferred from a combination of historical and current market information. As time goes on there will be fewer old books coming onto the market, though it is also true, of course, that as time goes on more books will become old. What part of today's production will become desirable in the future is a matter of conjectures, but the fact remains that the body of potentially available books printed before 1800 is diminishing by various degrees of rapidity, with diminution also increasing for nineteenth-century books. The rate of diminution, and therefore scarcity, depends on many complex factors—the general state of the economy, changing tastes and interests, the supply, and the development of new collectors, among others. It is difficult to believe that there may be a time when the desire to possess old books will not exist, although it is easier to perceive a time when there will be only a few desirable books available to be collected.

Although scarcity is an inexorable force, another condition attached to antiquarian books affects the way the market reacts to them. This might be called their "nonsingularity." Because multiple, genuine copies exist, the antiquarian book is unlike a painting or similar work of art that has a singular or sole existence. As part of a book's nonsingularity, it can be valued simultaneously for a variety of different reasons in different places. Thus the same physical object may be desirable for many different reasons. One of the functions of the market is to sort out the reasons and to adjust the book's location to the demands of the market.

As a physical object the book is subject to easy alteration. Past neglect or the wish to have the book conform physically to changing tastes can change its aspect and diminish its desirability and, consequently, its market value. There are good reasons for wanting a book in the best physical condition and as close to its original condition as possible. Obvious reasons are ease of handling and completeness. An original or contemporary binding is not only harmonious historically, it can also offer some assurance, though not absolute, that the copy has not been tampered with. The binding may also offer evidence of the copy's history. Condition becomes a premium in the market when copies exist in various physical states.

The antiquarian book is also affected by new knowledge. During the present century, powerful bibliographical techniques have been developed to examine the printing process and its effect on the transmission of the text. From these techniques we have gained a new understanding of priorities that exist for the printed text. Because priority often is linked to desirability by the collector, the market usually adjusts to changes in bibliographical knowledge, adapting them to its own devices in due course.

The foregoing suggests that an antiquarian book is seen as both a physical object and an idea. Its physical attributes may be defined, but these are elusive because of the large number of different books that exist. As an idea, the possibilities that exist for the collecting of old books seem infinite. In its own way, the antiquarian market attempts to grapple with both.

The Nature of Book Buying

The prime requisite for antiquarian book purchasing is a purse the size of which will determine the particular books a buyer might acquire. The antiquarian market as a whole offers a considerable price range though an individual price may not coincide with the buyer's interests or ability to pay. The potential buyer may forego one price for a book and seek another copy elsewhere, but this is done at the cost of time and effort. There is also the risk that the price may rise or that the opportunity to acquire the book may be permanently lost. The chances of paying less in the future seem to be quickly diminishing, given the constant removal of antiquarian books from the market. The only way a collector can avoid the increasing cost is to collect in the softer parts of the market, that is, where the price of books is more or less stable or, more challengingly, where the desirability of the books has yet to be recognized. This view not only applies to the desirability of the content but also relates to purchasing books in different geographical markets where the demand is less.

Because no standard method of pricing books exists, each price being fixed by the individual seller, there is always an implicit questioning of price. But questioning is one matter and acceptance is another, and this is what the buyer must decide. Perhaps a more delicate way of approaching the matter of price is to ask if it is appropriate, but this implies considerable understanding by the buyer. The buyer who understands the various factors that affect the price will know that a high price is not necessarily a bad price and, conversely, that a low price need not be a good one.

Supported with a purse and with a willingness to pay, buyers can prepare themselves for participation in the market in a number of ways. First, they should have some objective in the form of books in mind. Because the market requires some exploration for the possibilities that exist within it, the objective need not be closely defined, at least at the beginning. It can be assumed that an objective may be refined or altered to fit the changing views of the buyer and the conditions encountered in the market. Whether one pursues books from either a restricted or an open view, it is necessary to articulate each acquisition as part of the objective or goal. Otherwise the purchase of books can deteriorate into their mere accumulation. The worthiness of a collection can be related as much to the integrity and imagination with which it was created as it can to its cost.

Purposeful collectors will then have to know the sources that are most likely to satisfy their needs. This will be a matter of trial and error. Eventually collectors may choose to ally themselves with one dealer or a small group of dealers, but this will depend again on the nature of the objective and on personal inclinations. Aside from the commercial side of the market, books and their values have an ability to foster long and satisfying collector-dealer friendships. In fact, the economic aspects can become incidental.

The Antiquarian Book Trade

The antiquarian book trade differs from the trade in new books by limiting itself to books published in the past that are no longer available from the publisher. The potential number of books is therefore vast and incalculable. The age of a book is primarily one of degree, though the trade also sees a book as a matter of kind with the consequence that dealers in old books have assumed different titles reflecting both the age and kind of book dealt with. They conduct business under such names as antiquarian bookseller, rare book dealer, dealer in fine books, secondhand dealer, and used bookseller. One generally can assume that secondhand or used booksellers will be dealing with out-of-print books of recent vintage and that their stock will contain books of relatively modest cost, although occasionally older and possibly more costly books can be found in it. Such a stock may contain books that sometime in the future will be less common and more expensive. The antiquarian or rare book dealer, on the other hand, emphasizes books of greater antiquity or books having a recognizable distinctiveness. It might also be said that in recent years the antiquarian or rare book stock has tended to become more specialized, whereas the secondhand stock remains essentially undifferentiated. There are, however, various specializations among secondhand dealers.

But such attempts at categorization are not absolute and can defy the individual dealer's own image of his or her place in the trade. Books can flow from one class of dealer to another, and when they do the perceptions of the books are refined. The book itself, of course, remains the same.

GENERAL FUNCTIONS OF THE ANTIQUARIAN BOOKSELLER

In the process of selling antiquarian books, the bookseller performs three basic functions. The first of these is the identification of desirable books that the bookseller believes will be salable. The identification of such books requires a degree of expertise and information regarding both availability and demand. The source of this knowledge is the general body of bibliographical and other writings that are also available to the buyer of books, but, more than likely, the bookseller's knowledge comes from an experience of firsthand relationships with many books and from dealing in the market. In order to identify and locate marketable books, booksellers must travel to where they think antiquarian books are located or they must have the ability to attract such books. The books may already be in the market as part of the stock of another bookseller, or they may be off the market in the possession of some individual or repository willing to sell them. The ultimate objective of identification is a sale. Thus dealers may often pass up salable books, but they are usually books that *they* cannot sell, or books that are simply not worth their investment or risk. The prospect of profit is closely linked to identification, the profit being immediately apparent or dependent on subsequent research. The ability to identify salable books is of fundamental importance because only by doing so consistently can a dealer expect to maintain a viable place in the market.

Once a salable book has been identified, the dealer must decide whether to risk capital to secure it for stock. In essence, the stock is the embodiment of the dealer's knowledge, taste, and business acumen. He or she must give it space, and must control and service it. Some dealers prefer to maintain relatively small stocks with the expectancy of a lower turnover and overhead. Some, especially fledgling booksellers, have small stocks because of limited capital or because they stay close to a sharply defined stock. Extraordinarily large stocks may require warehousing. Access to the stock is obviously important, but the individual bookseller will manipulate it to suit his or her purposes. Some may prefer to seclude all or part of it from prospective purchasers, giving access through bibliographical descriptions or personally controlled circumstances. Many one-person firms give access only on appointment and use quotations and catalogues for presenting the stock to prospective buyers.

If the dealer has the stock, the final step in the marketing cycle is selling. The selling of books is often an extension of the dealer's personality, although it has been said that good books sell themselves. It has also been said that every antiquarian book has a buyer and that the sales talent involved is simply a matter of bringing the right book and the right buyer together. With this in mind, many dealers attempt merely to cultivate and attract potential buyers and allow the book to sell itself. In a similar manner, when dealers have customers of known interests and purse, they will merely *present* the likely candidate for purchase. Most dealers try to establish a more or less steady group of customers that yields greater satisfaction for the dealer while diminishing risk. Some dealers allow their reputation to do their selling, at least in bringing potential buyers to the door, while others must be more openly aggressive in reaching potential customers. Although there can be exceptions, normally the selling of antiquarian books is a polite and thoughtful exchange with deference and appreciation shown on both sides. Although booksellers are naturally interested in developing new customers, it is usually not done at the expense of secure, loyal relationships with regular buyers. Booksellers will sell directly from stock, by personally presenting individual books to likely purchasers, and by the issuance of periodic catalogues listing a part of their stock. Booksellers' catalogues not only serve as a sales medium but also as advertisement, keeping the dealer's name and reputation alive in the marketplace.

Although booksellers will have individual preferences, most must participate in all operations of business including its more mundane aspects. Antiquarian book firms rarely grow in size to more than a half dozen or so individuals, though some are large enough to require a formal division of labor. But whatever the size of the firm, the bookseller is acutely aware of maintaining a rhythm and balance between the various operations or functions. This need for personal control may be determined by economic necessity, but more often it is a matter of personal preference with the consequence that most firms remain small and run on an intimate, personal basis. They often remain individual or family affairs or a two-person organization that relies on temporary or part-time help for clerical assistance or to cope with special projects.

SOME GENERAL CHARACTERISTICS OF THE TRADE

Although the conduct of their business will be revealing of the character of individual booksellers, there are some general characteristics of the trade that are worth comment. The highly personal and idiosyncratic nature of each bookseller is apparent. Few are less than dedicated to their work and many see it as a not unpleasant calling rather than a simple way of making money. The effort is not without its pressures but allows for relative independence and individuality. Although booksellers may take pride in their individual distinctiveness, the nature of the trade also compels a strong sense of community. Books impose a certain like-mindedness because booksellers see their colleagues as potential sources of books and information. Booksellers usually respect one another, at least in their more public opinions, and rivalry is kept at a polite distance. When relationships become strained, it is usually over some breach of etiquette or sharp practice that deviates from the easy conventions that govern the trade. Inevitably, a few less than scrupulous booksellers appear, but such booksellers become quickly known and isolated by the main part of the trade. One reason for this is the rapidity with which information moves within the trade. The trade has its journals where formal news and information is transmitted, but because of the close association of booksellers, gossip travels quickly. The grapevine also acts as an important conductor of market news, especially concerning availability, needs, and prices. For a highly specialized trade, the vocabulary of bookselling is remarkably free of jargon. Much of its technical language comes from descriptive and historical bibliography, although this language may not be used with the precision of specialists in those fields. Perhaps the least precise part of the vocabulary relates to the description of the physical condition of books. The majority of booksellers are conscientious about describing physical condition especially when it has a noticeable effect on pricing, but such words as "mint," "fine," "good," "satisfactory," "as usually found" allow for some interpretation that may not be in the buyer's mind. The bookseller usually adjusts to this by permitting the return of books not in condition acceptable to the purchaser.

Types of Booksellers

Although booksellers may be typed by how well they conduct their business, by the size of their staff, by the extent and composition of their stock, and by the legal structure of their business, they may still resist classification. The strong instinctual qualities that accompany personal bookselling create different, less easy to define categories. Because the business is so personal, considerable vanity is displayed by some booksellers, especially as it applies to their stock. A prominent reputation can act as a stimulus to business, and it is something to be protected. Self-regard may manifest itself in the location and decor of the place of business, the format and presentation of catalogues, as well as with demeanor with customers. Although some dealers may show signs of being preoccupied with their image, others prefer to work away from the spotlight. The reputation of a bookseller may be localized geographically or may achieve national and international recognition; it can also depend on the dealer's specialization. There is a class of innovative booksellers who thrive on discovering new facts about a book or by presenting a book in an unusual light. Such booksellers tend to generate *new* antiquarian books although most booksellers follow basic patterns of marketing in established and quickly recognizable books. Two further classes of booksellers should be recognized: the old and the young, and the specialized and the general.

Formal training for the antiquarian book trade does not exist in the United States. Most entrants arrive at the trade through a thorough interest in books. Some find the prospect of selling antiquarian books attractive while pursuing academic studies. A collector or a librarian will sometimes cross to the selling side of the market. Some will begin selling new books, while some find themselves working for antiquarian booksellers through family connections or sheer chance. Young booksellers usually spend some years in apprenticeship learning the ropes; this ends when they believe they have sufficient capital and contacts along with some initial stock. There are no hard and fast rules on beginning, and often beginners will start while having another occupation. Experience is a prime requisite; the problem is getting it. There seems to be little or no antagonism between the old and the young because new antiquarian booksellers are usually taken as a sign of vitality within the trade. Although young booksellers' efforts are directed to establishing themselves, the older ones, as they reach the age of retirement (which often only comes with death), face the problem of regeneration. Most antiquarian firms die with the founder unless there are children who are attracted to the trade. Some family firms survive for generations, whereas others may go on for a period in name only because it is very difficult to transfer the strong personal imprint that a bookseller makes on his or her business.

Specialization has become increasingly prevalent in recent years, though firms having general stock can also be known for their specialties. For new dealers aiming at the prevailing currents in the market, specialization is a relatively quick way to establish themselves and to limit initial overhead costs because of the concentrated stock. It normally is linked to some subject—English literature, fine printing, architecture, technology, illustrated books, and so forth—that can be conceived in broad or narrow terms. Within the above examples, specialization may be confined to a particular time and place as well as genre. Although specialization has the advantage of bringing similar books together in the marketplace, the potential buyer should also be wary because books, like booksellers, tend to defy rigid definition and may be found in various specialized stocks. From the dealer's point of view the content of a specialized stock is more a matter of exclusion rather than adherence to strict terminology. It might be best to say that specialized dealers attempt to maintain a focus within their stock that expands and contracts according to circumstance.

THE BOOK TRADE AND ITS SOURCES

In the recent market, where demand for the ever-diminishing supply has increased, the locating of salable books has been the foremost task for the bookseller. Although the acquisition splurge of libraries has slackened, there are now more new collectors in the market. The new wave of collectors might simply be attributed to the presence of a new generation of collectors who would have supplanted the old as a matter of course. The demand is also the result of new markets linked to the expansion of higher education in foreign countries. Another factor is the more rapid diminution of the supply of other historically and aesthetically pleasing objects such as paintings and prints that has turned such collectors to books. And there is no doubt that antiquarian books more than ever are being seen as good financial investments.

To satisfy this demand, antiquarian dealers can look for their supply outside and inside the trade. The principal source outside the trade are collectors who wish to dispose of their books. The sale of duplicates from libraries also helps to replenish the market. Booksellers, of course, vie with each other for books from those sources, although when a collection has been created in collaboration with a bookseller there is some expectancy that he or she will have the first opportunity to repurchase.

Most dealers advertise a willingness to purchase books and collections. Such public solicitation is part of the appraisal process that can lead to referral to a more appropriate dealer. When a book is ready to be purchased by a dealer, the issue of a mutually agreeable price must be faced. This may not be a problem with the serious collector who is aware of market prices, but the unsophisticated owner of antiquarian books can be ignorant of prices and how they are set. Both the dealer and the seller have recourse to the auction records, but these require both insight and interpretation. If the seller does not have a price in mind, the dealer will usually make an offer; however, the dealer is chary of the person who moves from dealer to dealer in hopes of extracting the highest possible price. If the owner of books has no intention to sell, at least immediately, he or she can ask a dealer to make a formal appraisal for a fee. Auction houses and professional appraisers who specialize in antiquarian books are also available to render this service.

Within the antiquarian trade a dealer has two sources of supply: other dealers and the various auction houses. Some dealers rely heavily on these two sources, while others will use one or the other or both only occasionally. Very often it depends on prevailing conditions in the market and the particular books involved. In highly competitive fields that have strong demand, it is difficult for a dealer to purchase from another dealer with more than a nominal profit in mind. The geographical distribution of the book trade also contributes to dealer-to-dealer sales as books are sold from place to place to satisfy localized demand. Throughout this attempt to bring equilibrium to supply and demand, a process of refinement is taking place with a concomitant rise in price.

The auction has been a traditional and convenient method of bringing supply and demand together, but it accounts for a small proportion of antiquarian books sold in any given period. Because auctions have the ability to stimulate competition they can be attractive for the disposal of books in great demand. They are also useful for the quick disposal of books of indeterminate market value. Because an auction can bring together all gradations on the demand side of the market, it can be a perilous place for the uninitiated and even then it has its risks. It is usually left to dealers to act on commission for buyers or to participate directly when buying for stock. Aside from the movement of books, the auction is useful for gauging the mood of the market and for spotting new trends. Important auction sales are festive occasions that can be seen as contests and a celebration of the vitality of the trade.

Book fairs are another traditional marketing device that has been revived in the past decade. Sponsored by a body of antiquarian booksellers and held periodically, they can be aimed at international, national, or local participation. Booksellers converge for two or three days to display a representative part of their stock with the immediate result of intense buying and selling among the dealers. The atmosphere of most fairs is frenetic, as dealers also attempt to serve both old and new customers. Fairs have become a method of attracting both old and new collectors who are given the convenience of inspecting selections from wide-ranging stocks. For the fledgling collector a book fair can be a quick introduction to a cross section of the book trade.

Although books in demand can move quickly across the market, it should be remembered that most books move slowly and indeed may remain in a dealer's stock for years waiting to be *discovered*. Often it is dealers themselves who make the discovery as they see some of their books as part of a new demand. The buyer also has this opportunity, and in one sense buyer and seller contend with one another in an attempt to get the most out of a stock of books.

THE DISTRIBUTION OF ANTIQUARIAN BOOKS

The dealer's stock is the normal distribution point for the books he or she sells. Its location may be a matter of personal preference, or it may be imposed by the exigencies of business.

In the past booksellers tended to cluster, and this is still true, but many have dispersed to the countryside in order to live more pleasantly and to cut overhead. The location of stock is also affected by demographic changes, and recent years have seen the emergence of new centers of the trade, such as Los Angeles and San Francisco, and the decay of others.

Access to the stock is important for both seller and buyer because there may be no other way of knowing what is on the dealer's shelf. The dealer may maintain an inventory listing of some sort, but it is hardly adequate for efficient evaluation of the stock. The stock may be arranged in a number of locations depending on the space available as well as the price, subject, and condition of specific books. The main core of the stock is usually made most accessible to buyers; indeed it may be the only stock there is, although overflow and unprocessed books may be kept in adjacent or remote storage. How far into the stock a dealer will allow a buyer to inspect is partly determined by how well the various segments are controlled and by the dealer's familiarity with the buyer.

The organized portion of the stock is usually arranged by subject according to the bookseller's interpretation or whim. Consequently, browsing becomes important once the initial directions of the dealer are observed. Some buyers simply prefer to make a systematic survey of all or part of the stock to overcome the quirkiness of the location of likely books. This depends, of course, on the buyer's interests and willingness to give the process time and energy, plus the hope of luck.

To reach those buyers who cannot come to the stock, a selection from it is made available by dealers who issue regular or occasional priced catalogues. Some dealers' catalogues may contain minimal descriptive information or may be sumptuous publications replete with extensive notes and illustrations. The time and cost of description, printing, and distribution must either be absorbed by the dealer or passed on to the buyer. Most catalogues can still be obtained without charge, though a nominal price is sometimes imposed on unknown requests or when the production costs have been extraordinarily high. Some dealers will send advance or air mail copies to faithful buyers, whereas unresponsive buyers will be dropped from the mailing list. Catalogues not only offer an opportunity of acquiring books but are also a means of surmising what might be available in the dealer's general stock. Because of their content and the erudition of the notes, some catalogues have become standard reference sources, but the selling life of a catalogue is short. Within a short time after distribution, the most desirable books usually have been sold either by telephone, wire, or letter. Within a month or two sales from a catalogue will have diminished to a trickle depending on the vagaries of distribution. A quick reaction time is usually necessary by the buyer, although there is always the chance that a book has remained unsold or that another copy might have come into the dealer's stock. In any case, late orders inform the dealer of the particular wants of a buyer, which the dealer may be able to supply at another time.

Once a dealer has become familiar with the needs of a buyer, he or she may be willing to quote appropriate titles as they come into stock. When the need is pinpointed, the dealer may consciously seek out the specific titles for quotation to the customer. Want lists should be appropriate to the dealer's stock; otherwise there is little chance of a positive result. Although there is no obligation to purchase quotations or offers from want lists, it is implicit in the case of want lists that the buyer will purchase if the price and condition are right, provided a copy has not been acquired in the meanwhile. Distributing a want list indiscriminately is usually not effective; it is usually a better course to give it exclusively to a proven dealer who will then advise as to whether the books desired are available and in so doing perhaps recommend other booksellers. The key to the effective use of want lists is an affinity between buyer and seller and a prompt response when a book is offered.

PRICES AND PROFITS

After all has been said in considering the purchase of an antiquarian book, the price of the book must be faced. The price will reflect the dealer's various fixed costs, including the price he or she had to pay for the book (often coded into the book on a flyleaf), as well as dealer profit. The variations in fixed costs and what the dealer believes to be an acceptable profit allows for the range of prices one will find for a similar book. The price of each book is also usually marked in pencil on a flyleaf, although it is the practice for some European dealers, for various reasons, not to write the price in the book.

Although pricing and profit will naturally be influenced by the market, they are set by each dealer. When the demand is expected to be high and the costs low, the profit margin might be expected to be relatively larger than for a book where the dealer's cost coincides with the going market price. For the many books without reliable market indicators, the dealer will infer a price that he or she expects will fall within a reasonable range to attract demand. If the demand is light in the local market, then the dealer may knowingly price an individual book below the demand in another part of the market. Although supply and demand determine the market price, it is really the perception of the supply and demand that is important in the trade of antiquarian books because there are a vast number of variables at work.

Once the price of a book in stock has been set, it usually remains fixed unless a dealer maintains close control of the stock with periodic inventories. The chief exceptions to price changes in stock are books that the dealer recognizes as being in heavier demand than originally anticipated.

Although some dealers have a fixed view of price and resist any suggestion to lower it, others are willing to consider adjusting price upon demand. Almost all dealers, however, are willing to extend credit to regular buyers, and some occasionally offer a discount, usually 10 percent, which is the nominal discount received in dealer-to-dealer purchases.

Buyer-Seller Relations

The antiquarian bookseller may be looked upon as a collector of books who foregoes the pleasures of possession for profit. The bookseller thus shares many of the attributes of the buyer, and the wise buyer will do the same. There is much to be learned from the way a bookseller conducts business and the various values he or she applies to books. The keenness with which collectors observe the trade is a clue to the character of their collecting. The source of a collector's books can often be as revealing as the books themselves.

Aside from the many affinities that exist between the buyer and seller, the matter of profit and how it is taken separates them. Booksellers can never forget that they are in business, and they expect that the buyer will recognize this fact. They will expect payment according to the arrangements made at time of purchase. With understandable pride, they may expect some appreciation and intelligent use of their stock and services. In some instances, they may even expect a degree of loyalty.

On the other side, buyers will want sellers to inform them as fully as possible about the books they buy. They will expect that the book be accurately described and that a justifiable price be given to it. In return for loyalty, buyers may also come to expect an awareness and response to their needs. Buyers will want to assume that the advice the seller gives them is directed toward their benefit.

Although the seller and buyer have responsibilities to one another, the final word remains with the buyer. It is the buyer who must determine whether or not to purchase the book.

5

The Art and Craft of Collecting Manuscripts

Lola L. Szladits

"Oddly enough an American Adams wants to buy the MS of Flush—that foolish witless joke with which I solaced myself when I was all agasp having done the Waves," wrote Virginia Woolf to Vita Sackville-West on March 18, 1933. The American Adams was Frederick Baldwin Adams, Jr., the author of the Introduction to the book you are now reading. His delicate negotiation for the purchase of the original manuscript of *Flush*, a fanciful biography of Elizabeth Barrett Browning's cocker spaniel, deserves recalling in the fuller quotation that follows. Mr. Adams himself was to become a great public figure in the world of books and manuscripts, heading The Pierpont Morgan Library just 15 years after he revealed himself as a youthful private collector in the letter he wrote to Virginia Woolf on April 3, 1933 (the year after he graduated from Yale):

My dear Mrs. Woolf—
    Your letter arrived, and caused a great deal of happiness. I never really allowed myself to believe that you would not have already promised the manuscript of *Flush* to someone you know. As it is, I feel as though I had been given the piece of the birthday cake that contained the ring—That is, you must know, cause for excitement to bachelors of nine. (My engagement was announced this very April third, so I shall not long, thank God, remain a bachelor of twenty-three.) I don't know what to say about the business end of your letter. As an innocent con-

nected with INDUSTRY in New York, I should drive a very hard bargain. As a foolish boy who has spent a great abundance of his happiest hours reading, I should be anxious and willing to give anything you might suggest. As a combination of the two, I call you at 40 pounds and retire to hide behind the screen with Lady Teazle. There you will find me, awaiting with shudders (delicate conventional shudders) the outcome of your interview with Mammon. (I interview him daily on 42nd St. so that now I am less than afraid of *him*.)

Please be frank with me. I may have insulted you; I may have suddenly become a plutocrat in your eyes. Please tell me honestly how you feel about the price I mentioned. The fact is, you have never sold and I have never bought a manuscript. Perhaps you would be willing to consult one who professes to know. Whatever I *should* have said, it just seems that I can't valuate a manuscript in pounds. It is like weighing a soul before invoicing it to St. Peter, or trying to collect damages from a railroad that has crippled your wife. If £40 is all right, then a great transaction's done, and I shall be a proud god-father. If not, *tant pis*, I shall try again, if you permit me another chance!

I am, of course, delighted at the idea of it's being really a manuscript, not a typescript. That makes it a thousand times more real and living—a modern machine has not had a hand in its making. . . .

Very sincerely yours,
F. B. Adams Jr.

It so happened that Virginia Woolf's interview with Mammon did not encourage a sale. Her terms were unacceptable to Mr. Adams, and the transfer did not take place. Many years later, the manuscript of *Flush* together with manuscript and typewritten reading notes came to be a part of the Woolf archive in The New York Public Library's Berg Collection of English and American Literature.

The Literary Act

Virginia Woolf's surprise at having received an offer of a purchase is not unusual. How often do we hear: "Do you really want those manuscripts of mine?" It is not in disparagement of their own work or worth that writers repeatedly ask collectors that question. They are astonished that the leavings of their craft, the work in composition, with its deletions, additions, and rearrangements of passages, should be of interest to anyone other than themselves, the makers.

In his essay "The Poet," Emerson divides the progeny of the Universe into three offspring: the Knower, the Doer, and the Sayer. "The Poet is the Sayer," he writes. The practical answer, therefore, to the question repeatedly asked, "Why collect manuscripts?" is simply, "To know." In wanting to know what goes into the making of a literary work, the manuscript collector goes beyond that endearing statement quoted by E. M. Forster, that you cannot know your thoughts until you see what you say: He wants to *see* the Sayer say it. Beyond the fever of the hunt and the game of collecting, the collector prizes first this act of knowing, this joy in the maker and his "makings" (as one contemporary novelist, Tillie Olsen, describes the writer's original scraps and drafts). These revelations of the craftsman in action are the tangible evidence that rounds out one's knowledge of a work of art, of a life.

Even when it comes to the physical act of writing, to the trail of the writing instrument across the paper, we have many opportunities for enjoyment and investigation, and we need no graphologist to guide us, though the clues to personality that he or she follows may be of interest. Before we go into the somewhat formal and artificial terms that collectors and the trade use for manuscript description, perhaps we should first look at the writer's own confrontation with the process. From the sharpening of the quill pen to the mixing of ink; from the annoyance of a dry residue at the bottom of the inkwell to the freedom, later on, of the fountain pen; from the staring white virginity of the paper to the closely compressed lines of first drafts (or, for that matter, lines widely spaced in order to enable correspondents, as Edna St. Vincent Millay aptly put it, "to read between the lines")—all of these have been described and often cursed by the craftsmen of the literary act.

Forests of galley proofs, with mazes of manuscript additions and corrections, have to be made comprehensible to the printer. Publishing can still be thought of as a Renaissance operation involving two persons: the maker and the doer—the writer and the printer—even though the printing half of the team may have multiplied by dividing. But because, as Dr. Johnson once said, "the best part of every author is in his books," isn't an even better part in the genesis of these books?

The progress from draft to printed book carries forward the literary creative process. If artists' rough sketches either explain or add to our pleasure and understanding of the finished canvas, literary manuscripts can do the same—but with a difference: Only on rare occasions do they provide visual pleasure. The process of understanding is purely intellectual. No one would speak of "a pretty manuscript," and if the phrase "a good manuscript" is common, it is not used in the same sense as meant by "a good design" or "a good drawing."

Illuminated manuscripts are an act of beauty and of devotion, and—as we are often told by the scribes—an act of enormous physical achievement. Literary manuscripts, while less beautiful, are more the result of intricate intellectual processes often coupled with physical achievement. Descriptions of the author's health while completing a major work are plentiful, and reading them—preferably in the original manuscript letters—often leaves the reader gasping. One's respect grows with every recurrent complaint of eighteenth-century gout, nineteenth-century arthritis, plaguing headaches, and painful backs and ailing bodies. Perhaps no single act of creation in history was undertaken and completed in perfect health.

Prerequisites for Collecting Literary Manuscripts

When collectors embark on the voyage of adding literary manuscripts to a collection of printed works—the usual sequence of events—they undertake what is by its nature a sensitive activity. Before setting out on an uncharted sea, there are certain emotional and intellectual requirements necessary in order to travel safely. Passion and interest, knowledge coupled with curiosity, and (as has been said of Coleridge) "a mind growing to the last," are all needed. The inquiring mind (or if necessary, the prying mind) is in evidence in every growing collection.

However, passion and intellect will not suffice. To the basic quality of sensitivity another needs to be added—humility. It is useful to approach every new assignment with total loss of memory, because new, preliminary research will always be necessary, and it is done best if it is done from scratch. Collectors would do well to remind themselves that no matter how long and how well their memory serves them, they may know nothing about a new interest. Even if an association rings a bell, one needs to be reminded that memory is fleeting. The collector's humility ought to increase with the growth of the collection, and the first three commandments of manuscript collecting are: Buy what you love, buy what interests you, buy humbly.

Manuscript collectors need to have a good ear and ought to train themselves to become good listeners. As much information as can be gathered from reference books can be collected by a sharp ear that picks up temporal and eternal gossip. But the sifting of what one hears, either from the seller or from interested parties, calls for another necessary quality—objectivity. Final decisions in making any small or large purchase must be made in cold blood after assessing all the relevant factors that might have any influence on the value of the material. Once trained, the collector will recognize what sort of information bears upon any given case.

Although it is good to open one's ear, it is a basic requirement to keep one's mouth shut. Indiscretion often mars a transfer, either through premature boasts or inadvertent hints dropped at the wrong time and in the wrong place. Discretion at any stage, and on any level, involving important transfers ought to be demanded from any collaborator. Although everyone loves to tell, and to listen to, stories of successfully concluded transactions, there are many tales of woe that took the unforeseen turn because of indiscretions. Because delicate negotiations can at times continue for years, with or without interruptions, it is easiest and best to consider all of them as private as the material one considers.

Perhaps a reemphasis of the basic quality among all the contradictory ones is in order. All have one feature in common—sensitivity. Physical energy helps, money helps, patience is essential, common sense and good judgment are called for, but sensitivity is the key to success, because the collector moves in an essentially sensitive area. When live sensibilities, emotional or material, enter the picture, it may prove best to walk away from them. If an acquisition is destined to happen, it is going to happen, and if transacted in a professional manner, it usually does not end in tears or broken hopes on either side. The intangible factor in every acquisition is luck. All great purchases, like marriages, are concluded in heaven.

Keepers of other people's mail ought to know how to organize their own, and a great deal of time will be saved for generations to come if records of transactions are kept in an orderly manner. A log recording basic facts and figures kept up regularly helps to keep the record straight and available for immediate inspection; and, because whatever the collector collects is likely to survive our threescore years and ten, the tangible transfer in the form of contracts is (or ought to be) a written reminder to which coming generations can refer when the spoken word is a memory. Therefore, all bills and invoices, and all correspondence, even if considered trivial or temporary at the time, ought to be kept by private and public collectors. Unlimited funds except in a very few cases are not available, and even if they are, record keeping is part of the collecting process at any level.

From the intangible to the tangible, from the eternal to the temporal, the necessary qualities expected from the collector are sensitivity, interest, curiosity, humility, objectivity, and orderliness.

Defining an Area

If these personal qualities are important, material ones are going to influence the character of a collection equally. It is, therefore, advisable to define an area of collecting even before one sets out on the quest. The area, in some instances, is going to define itself. The collector's personal interest will certainly govern that, whether in building around a favorite author whose printed works are already on hand, or in collecting manuscripts of a period or around a certain group. Whatever the area might be, it is well if initially the collector delimits the field, because available space, expenditure, and time for acquiring and for sorting single pieces or archival material may not be unlimited. One can never buy even a single piece without having spent more or less time on studying it or the historical background surrounding it. If, within reasonable material definitions of limits, the collector knows what his or her main objective is going to be, the steady rise of the manuscript market, especially true during the past 20 years or so, ought not deter him or her.

There are two schools of thought on this subject. The advice that presently uncollected authors are good quarries for the beginner, because "sleepers" are always available, is not shared by those who know that in *any* market there are sleepers. The term is well defined by Mary A. Benjamin in her *Autographs: A Key to Collecting* (New York: Walter R. Benjamin Autographs, 1966). "Sleeper" refers "neither to a person nor to a Pullman car." It is "an autograph which has gone undiscovered, whether as one of a large miscellaneous lot or in a smaller group whose owner did not recognize its value." The market, like every other, is governed by supply and demand. Even these days, when vast bodies of archival papers have ended up (one could assume permanently) in public collections, one knows that there is a steady flow of material both through private transfers and public auctions.

The market ought to be viewed as a continuous pageant. Each generation in history sometimes tends to think of itself as the last of the great collectors, but this belief is a delusion. The market never dries up. Collecting may appear more or less interesting or stimulating, or it may appear more or less challenging, depending on the objective; but it is still a plentiful market, and it is going to continue to be one. The individual collector's personal experience, in the end, justifies which of two divergent schools of thought is subscribed to: (1) buy what you want most, regardless of competition; versus the more frequently heard (2) do not compete with what is already being collected. Everything is being collected, and there is going to be competition in any area. Every collector can proudly show items that were bought in the face of relentless competition. On the other hand, one remembers all losses, whether in the auction rooms or from dealers' catalogues. But in regretting all missed opportunities, one ought not dwell on them. They happen as a matter of course. One cannot win all the time. But one can, and does, win much of the time.

Help from Various Sources

In collecting rare books and manuscripts, the beginner and the established collector have several allies: members of the trade, fellow collectors, librarians, and archivists. Especially at the start, the collector is well advised to call for help. Specialist dealers know the market best; fellow collectors might share an interest and know the difficulties, some of which they may have overcome themselves during the course of their own collecting; the librarian and archivist can help in research and can produce examples with which to help resolve particular problems.

Dealers, in their own interest as well as in the collector's, often keep the individual's major field of collecting in mind, and although it is not always possible to supply members of the trade with want lists, it is advisable to do so where you can. The basic excitement is that everything is possible at any time; any item may turn up any day. When it does, it is nice to know that a friendly dealer is going to notify the collector as soon as the unexpected happens. Even if you lose interesting items repeatedly at auction, do not be discouraged. Next time you might carry off a similar item, perhaps alerted by someone in another city or even country. So, to restate the obvious: Friends among the trade are one of the keys to collecting success.

For practical purposes auction houses (which may seem very forbidding at first) are to be counted among members of the trade, and some of the collector's best friends are auctioneers. Just as dealers risk their own investment in buying for stock, the auctioneer, singly or corporately, risks much every time an auction is staged. Auctioneers have the primary responsibility to make sure that what is put up for sale is "as described." Their knowledge must therefore be extensive.

Large auction houses know their clients and usually try to make sure that auction catalogues reach them on time and sometimes will even provide galley proofs of forthcoming catalogues to enable the private or public collector to digest their information, do research, and have plenty of time to place bids.

If members of the trade are the collector's best friends, personal friends are even better. By a process of natural selection, each individual sooner or later finds another collector as a best friend. Even among collectors, public or private, there is the uncommon quality of generosity. Some items make their way from one collection to another, because "that is where they belong." Although there is much competition, and hunters and fishermen are by nature competitive, there is a brotherhood and sisterhood of collectors. The generous and wise collector, regardless of the big game hunter's competitive instinct, will "rejoice with them that rejoice [and will] weep with them that weep." The shared pleasure or distress is best established in communities where collectors congregate. Exchange of information or experience is a two-way street, and much can be gained by gathering around oneself, together with one's growing collection, a circle of like-minded individuals. Susan O. Thompson's chapter in this book on "The Book Collector in the World of Scholarship" describes many organizations and societies of book collectors.

The third partner in every collector's life is the librarian or archivist. Either one, even if in a specialist position, is more of a generalist than most collectors are. The help given is in the nature of first aid; the collector ought not expect any archivist to do more than to supply the tools. Librarians can light the trail, but no good collector or research worker will depend completely on the librarian's word. One's own conviction is what finally bears upon the decision, and not what the librarian—no matter how experienced—might advise. When it comes to authenticating handwriting, the archivist cannot be expected to pronounce the final word on the authenticity of a document. Any number of letters or examples can be placed side by side. The collector's eye or discernment must be the final judge. Shared information, and not shared opinion or advice, is what you must search for. The "have you heard" or "do you know" questions often asked ought to be rephrased as "can you help me find out," or "what do you have on . . . ?" Librarians and archivists are like trained bloodhounds. They can bring back documentary evidence, but they ought not to be expected to bolster an opinion or to make Solomon-like decisions that may end only in frustration for both sides.

Collectors are aware from the start that unless disaster strikes, their own decision in making a purchase, and the object bought, are going to outlast their lifetime. A collector owes it to his or her collection to keep an awareness of the market up to date and to keep lines of communication open. We are, therefore, not to limit ourselves to reading only those dealers' catalogues that might relate narrowly to our field of collecting. The ability to sift quickly through catalogues, even unsolicited ones, comes only after years of experience. Certainly at the start, every and any catalogue ought to be read carefully. Apart from the fact that to a collector nothing can be more interesting than catalogues, including the menulike column of prices, one will retain a residue of awareness of many different areas. Studying a catalogue is without question a time-consuming task, but the indifference with which one is likely to shove aside yet another catalogue, especially in a public position, can over the years result in many missed opportunities. That state of mind one cannot afford.

Reading catalogues is not an art that is difficult to master, but because some established forms frequently recur, it is proper here to give some descriptive definitions. We are indebted once again to Mary A. Benjamin for her *Autographs: A Key to Collecting* (New York: Walter R. Benjamin Autographs, 1966):

> *A*, or *Auto*, stands for autograph, meaning handwritten. This symbol does not, however, imply that there is any signature. Rather it refers solely to the fact that the body of the document is in the handwriting of the individual. When *A*, then, precedes any

description, that is, begins any series of alphabetical designations, it clearly asserts that the item is entirely handwritten.

L, the abbreviation for letter, denotes that the paper includes a formal salutation and ending, such as "Dear Sir" and "your obedient humble servant." When *L* is preceded by *A*, becoming *A.L.*, the combination specifies that the missive is entirely handwritten, but states nothing concerning a signature. Indeed the letter may, in fact, never have been signed, due to one cause or another, including absent-mindedness, or may have been, as frequently happened and still does, the draft of a letter kept for filing. Or, once signed, the signature may have been cut off. But when the letter is signed and the signature is on it, this fact is indicated by adding *S*.

S always signifies that an item is personally signed with the name of the individual. If he signed only with his initials, this fact must always be further indicated by cataloguers. An *A.L.S.*, then, is definitely a full autographed letter, written and signed by the individual with his full name. An *L.S.* states that he signed but did not write the letter itself.

N stands for note. An *A.N.S.* is occasionally used interchangeably with *A.L.S.* when the latter is very brief—only a line or two in length—and the contents of little significance. Strictly speaking, an *A.N.S.* differs from the *A.L.S.* in that the salutation and ending are omitted. An original telegram, for example, which bears the name of the recipient and his address, as well as the sender's name, is classed as an *A.N.S.* It may be referred to as an *A.D.S. D*, indicating document, and *N* for note are at times interchangeable, when representing a brief communication. . . .

Like the term "document," "manuscript"—abbreviated to *Ms.*—embraces a wide class. A manuscript may be a complete or incomplete page of writing from a book, one of its chapters or an entire book, a sheet of music or a poem. But the symbol *Ms.* seldom stands alone, for it needs further description. Combined with *A* or *Auto*—*A.Ms.* or *Auto. Ms.*—the declaration is that this is an autograph or handwritten manuscript. Adding, as in the case of an *A.L.*, the letter *S* to *A.Ms.*—thus *A.Ms.S.*—further declares that the manuscript is signed. It is then easy to deduce that *Ms.S.* means that this is a manuscript which is not handwritten but signed, as would be the case with a page from a book of printed poems which the poet had signed. More frequently, of course, such manuscripts are typewritten and signed, and in such instances, these facts are mentioned—"Typewritten *Ms.S.*". . . .

A.Q.S.—Autograph Quotation Signed—would indicate that the quotation is in the handwriting of a particular person and signed by him. . . .

There are three indications which apply to certain omissions in autographs—*n.d.*, *n.y.* and *n.p.* The first, which stands for "no date," means that the paper has no date whatsoever; *n.y.*—"no year"—that it bears the month and the day but not the year; and *n.p.*—"no place"—which says nothing about the date, but means that the letter does not show the place where it was written. In these days, when the general practice of letter-writers is to have printed or engraved stationery, it is not often that the place-designation is omitted, but some writers, still as formerly, attach little or no importance to a date or, if they do, often content themselves with noting "Monday" or another day of the week.

Once the novice collector has familiarized himself with these terms and their abbreviations, he can turn with some confidence to an autograph catalogue. He will next need to know the special meaning which is attached to the parentheses and brackets in this type of listing. The procedure observed can best be explained by considering a typical portion of a dealer's catalogue, like the following, minus the prefatory numbering:

1. Madison, James. A.L.S., 1p., 8vo, Washington City, 3 p.m., Feb. 24, 1811. To Washington Irving.
2. Madison. A.D.S., 2pp., fol., Philadelphia [1780].
3. (Madison). Auto. Ms. S., 3pp., 4to, 1810, of John Doe.
4. Madison, Dolly. A.L.S., 4pp., 8vo, Washington, Mar. 3, 1807. To Henry Adams.
5. Madison. A.Q.S., on card.

The use of abbreviations, *p.* and *pp.*, to indicate *page* and *pages* is familiar even to the layman. In the autograph profession, however, it must be noted that customarily it is the pages, not sheets, that are counted. If a sheet is written on both sides, each side is considered a page, and 5pp. would indicate either that there are five sheets, each written on one side, or that there are two sheets written on both sides and a third with only one side used. . . .

The collector needs to understand the meaning of two other words which are never formally abbreviated, but which are frequently encountered in autograph shop-talk. The first is "provenance" or "provenience." This term has somewhat the same relationship to a letter, a document or a manuscript as genealogy has to a person. It refers to the history of a paper in question and the identification of all those who have previously owned it. In cases of very rare and important items, a prospective purchaser advisedly ascertains the validity of title, just as one who proposes to buy land. And as land titles are traced back, from registered deed to registered deed, so the title to papers may be traced back, as far as possible, from generation to generation.

Some catalogues and library practice have made a fine distinction between *manuscript* (derived from the Latin) and *holograph* (derived from the Greek). *Holograph*, either as adjective or noun, means that the manuscript or marginal notes are in the author's own hand, whereas *manuscript* could be in anyone else's hand. If the writer of a manuscript cannot be identified, the statement might be amplified by "manuscript in an unidentified hand." *Typescript* is usually written out in full; but occasionally the abbreviated form *Ts.* can also be found.

Signatures, which to American collectors seem to be more important than to Europeans, can occur in pet names, pseudonyms, or initials. The informed collector might acquire some sleepers if he recognizes Sebastian Melmoth as Oscar Wilde, who also published *The Ballad of Reading Gaol* under his cell number, "C.3.3," or Sean O'Cathasaigh (the Gaelic form)—let alone John Cassidy—as Sean O'Casey. Some people, especially artists, prefer a pictorial signature to be recognized only by the cognoscenti. Fannie Hurst drew a lily, e.e. cummings an elephant, Whistler a butterfly. The zoological garden may be completed with the recently identified "Sp" for "sparrow" or "sparroy," which the youthful Virginia Stephen signed in correspondence with members of her family.

Hands and Some Characteristics

Although everyone knows of the danger of forgers at work, there are letters that might seem to be forgeries to the uninitiated, but which in fact are genuine. Thackeray used two hands, a slanted and an upright; sometimes he even combined both in the same letter. The Thackeray forger (and there has been at least one diligent one) gives himself away more in the spacing of his lines than in the slantedness or uprightness of his hand.

There are uncanny—and fortunately uncommon—similarities between the hands of total strangers, such as that of Charles Dickens and Charles James, whose hands resemble each other even to the flourish under their signatures. If the beginning collector fears forgeries, consolation can be derived from the fact that even the greatest collectors of manuscripts, as well as members of the trade, have been taken in by forgeries at one time or another. They stand as useful examples, because once recognized and remembered, the same mistake will not be made again.

Very often, especially in formal inscriptions, a writer's hand differs from that used in the informal letter casually tossed off. There might also appear to be a more self-conscious slant in a letter accompanying a presentation copy. Over the years hands change, and in old age, due to physical handicaps, a stroke, or weakened sight, a well-known handwriting can take on a different slant or even a different positioning on the page. The best advice collectors can follow is that, if in doubt, they should consult an archival collection. Side by side the same writing in the same period, or preferably same year, is not likely to vary enormously; decisions made on the basis of many examples are the wisest ones.

All periods and nations have characteristic writings. To a collector of nineteenth-century manuscripts, eighteenth-century hands might look almost alike and formal to the point of confusion. Similarly, national schools carry their individual marks. Bear in mind that English and American dating differs in the positioning of the month and the day, for example, the American March 21, 1941 versus the English 21 March 1941, or sometimes 21.III.41. These are practical matters that in due course become second nature to the collector.

Finding Out What One Has Bought

Intellectual use of a manuscript is implicit in its purchase, because no addition to a collection is made for unjustifiable reasons. More facts, at first hidden or unaccounted for, become apparent during the course of further study. If insufficient time has been spent before a purchase in finding out whether or not the item was published and in what form, research will have to continue. Documentation of facts needs to be collected and bibliographic references noted. The nature of a given document may change from "original research material" to "museum piece" once all available information bearing on it has been unearthed. With collections that grow fast, or if archival materials are acquired, it is often difficult to achieve ideal levels of documentation, though they ought to be attempted. Once collected together and digested in a concise manner, the documentation will save the collector time and trouble later on. No scraps or original traces, even if deemed ephemeral at the time of acquisition, ought to be regarded as trivial, because they have a habit of growing in importance as new facts and information come to light. Envelopes, because of postmarks, turn into documentary evidence. Address books, casually found among papers, might become important evidence in supplying the biographer with data. Telegrams can be illuminating, though not always as dramatic as the one Yeats sent to Lady Gregory informing her of his having won the Nobel Prize. Even library call slips can add a footnote in a quest for the reason why an author read a particular book at a certain point.

Because manuscripts are widely dispersed—both geographically as well as in private or public collections—a new owner should become acquainted with the ownership of manuscripts in a broader context. The collector should understand that if one letter is bought, perhaps the major repository of others ought to be found. If one draft of a work has been acquired, others might turn up elsewhere. Although a typescript was thought to be unique before acquisition, there may have been a carbon, or another uncorrected copy, even within the same community. May it never happen that any collector acquire a valuable letter in a fragment that cannot be reunited with the missing portion! Public collectors are often alerted to just that by wandering scholars who can bring two fragments or missing parts together during the course of their peregrinations. Great letter writers write them all day, or so it would seem to latter-day collectors. They often repeat themselves to different correspondents. The same subject, therefore, is likely to turn up in letters written either the same day or during a given period, and any owner should be curious enough to wish to track down all letters referring to the same subject. Therefore, soon after a new purchase, the collector himself becomes a correspondent.

When it comes to sorting large bodies of papers, the collector is confronted with a real challenge. A single masterpiece, delivered in unsorted drafts, and appearing at the start to be a ton of paper, might take months before, based upon the evidence of paper, ink, typewriters, and successive incorporated corrections, it forms a coherent whole. Before beginning an often overwhelming task, the printed work must be read, sometimes almost memorized, because it is only on the basis of that knowledge that even preliminary sorting can be attempted. Authors have been known to go from one typewriter to another, and not always even in the same locality; all traceable evidence must be brought to bear upon the cohesiveness of a draft. Internal evidence, dating supplied by the writer when beginning new passages during composition, or marginal scribbled notes that chart a course, all may be points of a compass. Long hours are often spent in discovering the direction. Each creator's technique and frame of craftsmanship during composition tends to vary from one work to the next. There are no rules. What is needed is knowledge and patience—and a large space in which to spread out papers!

In sorting large bodies of correspondence, of either one person or from various sources, the direction may be from the printed work to the originals, where the letters have been published. But more often than not, the correspondence is unpublished. Therefore, research into the vital facts is of paramount importance. The collector, one assumes, knows why the correspondence was bought in the first place. What he or she may not have had time to study are the ingredients; connections are not always immediately obvious. If available, biographical reference tools are helpful. Correspondences have a tendency to continue over a period of time and then stop for no apparent reason. Is there a reason for a break in a relationship? Did one overlook a death date? Is there a contribution in a little-known periodical documenting a particular connection? Often the correspondence itself answers fundamental questions, but just as often it does not.

As a collection grows, so do the sources of information revealed in related items. In order to make necessary connections readily, thorough collectors write a brief digest of each item. A salient fact in a letter; a biographical fact in a document; an additional or expurgated chapter from a manuscript—these points are noted, to be made available when associative powers get into action. Often the dealer or the auction house provides the clues in a printed catalogue, but the collector's point of view, or reason for purchase, might be different. A careful reading of each acquisition is bound to highlight the features of importance to the individual. A notation of these features may serve as a permanent guide and, during the course of time, can be enlarged.

Because collecting manuscripts is essentially an intellectual occupation, the use of one or a multitude of items involves a reading, researching, writing, and digesting process. Being concise is a virtue, because its opposite, elaboration, is a cardinal vice. There is no reason or need for being elaborate; more often than not, long notes serve only the ego of a collector who wishes to show off not only research skills, but also style. By the time the essentials are on paper in any form, or filed in any way, the collector could have written a research paper of his or her own. The writing of such a paper, indeed, might be the real test of whether or not the postacquisition work has been thoroughly accomplished. Of all the unwritten papers that great collectors could write while intellectually "fondling" their collections, one might build yet another collection. There is one major reward: The collector's life at best is a busy one.

Organization

To facilitate the use of a collection, the collector needs an awareness of organization from the start. Once again, there are no rules, but a framework within which manuscripts are housed and retrieved ought to be designed at the outset. Individual items can be kept in vertical files and filing cabinets, or individual boxes, and filed vertically. They are best preserved if filed flat in manila folders, in either custom-made boxes or ready-made containers available in quantity. Naturally, custom-made boxes are more expensive, but if money is no object, it is aesthetically pleasing to have a color scheme for each author or subject. Valuable single items can be housed in binders' cases designed to accommodate any number of pages or sizes. Each order to the binder ought to include instructions as to the lettering on the spine or front of the box or case. Drop-front boxes are useful, but, once again, financial limitations may have to govern individual decisions. Original manuscript letters mounted on mats suitable for framing may be visually rewarding. However, the wrong paper or the wrong paste may prove harmful in the long run. A knowledgeable technician can advise on safe materials, a subject treated at greater length in Willman Spawn's chapter entitled "Physical Care of Books and Manuscripts" later in this book.

When it comes to overall organization, especially for archival papers, each and every assignment is going to write its own plan. Given sufficient time and thought, papers have a habit of falling into their natural position, and it is best not to interfere with that. Manuscripts are best filed in alphabetical order by title or author, or correspondence under the name of the correspondent, and then chronologically. However, with that simple rule, the framework is not wholly defined, because the following factors interfere: chronological order of composition in manuscripts; discarded chapters or additions that for one reason or another may have to be kept separate; pages separated from drafts that might be better housed flat, while the main work is in a vertical case; critical works, or other related items best kept with a given work.

In the case of correspondence, although the core may be kept together, substantiating material or letters from other sources have to be accounted for and organized as well. Whether a correspondence is to be kept together or distributed according to writer or correspondent is another important decision that must be made.

A card file should be kept while the collection is growing. Such a file is useful, because any number of cards can be distributed in any number of relevant places, whereas the material itself can only be housed in one place. A correspondent file, a provenance file, a date file, and an address file all help in pulling together information that could otherwise be located only by consulting the originals. In spite of the saving of time or labor, reference to the originals for information ought to be avoided where possible; it cannot be emphasized sufficiently that wear and careless handling deteriorates paper. The card file has to coordinate with what will be contained in an abbreviated heading to identify the item itself. If an abbreviated title on the box or file is used, the descriptive entry on the card has to match it. On manila folders the information, as listed in dealers' catalogues or as designated by the collector, ought to be repeated. The outside of the folders can also be used to record data gathered in pre- and postacquisition research. Notes by earlier collectors may have been written on the originals themselves, or the recipients of letters may have penciled the date of receipt. Such notes may be helpful, but it is a reprehensible practice to add to them.

If a card file is kept, business information can either be interfiled with it or noted as a separate card. Date of purchase, source, price, any recorded expense such as binding, insurance, correspondence with other collectors or inquiring parties, can either be recorded on the face or back of the card or filed in back of it. If in a growing collection numbers or symbols help, they too can be used in various ways. Accession numbers can be useful to identify similar items or, ultimately, to keep a total count up to date. Symbols or shelf marks prove to be good guides in private collections. All of these ought to be reflected both on the materials' bindings or file folders and on the cards.

A basic framework is ultimately necessary in any intellectual enterprise. Large editions of letters, biographies, and historical works are usually supported by a card file containing pertinent information. Because there might come a point at which the collector and the writer become one, it is well to keep the card file or index file up-to-date and meticulous. Library catalogs can teach the neophyte research worker heading for a first (or even a third) academic degree a great deal about basic organization. Without documentation the collector's prized manuscript collection will turn once again into tons of paper, and the index cards into the pack of cards of *Alice in Wonderland*.

Care and Preservation

A manuscript collection ought to survive provided it is handled delicately, with awareness of the fragility of paper, and not negligently. How well we know the bundles of letters rolled up and held together for decades by rubber bands; the water- and coffee-stained letters, marked by their recipients or by disaster; notepaper repaired with perforated stamp margins, cigar rings, or tape. There are plenty of occasions to marvel at the survival of what is so fragile and perishable. The traces of pencil, ink, and the typewriter are also perishable. We have seen ink fade in front of our eyes both when exposed to sunlight for too long, and even in manila folders while lying flat in a box and not exposed to light. Care and maintenance of a collection is, therefore, of primary importance. Decay is often brought on by humans and it can be forestalled by humans. Although temperature and humidity changes do interfere, paper has survived under extremely adverse conditions, and human misuse can do more damage than the weather. Any private collector showing off his treasures knows that they are not to be handed around. Anyone sufficiently aware of the risks involved will not ask that they be. Although there is a thrill to be had from touching the original, only in rare instances is it necessary to allow a piece to rest in the lap of a visitor. Professional supervision of anything written on paper is most important in preserving it for the future. Loosely bound items fall apart in imperfectly bound sewings; dog-ears form when loose sheets are replaced in folders; fingerprints are superimposed on writer's cramps—an endless list of woe and terrors.

Accidents are most salutary and sobering. If the collector truly identifies with his or her collection, rough handling of the material can hurt as much as physical pain. The shudder running through one's own spine the first time a spine of a binding breaks is enough of a reminder for life. The first time one drops a rare item, and holds one's breath, is as unforgettable as the time one avoided a fatal accident.

There are, fortunately, trained persons who know what to do in case of an accident. A repaired item will, however, never be the same again, and neither will a precious document be like it once was, even though laminated to save it from complete dissolution. Proper respect for the material demands utmost care. If the collector's life is a busy one, it is also a hazardous one.

Literary Rights

"Where there are manuscripts, there is trouble," says an enduring and experienced library director, and one who knows the troubles he has seen. Unaware of legal matters involving all literary manuscripts, the collector might wander where angels, owners, and attorneys fear to tread. Although no attempt can be made here to cover the ground fully, a few signals may be useful as a warning about perils that the newcomer may not know about and need to avoid.

In land transactions, when title passes it is customary to define the property and to survey it. Other claimants might have legal title, or might believe they have. Abandoned property might turn into no-man's-land, and statutes of limitation might have to be considered. Manuscripts are movable objects, and like chattel, and unlike land, they can be transferred with relative ease. Do letters of intent to give constitute letters of deed? Are letters of acceptance legal? In buying in open market, has title been cleared before a manuscript reaches the dealer or the auction rooms? Loss, theft, or inadvertent gifts easily confuse the market even when one believes that the seller acquired the rights to sell. In the lost-and-found department of literary manuscripts there are endless pitfalls. Some hit the popular press. It is best, if in doubt, to take the matter to an attorney.

The right to *publish* a manuscript does not always automatically pass with transfer of ownership. Even the right to copy it photomechanically does not automatically pass with it. Therefore, copyright matters and statutory rights in unpublished manuscripts enter the picture. Whatever copyright act is accepted as law nationally and internationally will govern the actions of each generation. Once again, if in doubt, a specialized attorney ought to be consulted.

As is often the case, private collectors may be in a more advantageous position than public buyers; the latter are accountable at any time, and their records are open to public examination at any point. Litigation is costly and time-consuming, and there is only one piece of sound advice to follow: "Look before you leap." One cannot ask that every dealer supply one with written title. The need to trust someone, or a group, is very real, but sometimes responsible dealers make mistakes. The public buyer in particular must then remember that forgiving is divine, whereas errors are human. At the same time money is better spent on further acquisitions than on legal advice.

The right to publish can be passed on with a manuscript or a body of papers by the owner, provided that the owner has statutory rights. Well-intentioned families frequently believe that they do own them, though a distant claimant in fact has a perfectly clear title to them. In large families collateral descendants may believe that they alone own the publication rights. When an author's unpublished papers have received little attention for decades and then suddenly rise in importance, financial gain will often trigger off a search in family records with an eye to claiming rights—and royalties.

Even if legal title passes with the papers, laws of the right to privacy enter the picture. Those too change during the course of history, and a knowledgeable attorney knows the changes. We live in a period that maintains that everyone has a right to know. But that is often a privileged right, and passages in the private correspondence of public figures are often edited or censored before publication, and legitimately so. Who are public figures? How long does it take for a private person to go public? Does an author's written wish not to have his or her letters published constitute a legal or a moral prohibition? Is it legal for descendants or estates to wait decades before the public's claim to the right to know becomes, in effect, a legal claim? The collector's role is once again discretion, not in the sense that information ought to be withheld or suppressed, but discretion in giving access to others when in doubt. Because one cannot plead ignorance before the law, once again collectors are urged to read what they buy, both before and after the purchase is made. White papers turn purple, and ink is likely to jump off the page.

When giving access to written or taped archives, private and public owners have the right to ask readers to sign a statement that nothing is going to be quoted in print without the owner's written permission. There is legal recourse when such contracts are broken; once again one must consult a specialist. These are questions the collective mind of the collecting world is aware of; one ought to bear them in mind. If a collector's life is a busy, if a hazardous one, it is sometimes also an expensive one.

Editing

Once all rights are settled, collectors may consider editing some of their treasures themselves. The task is not overwhelming, if all the research has been completed, the nature of the publication determined, and the funds to see it through the press secured. Collections of correspondence, even small runs of letters cherished and handed down generation after generation in a family, often end up edited with knowledge and affection, printed on durable paper and in beautifully designed covers. Collectors can surround themselves with specialists eager to be appointed editors, and rich collectors have been known to acquire entire stables of experts, for they often do not have all the skills editing requires or lack the time. Public collectors often encounter typescripts of unpublished manuscripts, complete except for final editing, which await the attention of future generations. A private project can turn into a commercial success if the original manuscript is important and properly edited. An author's first unpublished work, or a last and unfinished one, are worthy candidates for such projects. Once again, more often than not the collector's judgment is of primary importance. A publication should not be designed to put a halo over the subject's head—or over that of the editor.

The editing must be objective: That is, the editor must keep in the background.

Technological developments in photolithographic printing permit the production of facsimile editions for important manuscripts and visually interesting material; facsimile production may permit lower printing costs. Royalties or honoraria for editorial labors may be additional expenses. By the time the project is ready to go to press, the collector may decide that a new acquisition may have been preferable to the expense of publishing the older one. But there is a special joy in aiding the publication of a worthy manuscript. And what better reason could a collector have for collecting? After all is said and done, the collector's life may be busy, it may be hazardous, it may be expensive—but it is the education of a lifetime.

Postscript

"Footprints on the sands of time" are what our collections can, at best, become. Collecting is an act of faith, but, even if it reflects the character of the person who performed it, it is a subsidiary act and an interpretive act, not a creative one. At its base is substance and not thought. The collector does not create out of nothing, but whereas a personality is reflected in a collection, the roles ought not be confused. It might seem superfluous to stress this point, but there might be a need to clarify it once. The ideal collector is the Miltonian servant who "also serves" because "he stands and waits."

If there is a moral to be drawn from the foregoing pages it is this: There are no easy prescriptions; there are no rules; there are no guides to collecting. One cannot design a framework into which all and any circumstances might easily fit in an established pattern. There are only circumstances, some advantageous, some not. There are people, representing the moving spirit behind lifeless objects that might come to life provided they are being used the right way. Even a definition of a "right way" cannot be supplied, because one day's or one year's "right way" might become the mistake of the next.

Manuscripts and books do indeed have their destiny that relieves conscientious collectors' minds from the inevitable questioning of the rightness or wrongness of an ultimate location of valuable papers. For many years the physical housing of great works of art created a crisis of conscience. Ought the Elgin

Marbles be in London? Ought the Victory of Samothrace grace the staircase of the Louvre? Why find the most beautiful head of an Egyptian queen in Berlin? The list of questions is endless, and the answers provided by history are circumstantial. If, in a shrinking global world, national boundaries could be ignored, and the kingdom of the creative spirit were established as exemplified in objects and written traces, then indeed the questions would not be raised. If sensitive minds, coupled with an optimal 20/20 vision, were brought to bear upon a global heritage, even the most poetic question printed below would not wait for an answer.

In a letter sent at the end of 1885 to William Sharp, who compiled an anthology of sonnets, Oscar Wilde incorporated one of his own sonnets. If only collectors of literary manuscripts could engrave the postscript on their walls in durable matter!

ON THE SALE BY AUCTION
OF KEATS'S LOVE LETTERS

These are the letters which Endymion wrote
   To one he loved in secret, and apart.
   And now the brawlers of the auction mart
Bargain and bid for each poor blotted note.
Ay! for each separate pulse of passion quote
   The merchant's price: I think they love not art,
   Who break the crystal of a poet's heart
That small and sickly eyes may glare and gloat!
Is it not said that many years ago,
   In a far Eastern town, some soldiers ran
   With torches through the midnight, and began
To wrangle for mean raiment, and to throw
   Dice for the garments of a wretched man,
   Not knowing the God's wonder, or his woe?

I wish I could grave my sonnets on an ivory tablet. Quill pens and notepaper are only good enough for bills of lading.

6

Descriptive Bibliography

Terry Belanger

This chapter is concerned primarily with descriptive bibliography, especially with the terms that the book collector must master before he or she can use descriptive bibliographies intelligently and read booksellers' catalogues wisely. For this purpose, we need to sharpen the definition of such a common word as *edition*. Publishers tend to use the word rather loosely, but *edition* has a precise bibliographical meaning. An *edition of a book* is *all copies printed at one or later times from the same setting of type*. Within an edition, all copies printed *at any one time* are called an *impression*. A number of impressions from the same setting of type may be produced over a period of many years, but they are all part of the same edition, because the type itself is identical in each of these impressions. In 1866, for instance, Thomas MacKellar wrote and published a manual of typography called *The American Printer*. He had electrotype plates made from the original setting of type, and over the next dozen years or so, he issued nine further impressions of *The American Printer*, making only the occasional minor correction between one impression and the next. These nine later impressions were identified on the back of the title pages as the second through tenth editions; but only in 1878, when he thoroughly revised and reset his text, did he produce in bibliographical terms his second edition— called on the title page the eleventh edition. Again electro-

97

typing the setting of type used in this edition, MacKellar put out seven further impressions of the second edition—labeled the twelfth through eighteenth editions on the back of the title pages.

An *issue* is that part of an edition offered for sale at one time, or as a consciously planned unit, and an edition is occasionally sold by means of several different issues. Different issues within an edition will be largely the same, but they might, for example, have different title pages, one giving the name of a New York publisher for distribution in the United States, the other giving the name of a London publisher for distribution in Great Britain. Sometimes books are later remarketed with slight additional matter or with a new title page date. In 1842, the London publisher Henry G. Bohn reissued Charles Timperley's *Dictionary of Printers and Printing*, which had originally been published in 1839. Bohn replaced the original title page with a new one and changed the title of the book to *An Encyclopaedia of Literary and Typographical Anecdotes*, and he added a 12-page supplement at the end. In all other respects, the two issues—both using the same sheets printed in 1839—are identical.

Issues are usually determined by the publisher or publishers *after* the book has been printed. Where there is a substantial difference in the printed text of two copies of a book, we are dealing, not with different issues, but with different editions.

State refers to the minor differences in the printed text between one copy and another of the same book. When an error in the text is discovered during the printing of the pages, for example, the press is stopped long enough to make the correction. Sheets printed before the error was noticed constitute the uncorrected state; sheets printed after it was caught constitute the corrected state. Thus in the first Shakespeare folio of 1623, page 277 is incorrectly printed 273 in a few copies. Clearly, the error was caught early in the pressrun, because most surviving copies have the correct page number. Variant states generally occur in the printed sheets, before they go to the binder, and before publication. Variant states are caused *before* publication, just as variant issues are caused upon or after publication.

These terms—edition, impression, issue, and state—are important to the book collector because they help describe priority of publication. Collectors tend to desire the earliest form in which a book was published, preferring the uncorrected state of the first issue of the first impression of the first edition to all later ones. From the general *reader's* point of view, this attitude is silly: Why not collect the most correct edition, rather than the earliest one? William Matheson has dealt with the logic (and illogic) of book collecting in Chapter 1 of this book, however, so my task here is not to defend the sometimes seemingly indefensible preferences of collectors, but rather to lay out the vocabulary used to determine and describe these preferences.

To the book collector, the word *bibliography* properly means *the study of books*; a *bibliographer* is one who studies them. But the word is shopworn. *Bibliography* has many common definitions, and because collectors, scholars, and librarians too often use the word indiscriminately, it lacks precision. For this reason, *bibliography* generally attaches itself to qualifying adjectives like *enumerative, systematic, analytical, critical, descriptive, historical*, or *textual*.

Some definitions of the resulting, frequently found compounds are in order. The two main sorts of bibliography are:

1. *Enumerative bibliography*: the listing of books according to some system or reference plan, for example, by author, by subject, or by date. The implication is that the listings will be short, usually providing only the author's name, the book's title, and date and place of publication. Enumerative bibliography (sometimes called *systematic bibliography*) attempts to record and list, rather than to describe minutely. Little or no information is likely to be provided about physical aspects of the book such as paper, type, illustrations, or binding. A library's card catalog is an example of an enumerative bibliography, and so is the list at the back of a book of works consulted, or a book like the *New Cambridge Bibliography of English Literature*, which catalogues briefly the works of English writers and the important secondary material about them. Many examples of subject-oriented enumerative bibliography are given in G. T. Tanselle's chapter "The Literature of Book Collecting" in this book.

2. *Analytical bibliography*: the study of books as physical objects; the details of their production, the effects of the method of manufacture on the text. When Sir Walter Greg called bibliography the science of the transmission of literary documents, he was referring to analytical bibliography. Analytical bibliography may deal with the history of printers and booksellers, with the description of paper or bindings, or with textual matters

arising during the progression from writer's manuscript to published book. Analytical bibliography (sometimes called *critical bibliography*) may be divided into several types, as follows:

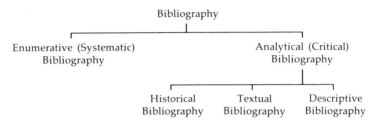

Historical bibliography: the history of books broadly speaking, and of the persons, institutions, and machines producing them. Historical bibliography may range from technological history to the history of art in its concern with the evidence books provide about culture and society.

Textual bibliography: the relationship between the printed text as we have it before us, and that text as conceived by its author. Handwriting is often difficult to decipher; compositors make occasional mistakes, and proofreaders sometimes fail to catch them; but (especially in the period before about 1800) we often have only the printed book itself to tell us what the author intended. Textual bibliography (sometimes called *textual criticism*) tries to provide us with the most accurate text of a writer's work. The equipment of the textual bibliographer is both a profound knowledge of the work of the writer being edited (and of his or her period) and an equally profound knowledge of contemporary printing and publishing practices.

Descriptive bibliography: the close physical description of books. How is the book put together? What sort of type is used and what kind of paper? How are the illustrations incorporated into the book? How is it bound? Like the textual bibliographer, the descriptive bibliographer must have a good working knowledge of the state of the technology of the period in order to describe a book's physical appearance both accurately and economically. Descriptive bibliographies are books that give full physical descriptions of the books they list, enabling us to tell one edition from another and to identify significant variations within a single edition. Good descriptive bibliographies are therefore indispensable to book collectors, whatever their fields of interest and whatever the time period their collections cover. Unfortunately, good descriptive bibliographies do not exist for all fields and for all periods, and, as a result, collectors must frequently do their own spade work, learning enough about the techniques of descriptive bibliography to distinguish among editions, issues, and impressions without outside help. The bulk of this chapter therefore concerns itself with the vocabulary of descriptive bibliography, concentrating on the earlier periods of bookmaking (because a chronological understanding of the structure of books is essential), but also sketching in the relationship between the handmade and the machine-produced book.

Analytical bibliography is concerned with the whole study of the physical book: its history, its appearance, and the influence of the manner of production on its text. The three types of analytical bibliography—historical, descriptive, and textual—are all closely interrelated. It is lunatic to attempt to draw overly precise distinctions among them. They are equally important as aids to our understanding of books.

Further discussion of the various sorts of bibliography may be found in Roy Stokes' *The Function of Bibliography* (London: Andre Deutsch, 1969).

In the creation and dissemination of a printed book, many persons take part: to move from book production to distribution, they may include (besides the writer) the typefounder, the papermaker, the printer, the illustrator, the binder, the publisher, the retail bookseller (or librarian), and the book collector (or library reader). Each of these individuals can affect the physical book as it comes to us—some more than others, to be sure. But all need to be accounted for if the complete history of a book is to be known and described.

The Typefounder's Role

In the first half century or so of printing (the period before about 1500) printers frequently cast their own type, but specializations within the graphic arts industries developed quickly, and by the end of the sixteenth century, most printers were buying their type from typefounders, who issued specimen sheets of their wares for the printers to choose from. Gutenberg used black-letter type, but in most countries except Germany, the Roman letter quickly superseded black-letter types, and it is with various forms of the Roman letter that we are concerned with in the printing of most books.

Descriptive bibliographers attempt to describe early and later typefaces exactly, and there is an extensive literature on this complicated subject; one might begin with *Printing Types: An Introduction* (Boston: Beacon, 1971) by Alexander Lawson. But most book collectors are unconcerned with the minutiae of type description unless they collect very early printed books, for which a knowledge of type styles is essential in dating and in the determination of the place of printing.

The Papermaker's Role

Before the early nineteenth century, all paper was made entirely by hand on a mold, one sheet at a time. The sheets used in book work varied in size from about 12 × 15 inches to about 19 × 27 inches; larger sizes (though they were very expensive) were available for special work. Most paper made before 1800 contains *chain lines*, the faint, parallel lines, about an inch apart, revealed when the sheet is held up to a light. The chain lines are a reflection of the ribs of the paper mold; the paper is thinner at the points directly over these ribs than it is elsewhere on the sheet. The dimensions of printing papers are almost always in the ratio 3:4. If, for example, the shorter side of the sheet is 15 inches, then the longer side will be about 20 inches. The ribs of the paper mold creating the sheet are always parallel to the short side of the sheet, and—whatever the size of the sheet—the pattern of chain lines on it will always appear as in Figure 1.

A sheet of handmade paper often contains a *watermark*, a design (like chain lines, revealed when the paper is held up to a light) caused by a corresponding wire pattern fastened to the surface of the paper mold. There may also be a *countermark*, caused on the surface of the paper by a corresponding wire pat-

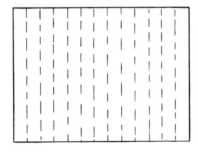

FIGURE   1

tern fastened to the end of the mold opposite the watermark, which sometimes gives the name of the maker of the paper or the date of manufacture or licensing. The most usual position of the watermark and the countermark are as shown in Figure 2.

The standard introduction to the history of paper and papermaking is Dard Hunter's *Papermaking: The History and Technique of an Ancient Craft* (2nd ed.; New York: Knopf, 1947); this is the first book you should read on the subject, perhaps skipping the long sections on non-Western paper the first time through. Only one further point needs to be made here. Beginning in about 1760, papermakers learned to produce wove paper on molds of wire mesh; paper made on such molds does not have chain lines (though it may have watermarks and countermarks), and it tends to have a somewhat smoother surface than *laid* paper (that is, paper with chain lines). Technological developments in the early nineteenth century allowed wove paper to be manufactured in endless webs on large, automatic machines. These machines created paper without chain lines; but (for aesthetic reasons) false chain lines were occasionally pressed into the paper with a dandy roll.

Machine-made paper can be cut to any size for printing, but sheets so made differ from handmade paper in that they have no *deckles*, the uneven, feathery edges always found on all four sides of handmade sheets and produced by the peculiarities of the hand paper mold. Books printed on handmade paper are frequently trimmed after the folded sheets have been sewn together, to remove the deckle and produce neater edges. A book whose leaves have not been trimmed is called *untrimmed* or *uncut* (the words are exactly synonymous), terms not to be confused with *unopened*, which describes a book having the folds of the sheets still intact at the top and outer edges. An

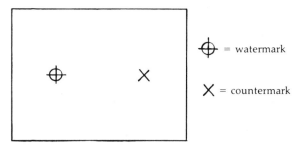

FIGURE 2

unopened book cannot be read, because the folds prevent you from opening certain of the pages; an uncut book will nevertheless have opened pages and can be read very easily.

The Printer's Role

The great watershed in printing, as well as in papermaking and binding, is the beginning of the nineteenth century. The period before about 1800 is generally called the handprinting period; the later period is called the machine-printing period. Terms like *folio*, *quarto*, and *octavo*, although still frequently (and imprecisely) used today to refer to the size of a book, have specific bibliographical meanings reflecting the practices developed during the handprinting period.

Pre-1800 printers first had to determine the *format* of the book—the manner in which the whole sheets of paper were to be printed. They might decide to print the sheets in such a manner that the binder would be presented with piles of printed sheets each of which was to be folded once down the middle, parallel to the short side of the paper, forming sections or *gatherings* each of two leaves totaling four pages. Because a book is made up of a number of these folded sheets or gatherings, the printer would often identify each sheet with a letter or number at the bottom of the first page; these marks are called *signatures*. By assembling the folded sheets in the order indicated by the signatures, the binder could be sure that the book was put together in the right order.

A book made up of sheets folded once, with two leaves totaling four pages per sheet, is called a *folio*, abbreviated f° or 2° (that is, two leaves/sheet).

The size of the sheet determined the size of the resulting book. If the printer wanted a large book he would start with a large sheet, and with a smaller sheet if he wanted a smaller book. Not all large books are folios; only books made up of whole sheets folded once can properly be so described. The sloppy tendency to describe any large book as a folio must be avoided. The word has a specific and unvarying definition: a book made up of whole sheets folded once. If the original sheet is 20 × 28 inches, the size of the book will be 20 × 14 inches; if the original sheet is 12 × 16 inches, the size of the book will be 12 × 8 inches—but both books are folios.

A folio book consisting of 280 pages contains 70 sheets of paper folded to make 140 leaves. The binder would receive the book from the printer as 70 different piles of printed sheets. To produce one copy of the book, he would take one of each of the 70 different sheets, fold each of them once, and sew them together one at a time through the folds. Because this meant a lot of sewing, printers frequently arranged the printed pages in such a way that the binder was to put two or more gatherings one inside the other *before* sewing. That is, instead of gatherings each of one sheet, two leaves, and four pages, each gathering would consist of (say) three sheets of six leaves and twelve pages. In this instance, the first leaf of the second sheet would be signed A2, and the first leaf of the third sheet would be signed A3, so that the binder would be sure to put one folded sheet inside the others in the right order, as in Figure 3. The three sheets of the second gathering would be signed B1, B2, and B3 and assembled in the same manner, and so forth through the entire book.

A book in folio format made up of gatherings each containing three printed sheets is called a folio in 6s, because there are six leaves in each gathering; a folio made up of gatherings each containing six printed sheets is a folio in 12s, and so forth. A folio book of 400 pages where each gathering contains two sheets would contain 100 sheets ($\frac{1}{4} \times$ 400 pages) and 50 gatherings (2 sheets/gathering); the same book in which none of the sheets were quired together would contain 100 gatherings.

When the printer wanted a smaller and more convenient format than folio, he could set his pages in type and *impose* them (lock them up for printing in the right position) in such a way that the binder had to fold each of the printed sheets twice, creating gatherings of four leaves totaling eight pages. This format is called *quarto*, or 4°. Most quartos are smaller than most folios. But if the original sheet is a large one of 20 × 28 inches,

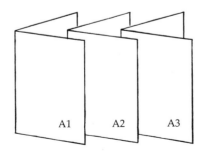

FIGURE 3

for example, each single folio leaf produced from the sheet will be 20 × 14 inches and each quarto leaf 14 × 10 inches. If the original sheet is a small one of 12 × 16 inches, then each folio leaf will be 12 × 8 inches in size. The quarto leaf in the first case is larger than the folio leaf in the second. But the difference between quarto and folio and the other formats is generally easy to determine during the handprinting period, for the evidence provided by chain lines and watermarks enables us to distinguish among them. Because the chain lines in laid paper are always parallel to the short side of the sheet, folio format will *always* produce gatherings where the chain lines run vertically up and down the leaves; the watermarks and countermarks (if present) will appear approximately in the middle of the page, as in Figure 4. In quarto format, the sheet is folded twice, the chain lines are horizontal, and the watermark will be in the gutter of the gathering, halfway up the leaf, as shown in Figure 5.

It is much more difficult to determine the format of books made of wove paper, especially if they have been trimmed, removing the deckle. Because format is decided not by the size of the leaf but by the evidence of chain lines, watermarks, and

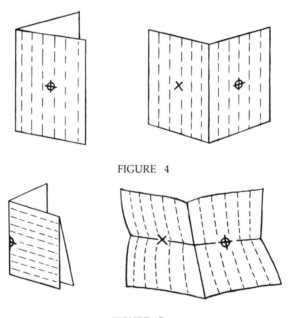

FIGURE 4

FIGURE 5

deckles, it is not usually possible to determine the format of nineteenth-century books that lack these features. Books printed on paper produced in endless rolls are not given a format at all—the best one can do is to give the exact size of the leaf in inches or centimeters.

The Collational Formula

The details of the physical makeup of sheets in a printed book are called its *collation*, and the format and collation of books may be (and frequently are) expressed by means of a shorthand formula. Thus a book in folio made up of nine gatherings signed A, B, C, D, E, F, G, H, and I can be succinctly described as follows:

$$2°: A-I^2; \text{ 18 leaves}$$

The leaf count properly is always present, given after the collation; the one serves as a check on the other (9 gatherings times 2 leaves equals 18 leaves).

The letters J, U, and W are latecomers into the Roman alphabet, and printers have traditionally left them out when assigning signatures to their gatherings of folded sheets. Thus the following formula:

$$4°: A-Z^4; \text{ 92 leaves}$$

is the one you would expect to find for a book containing 23 quarto gatherings. Where the book has more than 23 gatherings, the signatures may proceed by doubling: after signatures X and Y and Z, we find signature AA (or Aa or a variant). The attempt of the collational formula is always to be as brief as possible; thus instead of:

$$2°: A-Z^2AA-ZZ^2AAA-BBB^2; \text{ 96 leaves}$$

the following simple condensation is used:

$$2°: A-3B^2; \text{ 96 leaves}$$

Some lengthy books must use five or even more complete alphabets in giving every signature its unique designation. American printers often simplified the signing of their gatherings by using numbers instead of letters. The formula:

$$2°: 1-48^2; \text{ 96 leaves}$$

describes a book with exactly the same format and collation as

$$2°: A-3B^2; \text{ 96 leaves}$$

The printer's tendency, especially when working on the first printed edition of a book, is to begin the setting of type and the printing of the sheets with the first page of the text proper, saving the preliminary pages containing the title page, the table of contents, the dedication, the list of subscribers, and so forth, until after the text is completed. By this method the author has until the last possible moment to make up his or her mind what to say in the preface, or to whom to dedicate the book, and so on.

This manner of proceeding is reflected in the collation of a book. The printer will often arbitrarily assign the signature B or C (or 2 or 3) to the first gathering of printed text proper, reserving the letters A or A and B (or the numbers 1 and 2) for the preliminary gathers to be printed later. But the preliminaries frequently take up more pages than the printer has allowed gatherings. So he may sign the preliminaries with lowercase letters:

$$4°: \text{a--d}^4\text{B--I}^4\text{K}^2; 50 \text{ leaves}$$

Sometimes the very first gathering is not signed at all; it may be the title page, which the printer prefers not to deface with a signature:

$$4°: [\text{a}]^4\text{b--d}^4\text{B--I}^4\text{K}^2; 50 \text{ leaves}$$

Either brackets or italics may be used to indicate unsigned gatherings, where there is no question what the signature should be. Where the signature cannot be inferred, the Greek letter π (pi) is used to indicate a *preliminary*, unsigned gathering:

$$2°: \pi^2\text{A--R}^2; 38 \text{ leaves}$$

that is, an unsigned gathering of two leaves before 18 signed gatherings; or

$$2°: \pi^2 2\pi^2\text{A--I}^2; 22 \text{ leaves}$$

that is, for two preliminary unsigned gatherings before nine signed gatherings. Another Greek letter, χ (chi), is sometimes found in a collational formula. It indicates an unsigned gathering found elsewhere than at the beginning of the book:

$$2°: \pi^2\text{A--G}^2\chi^2\text{H--I}^2; 22 \text{ leaves}$$

Such gatherings may occur simply because the printer forgot to indicate the signature, or because the author had afterthoughts that needed more space than the original plans called for. The binder may not be pleased when he encounters the unsigned gatherings, but he does have the page numbers of the book to help him—if the book is paginated (early printed books frequently were not). He also has the *catchword*, the first word of the following page printed after the text at the bottom of the preceding page, as a check that he is assembling the book in the proper order. Catchwords were commonly used until the end of the eighteenth century; they are uncommon during the machine-printing period.

If the printer chooses to use *octavo* format, he will impose his pages in such a way that the binder must fold each sheet three times, creating eight leaves and 16 pages in each gathering. The collational formula describing a typical octavo (abbreviated 8°) book might be:

$$8°: a–b^4B–H^8I^2; 34 \text{ leaves}$$

In octavo format, the chain lines on each leaf will always be vertical, and the watermark if present will be divided among various leaves in the upper inside corner of the gathering, as in

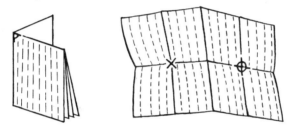

FIGURE 6

Figure 6. A more complicated octavo book might have the following formula:

$$8°: \pi^22\pi^4*^2B–F^8\chi^2G–R^8S^4; 142 \text{ leaves}$$

that is, a book in octavo format consisting of an unsigned first gathering of two leaves, a second unsigned gathering of four leaves, a third gathering of two leaves signed at the bottom of the first page with an asterisk, five gatherings signed B through F of eight leaves each, an unsigned gathering of two leaves, eleven gatherings of eight leaves each signed G through R, and a final gathering of four leaves signed S. In all cases, the chain lines of the gatherings would be vertical. Thus the first π gathering is made up of a quarter of a whole sheet, and the final S gathering is made up of a half sheet—but both are octavo in format.

Why would the printer bother with the complicated preliminaries:

$$8°: \pi^22\pi^4*^2$$

when he could simply have one gathering signed A of eight leaves? There could be many reasons for this apparent inefficiency: π^2 may be the half-title and the title page, printed at the very last minute; $2\pi^4$ might be the dedication, the text for which was prepared long in advance and that was set into type and printed at once, before anything else. The two-leaf asterisk gathering might be the table of contents, a substitution for an earlier, *canceled* pair of leaves in which a major mistake had been discovered, necessitating the change. The leaf or leaves removed is called the *cancellandum*; the leaf or leaves replacing the cancellandum is called the *cancellans*.

To continue with standard formats, we next have the situation where the printer imposes his pages in such a way that the binder must cut or fold the sheet parallel to its long side into thirds, and then fold the sheet twice the other way, creating 12 leaves totaling 24 pages. The chain lines will be horizontal and the watermarks, where present, will appear on the outer margin, about a third of the way from the top or bottom edge of the leaf. This format is called *duodecimo*, or 12°. The collational formula describing a typical 12° book might be:

$$12°: \text{A–H}^{12}; \text{96 leaves}$$

Frequently duodecimo books are printed on half sheets of paper, producing gatherings of six leaves:

$$12°: \pi^2\text{A–T}^6; \text{118 leaves}$$

The intricacies of duodecimo and other formats not mentioned here may be studied in detail in such books as Philip Gaskell's *New Introduction to Bibliography* (corrected edition; Oxford: Clarendon, 1974). During the handprinting period, folio, quarto, octavo, and duodecimo were the major formats; but there were many others: 16°, 24°, 32°, and so forth. After the introduction of large metal printing machinery in the nineteenth century, very large sheets of wove paper cut from endless rolls were used in printing, and the sheet might be imposed in such a way that it was meant to be folded many times, creating gatherings of 32 or even 64 pages. But there is a law of diminishing returns: If there are too many folds to be made, the binder will have a difficult time beating the gatherings into manageable shape. A typical nineteenth-century book might have as its collation:

$$9" \times 6": \text{[A]}^8\text{B–R}^8\text{S}^4; \text{140 leaves}$$

Because there are no chain lines or deckle, and because the paper in the book is likely to have been machine-made, we cannot give the format, only the size of the leaf. This book has a preliminary unsigned gathering of eight leaves which we infer as the A gathering, followed by 16 gatherings each of eight leaves, concluding with a final gathering signed S of four leaves, for a total of 140 leaves.

The printer is always interested in imposing his pages of type so as to produce an economical and logical format and collation. But simplicity is not always possible in first editions in particular, the more so when the author insists on extensive corrections in proofs, causing the canceling and the replacement of individual leaves or whole gatherings. But although the first edition of a book might have as its collation the following:

$$4°: \pi^2 2\pi^2 \text{a--c}^4 \text{d}^2 \text{B--M}^4 \text{N}^2 \text{O--R}^4 \text{S}^2; \text{ 82 leaves}$$

later editions of the same book, containing an exact resetting of type in a page-for-page reprint, would be reimposed more simply, producing a collation like the following:

$$4°: [\text{a}]^4 \text{b--d}^4 \text{e}^2 \text{B--R}^4; \text{ 82 leaves}$$

where the text proper in both instances begins with the first leaf of the B gathering. The reader of these two editions would not be likely to notice the difference in collation—but the book collector is very much interested in the difference, because the first is very much more likely to be the first edition (whether or not it is so labeled) than the second.

Without having recourse to page numbers (for there may not be any or they may be inaccurate), each page of a book may be described in bibliographical terms, using the collation. In the following:

$$8°: [\text{A--B}]^8 \text{C--Y}^8; \text{ 176 leaves}$$

the eight leaves of, for example, the D gathering are called D1, D2, D3, D4 . . . D8. Right-hand, or *recto*, pages may be distinguished from left-hand, or *verso* ones: D1^r, D1^v, D2^r, D2^v, D3^r . . . D8^v. Thus F8^v will face G1^r. In all of these gatherings, the first and eighth leaves will be connected to each other through the spine, as will the second and seventh, the third and sixth, and the fourth and fifth leaves. These pairs of leaves are *conjugate* with each other, joined by the fold. In a standard quarto gathering, leaves 1.4 and 2.3 are conjugate.

Canceled leaves may be indicated in the collational formula:

$$8°: [A]^4B–C^8D^8(\pm D7)E–H^8; \text{ 60 leaves}$$

indicating that the original seventh leaf of the D gathering has been removed and replaced, usually by pasting the cancellans (or replacement leaf) to the stub of the cancellandum (or removed leaf).

A final, important point about collations. They are used to indicate the *ideal copy* of a book, that is, the complete book as intended by the printer, when his part is done. Sometimes the binder will remove final blank leaves, or conjugate leaves containing advertisements, and a book which began life as:

$$4°: a–b^4B–M^4; \text{ 52 leaves}$$

might in many copies be lacking a1 (a blank leaf) and M3 and M4 (four pages of advertisements). The collation of the book is nevertheless as given here, and *not*:

$$4°: a^3b^4B–L^4M^2; \text{ 49 leaves}$$

Because the collation indicates the ideal copy of the book, and because the copy in front of us may be imperfect, we may have to look at several or even many other copies of the same book, before we can be sure of the collation. Thus the utility of descriptive bibliographies to the collector. The competent writer of a descriptive bibliography will have studied as many copies as possible of all of the books described, helping us to understand the makeup of each individual copy, when seen in isolation.

When first encountered, collational formulas can seem forbidding, but even with the basic information provided in this chapter, the following formula can be understood:

$$4°: [a]^4b–c^4d^2B–D^4E^4(\pm E^4)F–2F^42G^4(\pm 2G4)2H^4(\pm 2H^4)$$
$$2I–3P^43Q^4(\pm 3Q2)3R^2; \text{ 260 leaves}$$

This is the collation of the 1713 edition of Newton's *Principia mathematica* (the entire E and 2H gatherings were canceled).

These are the major shorthand symbols used in constructing collational formulas, though there are other ones used under special circumstances. Readers who have become infatuated with the subject are referred to Fredson Bowers' *Principles of Bibliographical Description* (Princeton, 1949) for a much more detailed exposition of format and collation, with many examples. Although matters of format and collation can quickly become abstruse, a basic knowledge of the subject is advantageous to the book collector. Determining collation gives us a much better picture of the way in which a book was printed, frequently enabling us to determine priority of editions, and providing us with clues about variant states and the reasons for them. Collectors prefer copies containing uncanceled leaves and all blanks; having the collation of a book before us allows us to center our attention on such matters efficiently.

The Publisher's Role

Behind the publication of most books is an *entrepreneur*—the person who assembles capital, secures a manuscript, and causes it to be printed, illustrated, assembled, bound, and distributed. During the earliest period of printed books, the entrepreneur was most often the printer himself, but by the beginning of the sixteenth century, the publisher's role became increasingly distinct as a trade separate from that of the printer.

The publisher acquired a manuscript and sent it off to be printed. Meanwhile, the publisher might decide to have the book illustrated and hire an artist to execute the illustrations, sending the resulting blocks or plates to be printed, perhaps to an entirely different shop than the one responsible for the *letterpress* or text of the book. While the printer deals with matters concerning the format and collation of a book, the publisher's concern is a broader one. Bibliographically speaking, the point is important, because the collational formula of a book deals solely *with the folding of the sheets of text and the leaves conjugate with them*. It does *not* take account of separately printed illustrations or maps or fold-out sheets tipped into the book in various places. In a complete bibliographical description of a book, the account of the illustrations is reserved for a section of its own that follows the collational formula. Separately printed illustrations may be inserted in any number, anywhere into a printed book, and we cannot tell from the collation of the printed sheets where they are to go, or how many there are to be.

The publisher will advertise the finished book and superintend its distribution to the retail bookseller (or librarian), so that the public may acquire copies. The publisher must also decide whether there is to be more than one issue of the book; perhaps one issue will be illustrated, another not. Furthermore, a decision must be made whether to market the book in various kinds of bindings, some more elaborate and expensive than others.

The Binder's Role

Again, the early nineteenth century is the great watershed. Before the end of the eighteenth century, the publisher stored most of his books in flat, unbound sheets. Retail booksellers bought their books in sheets and had only a few copies at a time bound up for sale in their shops. More elaborate bindings would be ordered individually by the customer to his or her own specifications: bound in calf or morocco, with or without gold tooling, and so forth. For the sake of convenience, the bookseller might provide books with their sheets folded and cheaply stitched into paper covers, or paper-covered boards. But these bindings were considered to be temporary, to be replaced with more permanent coverings after purchase. About 1,000 copies of the first Shakespeare folio of 1623 were printed; if we could reassemble them all, we would expect to find every one of them in a different binding.

With the introduction of cloth for bookbinding in the 1820s, publishers began to bind up much or all of an edition in identical fashion *before* releasing any copies to the retail booksellers; cloth lends itself to *edition binding* (as this practice is called) in a way that leather skins, each one unique, do not. A cloth binding is usually less splendid than a leather one, and, especially in the earlier decades of edition binding, many book buyers replaced the original cloth bindings in which their books were purchased with more elaborate ones. Present-day collectors, of course, generally prefer the original binding (however temporary it was intended to be) to a later one (however splendid); and a Jane Austen novel in original boards is worth several times one that has been rebound magnificently in morocco. There are bibliographically sensible reasons for this preference, because we always want to get back as close as possible to the book as originally marketed. A later binding may be very beautiful, but the later binder may have trimmed the leaves, removed blank ones, replaced defective leaves or whole gatherings with substitutes from other copies (and possibly other editions), or otherwise tampered with the original.

Furthermore, later bindings may obliterate evidence of *provenance*, or previous ownership. We are always interested in knowing who owned a book, through evidence of bookplates or names in the end leaves—evidence that later owners (or their binders) may not have been concerned to preserve. For all these reasons, the magical words in the description of bookbindings are *as originally issued*. Bear in mind, however, that these words make the most sense in the period after about 1770; before that time, the distribution of books to retail booksellers in sheets required individual, bespoke bindings.

For books produced during the handprinting period, collectors prefer *contemporary* bindings, that is, bindings executed soon after publication. Bindings tend not to be either signed or dated, but an expert can usually date them to within a couple of decades. There is no single, good, general introduction to the history of bookbinding where you can go to learn dating techniques, but one of the best places to start is with the Walters Art Gallery exhibition catalogue *The History of Bookbinding 525–1950* (Baltimore, 1957).

I have emphasized several times in this chapter that the vocabulary used in descriptive bibliography attempts to be precise, and that the cause of precision is not helped by the existence of both specialist and common definitions for the words we use in descriptive bibliography. The word *collation* is an example of such a word; it is properly used to describe the order of the printed and folded sheets of letterpress. But booksellers frequently use the phrase "collated and perfect" to mean that they have gone through a book page by page to ensure that all leaves are present in the right order and that all illustrations are also present. This phrase is sanctioned by long usage, and so long as we know what is being talked about, there is no harm done.

Serious-minded bibliographers occasionally issue injunctions against the slipshod use of their favorite words: issue, state, impression, edition, signature, gathering, and the rest. These Canute-like injunctions are to be taken seriously—but not too seriously; it depends upon one's audience. Still, a knowledge of the exact vocabulary of descriptive bibliography is a useful adjunct to the book collector's education, for the complete descriptions of printed books can necessarily become very elaborate, dealing with matters of type, paper, printing, illustration, and binding, as well as with the circumstances surrounding writing and publication. The better a book collector can interpret the vocabulary of descriptive bibliography, especially that which most concerns the periods of his or her interest, the better the quality of books likely to be bought, and the better the quality of the collections formed.

7

Fakes, Forgeries, Facsimiles, and Other Oddities

Joan M. Friedman

Iᴛ ɪꜱ ᴀɴ ᴜɴᴘʟᴇᴀꜱᴀɴᴛ ᴛʀᴜᴛʜ that whenever an object or service is seen by some as having value, which generally translates into monetary terms, unscrupulous or naïve people are apt to appear on the scene with ersatz versions of the same product or service. Such is certainly the case with collectible books, and thus the collector must be armed against deceptive practices with knowledge that will enable the detection of fakes and forgeries when they are encountered.

It is fashionable in some circles to question what harm fakes and forgeries cause, if it takes scrutiny by an expert (who even then may continue to be fooled) to detect them; should not average collectors be just as happy with a fake as with the original, if they cannot tell the difference? Such arguments are specious for a variety of reasons. Apart from the desire not to be a victim of fraud—the extortion of a high price for an "authentic" old or rare object that is, in fact, nothing of the kind—there are a number of considerations that *do* make a difference, which are of interest to collectors and scholars and which justify the higher value placed on an original book.

The scholar's case is perhaps the most clear-cut. Original editions and other early works provide historical evidence upon which conclusions can be drawn about the author's intentions and the evolution thereof, about the nature of the book-buying public at an earlier period, about the manufacture of paper or leather bindings, about practices in printing houses. These and other uses have been enumerated in Terry Belanger's chapter entitled "Descriptive Bibliography" in this book. For valid conclusions to be drawn from bibliographical evidence, it is, of course, essential that the source material itself be authentic. For some purposes facsimiles may be adequate, but as a rule serious scholars will want to be certain of their evidence in a bona fide original work.

For collectors who own books solely for their own enjoyment, for the delight of ownership and the pleasure of reading, the case for authenticity may be less clear. Most collectors, though, collect original works because the physical object itself provides a part of the enjoyed activity—an evocation of a time past, a link with an author, replication of an experience belonging to a particular time, place, or person. Enjoyment of, say, *The Mysteries of Udolpho* may be immeasurably enhanced by the knowledge that the edition in one's hands is the same Jane Austen read when writing *Northanger Abbey*. To a lover of books, such experiences are worth paying for.

A further cause for seeking only authentic books is the protection of one's investment, for, in the long run, fakes tend to be unmasked. Although the primary motive of most collectors of books is not financial, it is nonetheless true that old or important books usually increase in value over the years and thus represent a sound area of investment (albeit one with high overhead in costs of storage, moving, and maintenance—but as for a house, these costs are returned in use).

Even if only a small amount of money is spent without any motive of financial return, a collector is entitled to get what he pays for. Although in a few celebrated cases, notably that of T. J. Wise, to be discussed below, forgeries can come to have a monetary value of their own,[1] they can never have the same value as the original they claim to be; and despite market factors, to many individuals they have no value at all. The rule here must be, know what you are buying and pay for it according to the worth of the known object to you.

Some Definitions

There are essentially three types of nonauthenticity one encounters in the bibliographic world: true forgeries, fakes, and facsimiles. The true forgery, the production from scratch of a new work—an edition that never had previous existence but purports to be the product of a different time or a different hand than is actually the case—is very uncommon in the world of books. There have been a few notorious practitioners of bibliographic forgery, but by and large true forgers find more fertile ground in the fields of literature and art than in the printed product.

Fakes, on the other hand, are rather more common. A fake, in the case of books, is the exact copying of a work that has a legitimate existence, with an intent to deceive the buyer into believing it an original. An exact copy made without the intention of deception is properly termed a facsimile; however, it is not uncommon for facsimiles honestly made to be passed off or mistaken for originals, at which point they become fakes. Both facsimiles and fakes are often used to complete imperfect copies of genuine works, producing a "made-up" or "sophisticated" copy.

True Forgeries

A true forgery of a printed book would have to be a printing of an edition never actually in existence, but one that might plausibly have existed. In such cases the text printed may be the perfectly authentic work of a reputable author—it is not literary forgery, the ascribing of work to one other than the true author, that we are dealing with here. Extraction of a poem or essay from a collected edition of an author's works, and printing it in what purports to be an earlier, separate edition, is one way of producing a forgery. Legitimate separate printings of this nature do exist, but obviously not for all works by all authors, and such that are found are necessarily scarce. An author may be little known early in his or her career; early published works thus appear in small editions and may be discarded as ephemera. Surviving copies are rarities bound to be especially prized by collectors.

Fabrication of this sort of early edition was the course taken by the most notorious of bibliographic forgers, Thomas James Wise (1859–1937). Wise, a London businessman in the essential-oil trade, was by avocation a bibliographer and book collector who assembled a distinguished collection of English literature of the seventeenth through nineteenth centuries, including one of the first serious collections of the Romantic poets. He was able to add to his collection extremely rare works of the Romantics by seeking out their friends and children and buying association copies (with the author's inscription) and manuscripts still in family possession. Wise produced an eleven-volume catalogue of his library,[2] as well as bibliographies of Ruskin, Swinburne, Tennyson, Robert Browning, and Wordsworth, which remain standards to this day. So well known as a connoisseur of Victorian editions did he become, that he was called upon by the Browning and Shelley societies to oversee the production of their facsimile reprints of those author's works.

These reprints were type facsimiles (which will be treated in the following section) intended for the use of the members of the societies, many of whom were scholars who could not afford or obtain original early editions of Romantic poetry. This work provided Wise with much valuable experience in the production of books intended to look 50 or more years older than they really were and gave him unquestioned access to the London printers Richard Clay and Sons, who did the printing. They, in turn, became accustomed to Wise and his projects, with title pages bearing fictitious imprints; they knew that these printings would subsequently be accompanied by editorial matter including a clear statement that they were reproductions. No suspicion was aroused when Wise continued to provide Clay and Sons with this type of work.

In this fashion Wise was able to have printed more than fifty pamphlets purporting to be earlier editions of the works of Victorian poets and writers—the Brownings, Tennyson, Dickens, Ruskin, Rossetti, Kipling, and even George Eliot, among others. His forgeries were exposed in 1934 by John Carter and Graham Pollard in a masterpiece of bibliographic detection modestly titled, *An Enquiry into the Nature of Certain Nineteenth Century Pamphlets*.[3] The means by which Carter and Pollard proved the case against Wise were technical and will be discussed below, but the circumstances that aroused their suspicion in the first instance bear scrutiny here, for no technical studies would have been undertaken had not suspicion existed.

The work that first raised question was what alleged to be a private printing of Elizabeth Barrett Browning's *Sonnets from the Portuguese*, bearing the imprint, "Reading, Not for Publication, 1847." Before this pamphlet turned up in 1888, the earliest printing known of these sonnets was that in the 1850 edition of Mrs. Browning's *Works*.[4] At the time the Brownings were honeymooning in Italy, Mrs. Browning's close friend Mary Russell Mitford was living near Reading, and the story circulated about the pamphlet was that Mrs. Mitford arranged to have them printed for private circulation only, after Robert Browning insisted that his shy wife's masterpiece deserved a wider, if restricted audience.

The odd fact about this pamphlet, though, was that no one had ever heard of it prior to 1888; the copies extant were all in mint condition, unbound, whereas one might expect them to have been lovingly, even preciously, bound and read often. No copy had been in the sale of Robert Browning's own library. None bore presentation inscriptions, which was particularly odd for what was, after all, a private printing, presumably intended in entirety for presentation by the author to her close friends. Wise's story of the circumstances of the pamphlet's production was substantiated by Edmund Gosse, who had been a personal friend of Robert Browning's and who was easily taken in by Wise's account in his eagerness to be associated with the "find." Later, Wise provided a provenance for the copies that had passed through his hands, in the person of W. C. Bennett, a friend of Mrs. Mitford's; but that part of the story was not revealed until after Bennett's death in 1905. And the final odd circumstance was that all copies that had turned up could be seen to have passed through Wise's hands.

This provenance was held in common with a number of other pamphlets of the same sort: all early separate editions of poems of nineteenth-century writers, all in mint condition and without presentation inscription, most unbound. And a very large number of them passed through a single bookseller in London, Herbert Gorfin. It turned out that Wise had helped Gorfin, who had been a clerk in his firm, set up his bookselling business and had sold him a stock of the forged pamphlets, explaining that they were a cache of "remainders" he had acquired.

A seal of respectability had accompanied Wise's forgeries before Carter and Pollard intervened, through a particularly clever set of circumstances. From time to time Wise would present the British Museum Library with books from his collection, including many of the forgeries. These would be cataloged and would appear in the British Museum Catalogue, then, as now, a standard source for verification of printed books.[5]

The episode of Wise and his forgeries shows the importance of attention to the circumstances in which a very rare book appears on the market. Very few will ever deal in the kind of absolute rarity Wise produced, and even extreme caution, the checking of provenance and consultation of bibliographies and library catalogs, cannot guarantee against a dishonest person in the right position. Once there is suspicion, though, technical study will confirm what circumstances may suggest. Ironically, Wise himself recognized that bibliographic deception cannot succeed in the long run—the *Enquiry* itself opens with a quotation from Wise's bibliography of Swinburne, "The whole thing proves once more that, easy as it appears to be to fabricate reprints of rare books, it is in actual practice absolutely impossible to do so in such a manner that detection cannot follow the result."

Fakes and Facsimiles

A faked book purports to be a copy of one quite legitimately in existence, while it is in actuality a later replication of the book. There are a number of methods of producing a reproduction of a book, each with its own virtues and faults.

The earliest facsimile-fakes were manuscript copies of the printed page. These can be quite skillful and accurate in the minutest details, because they are copied from an actual model, and perpetuate all the printed imperfections that may appear. In this way they are superior to type facsimiles, fakes where a font of type as close as possible to the original is used to print copies; such reprintings will rarely stand up to scrutiny next to an authentic original. A third method is photographic replication of the printed page, usually by photo-offset lithography.

Facsimiles of entire books are often produced openly and with honest intentions. As was seen in the Wise case, learned societies sponsor facsimiles of early, rare editions for the purpose of scholarly study. In recent years the reprint industry has come to play a major role in publishing, providing the university and research library market with photographic facsimiles of important works in all fields, works that were formerly obtainable only at the oldest or wealthiest institutions. These works are sold as reprints and priced accordingly. They have title pages appended with the modern imprint and with the information that they *are* reprints of a particular edition. These books can themselves go out of print and begin to appear in

booksellers' catalogues; one expects them to be described as reprints and would be justified in returning any reprint not so
described.

In a few cases such reprints do not carry a modern title
page; and sometimes an unscrupulous dealer will remove the
modern title page. When this is the case, and the facsimile is
passed off as an original, it has become a fake. It is not often
hard to detect such a fake, provided one is alert to the possibility. Familiarity with authentic examples of the sort of book
involved will develop sensitivity to the inherent shortcomings
of counterfeits.

Made-Up Copies, Sophistications,
Doctored Books

Collectors are more likely to encounter, and be fooled by, a
genuine but imperfect copy of a book "made up" with facsimile
sheets or leaves from another copy than they are to meet with a
complete fake. Such a made-up copy, provided that the facsimile or other sheets used to complete it derive from the same
edition as the imperfect book, may have legitimate appeal to a
collector, provided that the collector recognizes it as a made-up
copy when purchasing. But, in the words of John Carter, "Mak-
ing-up with leaves from a copy of a different (usually later) edition—i.e., faking-up—is a bibliographical felony and valid
grounds for divorce between buyer and seller."[6]

An infamous example of a book made up with sheets from
a different edition was the Jerome Kern-Baron Rothschild copy
of the first edition of *Tom Jones*, published in six volumes in
1749. Described in glowing terms in the famous catalogue of the
Kern sale in 1929, including the statement that turned out to
have an unintended truth, "Such another copy cannot exist,"[7]
the book later was revealed to have been made up with twelve
leaves from the second edition. John Hayward, Rothschild's
cataloguer, uncovered this unwelcome insertion in 1940, when
he was preparing the printed catalogue of the Rothschild collection.[8] Rothschild subsequently sued the dealer who had sold
him the book, on the grounds that it had been represented to
him as the copy described in the Kern sale catalogue, which,
needless to say, had not mentioned the sophistication. The case
was settled out of court in 1944, in Rothschild's favor.[9] It set the
important precedent that booksellers are expected to have the

requisite expertise to know their wares and are responsible for accurate description of their stock. Collectors have redress against dealers who mislead them.

The notorious T. J. Wise was also responsible for sophisticating a number of books in his library and books he sold to the Chicago collector John Wrenn. In his case the doctoring was all the more heinous because he removed the needed leaves from copies in the British Museum Library, thus committing theft as well as fraud. The whole affair has been chronicled by David Foxon.[10]

Made-up copies can be acceptable when the book made up is an especially rare one, and the collector is not likely ever to encounter a perfect copy. This is apt to be the case when dealing with incunabula, many copies of which were routinely provided with manuscript facsimiles of their missing pages during the nineteenth century. Certainly one would not turn down such a book on the grounds of imperfection, but the price paid ought to be less than for a complete copy, were it available.

Sophisticated books can turn up in a number of other forms collectors must be alerted for. Hardest of all to detect, especially if a book has been rebound or rebacked, is an imperfect copy made up with leaves from another original, even more defective copy. Provided both copies of the book are of the same edition and issue, many uses are well satisified with such a copy, and only the collector concerned specifically with bibliographic history will reject such a book out of hand. Nevertheless, one would hope that dealers would accurately describe such doctoring, and a collector is justified in shunning dealers known to make up copies in this way without stating so. It is once again a matter of being entitled to know what you pay for.

Detecting Fakes Bibliographically

Now that one is aware of the sorts of fakes and forgeries that can be found, the next step is to learn to identify them when encountered. Some of the methods described will become second nature to collectors, performed automatically whenever a book is examined; others are more involved and can only be applied when suspicion is aroused. Ideally, the automatic actions will alert to the need for more concerted analysis.

The most evident way of judging the authenticity and completeness of a book is by collation, that is, by the gross physical makeup of the book. Collation, particularly for books of the handpress period, will tell how many pages there ought to be and whether all leaves present in a gathering derive from the same printed sheet. Stubs, with or without leaves attached, should alert one to something odd: They could be genuine cancels, but they might be facsimiles supplied for missing leaves.

Format is important in detecting facsimiles of entire books, which are sometimes printed on modern paper "laid" with chain lines. However, since these modern chain lines are machine-produced on rolls of paper, they bear no relation to a sheet in an original work, and so will sometimes end up oriented the wrong way for the format indicated by signatures. Other modern facsimiles, although reproducing original signature letters, make no attempt to reproduce the original format; a quick inspection of the gatherings reveals them for what they are.

Another simple bibliographic way to verify the authenticity of a book is to compare it with a printed description of a known original in a bibliography or library catalogue. As the Wise case proved, such listing does not absolutely guarantee the authenticity of a book, but it reduces the probability of simple fakes—and few fakers can be as well placed as Wise was. Listings in the National Union Catalog and the printed catalogue of the British Museum Library are particularly useful for confirming "first editions," a phrase sometimes optimistically employed by booksellers who have overlooked earlier printings. Obviously, a book described as "unrecorded elsewhere" ought not to be found in these places; such a claim, though it may be perfectly true of a genuine work, should put the buyer on guard. Printed bibliographies can confirm the existence and correct collation of a book, but the best ones can do more.

"Points," or peculiarities present in most books printed in the handpress period and a great many in more recent eras, can help identify genuine editions. Examples of points include misprints, dropped letters, misplaced signatures, cancels, and the like—accidental events in the book's history that might be overlooked by a counterfeiter. Of course, fakers, too, have access to bibliographies and can reproduce such points if they take the trouble, so their presence alone cannot absolutely guarantee the book in hand.

The best bibliographies provide still more information, some of which is nearly impossible to fake. A standard method for characterizing a book's text, for example, is the measurement of 20 lines of type. Such a measurement tends to be unique to a particular setting of type, due to variable factors such as the lead spaces usually placed between lines of type. Even the best type facsimiles might not reproduce this accurately. Other "fingerprint" information, such as indication of the position of a signature letter in relation to the text above, can identify absolutely a particular setting of type. This information, of course, would apply equally to a photographic facsimile as to an original, but photographic facsimiles are easily detectable by other means.

Detecting Fakes by the Study of Type

Technical examination of a suspected book itself will often reveal anomalies that can only be explained as the work of a faker. Luckily, collectors need only rarely resort as far as laboratory analysis; most problems will resolve themselves before reaching that stage, by visual analysis. In extreme cases, scientific analysis can prove a case definitely.

The most striking feature of a book is its printed text, and examination of the type and its printing is one of the quickest ways to determine fakes. A superficial examination of a page of type reveals immediately, for example, whether the page has been printed by letterpress or, in facsimile, by offset lithography.

Letterpress, in which type metal comes into direct contact with each sheet of paper, leaves a characteristic impression, or "bite," in the paper; running a finger over the page will confirm that metal has been pressed into the paper. On the other hand, offset lithography, the method used for most photographic facsimiles, transfers ink to paper via an intermediate rubber mat; the ink lies smoothly on the surface of the paper, and there is no bite.

When a copy of a book is particularly dingy, the sheets may be chemically washed and pressed to brighten it up; if this has been done, the bite will be nearly pressed out. Such washing of the leaves can be a warning that facsimile leaves have been inserted and disguised by the overall pressing. In any case, the degree of bite to be found in letterpress varies from pronounced to faint; experience will develop the ability to detect it, and some find that visual inspection does as well in revealing photographic facsimiles—they never look quite as fresh as a letterpress product. Most contemporary books have, for about a decade now, been printed by offset lithography in the first instance, so the detection of photographic facsimiles of modern books may prove to be more difficult in the future than is now the case.

Visual examination of text is a relatively easy way to detect manuscript facsimile pages. The quality of ink used in a pen is very different from printer's ink, having a water or eggwhite rather than an oil base. As a result, such a page will reflect light very differently from a printed page. A manuscript facsimile will also lack the bite characteristic of letterpress, and slight magnification of manuscript letters will reveal the smooth edges of pen lines instead of the irregular edges of printed type.

Typefaces themselves provide some of the most irrefutable bibliographical evidence, particularly useful when dealing with type facsimiles or with forgeries. Although certain few general varieties of typefaces have prevailed in Western printed books since the seventeenth century, variations in fonts, some more noticeable than others, have obtained throughout typographic history, and most fonts have been in use over limited periods. Although there are varieties of modern fonts based on earlier designs, often bearing the name of the earlier design—for example, Monotype Caslon—these are always distinguishable from their models. Even recuttings of the same design can be detected by experts. Unless one has access to the same cold type or matrices used in an original, a type facsimile is destined to differ from its model. Thus it is often possible to identify faked pages of type by the use of an anachronistic typeface.

The evidence of typefaces was one of the prime pieces of information marshaled by Carter and Pollard in proving the Wise forgeries. Certain letters of the alphabet have natural forms that overlap the rectangular form of a piece of type: the top of a lowercase "f" and the bottom of a lowercase "j," if designed to fit in smoothly next to other letters, ought to extend over the body of the type onto the shoulder of the adjacent letter in a projection called a *kern*. However, such kerns tend to be fragile and prone to breakage, and so in the late nineteenth-century typefaces were designed that fit these letters onto the body of the type, by introducing a backward bend into the looped part of the letters. Such an improved font was used by Richard Clay and Sons in printing some of the Wise forgeries, including 16 of them dated before 1873. Yet the kernless fonts, designed by the typefounders P. M. Shanks & Co., were first introduced in 1880–1883.

Furthermore, Carter and Pollard were able to trace the font used in Wise's pamphlets to the particular printing house (for typefounders sell their products to many printers) by an additional typographical quirk they recognized: In some of the pamphlets, a question mark belonging to a different style and size of type altogether appeared now and then. Apparently, the piece of type had migrated into the wrong case, and although such examples of "foul case" are not at all uncommon in printing houses, the odds against the same piece being misplaced in the same way in more than one shop are astronomical. Thus, when they discovered a legitimately printed work with the same typographical oddity, they were able to trace all the Wise pamphlets to the printer of that work.

Other type facsimiles can be easily distinguished without resorting to the subtleties of kerns. In the nineteenth century a number of type facsimiles of incunabula were produced. Because the black-letter typefaces used in the printing of fifteenth-century books had long since passed out of use and existence, it was necessary to design and cut new typefaces imitating the originals. In many cases this was done exceedingly well; such type facsimiles, when the paper and collation has been given similar attention, are, in isolation, hard to distinguish from an original. However, comparison of such a work with its original model will immediately reveal the facsimile.

Early typefaces had many more characters than the 26 letters in upper- and lowercase: There were a great number of ligatures, or joined letters, as well as symbols for abbreviations common in medieval writing and variant forms of many letters. The newly designed fonts, however close to the originals they came, could not always be set in exact faithfulness to the original's usage of the ligatures, variant forms, and abbreviations. Furthermore, modern inking and presswork is apt to be more even and reliable than that of the fifteenth century. In general, these type facsimiles present an altogether more uniform page appearance than is to be found in genuine incunabula; a collector who deals in incunabula will soon learn to recognize the irregularity of a genuine fifteenth-century book.

These typographical distinctions may not be immediately discernible to beginning collectors, but it does not take too long a period spent consciously looking at type to become sensitive to its variations. Some good books can help one learn type-faces;[11] it is one of the fields of bibliography that many collectors find most fun in its own right. However, many of the convicting characteristics of anachronistic typefaces that are used in type facsimiles are more subtle than those described above; a collector may only be able to suspect a font's authenticity.

Detecting Fakes by the Study of Paper and Ink

Paper as well as type can often reveal an inconsistency between what a book purports to be and what must have been its production history. I have mentioned above how the evidence of chain lines, if not consistent with format, can indicate a modern facsimile. Chain lines and watermarks, or the absence thereof, can also indicate that certain leaves are fakes or inserted from different editions when they do not match the company they keep. Watermark evidence must be used very carefully, though, because in the handpress period it was not uncommon for a printer to use more than one lot of paper in printing a given book; perfectly legitimate copies will often change watermarks in mid-book. However, this is not the case for modern machine-produced books, where one does expect a single lot of paper to have been used, and a change does indicate tampering.

Nevertheless, the study of watermarks can lead to the detection of anachronisms very similar to the anachronisms found in type facsimiles. Clever fakers do take the trouble to obtain stocks of old paper on which to print their copies, but often the paper is not old enough or comes from the wrong geographic area to match the original publication. In one well-known case, a fake was made of the first printed map of an American city, Mexico City, which was originally issued in 1524 in Nuremberg. The engraved facsimile was printed on old paper, but it bore a watermark dating it to 1584. Once the watermark evidence had provided the suspicion, superimposition of the fake with a copy of the original revealed other slight differences inevitable in reproducing a thing so nonmechanical as an engraved line.[12]

It is worth noting that the evidence of the watermark alone cannot convict a fake. In the nineteenth century in particular (when watermarks are often obliging enough to include a date), it was very common for both type and plates to be saved and reprinted at a later date; when stereotype plates came into use this procedure became more common. Type originally set in 1804 but reprinted in 1830 may appear on paper dated 1829; in this case one is dealing with a reprinting rather than a faked edition, and comparison with an early issue will confirm that the setting of type (or engraved plate) is identical.

The chemical makeup of paper can provide useful evidence. Until the third quarter of the nineteenth century, all paper was manufactured from pulped cloth, cotton or linen. In the mid-nineteenth century, experiments resulted in paper manufactured first from a plant, esparto grass, and eventually from wood pulp, the source of most paper today. The procedures for making paper out of wood pulp have also changed over time: Different methods of grinding the chips and different admixtures of chemicals have resulted in a large variety of different papers, each introduced at a known date. Some of the Wiseian forgeries were printed on esparto grass paper, although they bore imprint dates as early as the 1840s, 40 years prior to the introduction of usable esparto grass paper.

The detection of esparto grass or chemical wood paper can be accomplished only by chemical tests that few collectors will be equipped to carry out. When there is suspicion, collectors may want to consult paper chemists in industry or in research institutions.

The chemical composition of ink, too, has varied over the centuries. Particularly in the last 100 years, synthetic compounds have found their way into printing ink. The presence of such compounds in books claiming to date before the compound's introduction is clear evidence of foul play. Detection of these compounds also requires laboratory analysis and is not likely to be useful to most collectors: Fakes usually reveal themselves long before ink tests become necessary.

Other Visible Signs

The imperfections expected in old books can point the way to leaves that have been supplied to an incomplete copy. For example, many old books have been eaten at by vermin—"bookworms"—leaving small telltale holes where they burrowed. Provided that there are no insects alive and active in a book when bought, and no better copy is available, such a copy may be acceptable to a collector. If the book has been made up with facsimile leaves or leaves from another copy, though, the worm holes will not be found in the proper positions on the supplied leaves, because they will not have been part of the book when the vermin were eating at it. The same is true of water and other stains often found: The newly supplied leaves will not have been with the book when the glass was spilled or the basement flooded, and thus they will lack the stain.

A Word about Bindings and Illustrations

Because they have value to collectors, bindings and illustrations are quite as likely to be faked as is printed text. And, as in the case of text, faking can include doctoring and making up as well as substitution of facsimile-fakes and forgery of new bindings or plates. Both are too complex for detailed treatment here, but a few remarks will serve as a warning.

The field of doctored bindings is a tricky one, because it is common accepted practice for dealers or owners to have bindings repaired in a style consistent with the original when a book has become too ragged to read. Usually this will take the form of a rebacking, and most dealers will include the information that a book is rebacked in their description of it. In fact, booksellers' catalogue descriptions nearly always include a brief indication of the binding on a book, and it is only when the book in hand does not conform to that description that fakery becomes an issue.

Collectors who are interested in bindings per se and are willing to pay for them must be prepared to learn through experience what bindings are "right," for there are few good books about historical binding. Exhaustive study of leather tools and other technical factors can help, but ultimately the judgment of bindings is more akin to art connoisseurship, where problems of authenticity are more often resolved by subjective factors than by hard and fast rules.[13]

Illustrations present a somewhat easier case, but they too are more problematic than printed text. Because most illustrations until the past 100 years were printed by different methods than text—usually engraving or etching—they had to be an addition to the letterpress sheets. The evidence of collation is not significant in verifying such plates, for they can never be conjugate with the text sheets; they are always insertions. Modern machine-printed illustrations and earlier wood engravings and line cuts can be and are printed along with text, and they are thus exceptions: Whatever has been determined about text and paper in books so illustrated applies equally to the pictures. For most older "plate" books, though, the book's makeup alone cannot reveal whether it has all its illustrations or whether those present are genuine.

Examination of illustrations themselves can provide some information about their authenticity. Photographic reproductions of illustrations, whether or not a screen has been used, will lack the raised ink characteristic of etchings and engravings (counterpart to the bite of letterpress). Even the lithographic illustrations of some nineteenth-century books can be detected in facsimile, if photographic methods have been used: Under slight magnification, the dots characteristic of the photographic screen will be revealed. If the original process itself has been employed, though—via reengraved plates or new lithographic artwork—one must again have resort to printed bibliographies and comparison of copies.

As the measure of 20 lines of type is characteristic of a given setting of type, so the size of a platemark is characteristic of an individual plate. It is easier to reproduce the size of a plate than of a complex setting of type, but it can be overlooked by makers of facsimiles. Good bibliographies and exhibition catalogues (illustrative matter often figures in exhibitions) will provide the size of platemarks for some, but rarely all, the plates of a book.

Because collation cannot be a guide, bibliographies must also be consulted by those who collect illustrated books and want to be certain of obtaining complete copies. Many of the best bibliographies list the titles or subjects of every plate in a book. Illustrations with captions that differ from those cited in such a bibliography may be supplied from a different edition or from a different book altogether.

Book illustrations are printed, by whatever means, on paper, and so the evidence of paper discussed above is equally valid in the study of plates. However, one cannot expect text and pictures to have been printed on the same or even similar papers: Different printing houses may have been responsible for them, and even the same printer will vary the paper used according to the type of printing employed.

Ultimately the most clever facsimiles, those produced by the same printing process as the original and by skillful counterfeiters, will respond only to aesthetic judgment. Familiarity with the illustrations in the type of book you collect, knowing your field, will eventually develop a sense of what is authentic. Comparison with undoubted originals, when possible, is also helpful when a plate is suspected.[14]

Piracies and False Imprints

Piracies and false imprints, deceptions that occurred in the past history of a book, do not really fall into the category of fakes. Nevertheless, modern collectors will want to be alert to their existence, to know what they are buying.

Piracies were especially prevalent before copyright regulations became enforceable in the mid-eighteenth century, though they continue to occur today. A popular book would be reprinted by a printer other than the one authorized by the author and issued to share in the proven market. Not only would authors be deprived of their earnings (in any case, authors have rarely made much money and often underwrite publication of their works), but the risk undertaken by the original printer or publisher would be inadequately repaid. Obviously, begetters of piracies do not reprint the many worthy books that do not sell well. Within given jurisdictions and countries, regulations might be strictly enforced, but until modern times copyright laws were not reciprocal, and there was nothing to prevent printers from setting up in a foreign country to produce piracies. Sometimes, in fact, piracies would be printed within the country of the original edition, but provided with a false foreign imprint to protect the illegal printer.

Piracies are of the same date and general bookmaking practices as the authentic editions they copy, but they do not necessarily attempt to mimic the original in the way that modern facsimiles do. Thus they may confuse collectors. Consultation of bibliographies can confirm that a piracy is *not* the original edition, but often a piracy will have eluded a bibliographer and thus be unrecorded. Identification must then be based on physical evidence that proves it genuinely old, and the negative evidence that it is not the recorded original. Of course, piracies in themselves may be greatly prized by collectors.

False imprints can also result from political or religious suppression. When a given viewpoint is censored by authorities, an author may publish as if in another jurisdiction. Such publications are not fakes at all and may be greatly desired by bibliographers and collectors.

A Postscript about Booksellers

The tone of this chapter has necessarily been suspicious and monitory, but it must be admitted that the book world, both buying and selling, is made up of some of the most honest and amiable people on earth. Most dealers strive to be honest, and although anyone can fail to spot occasional wrong items, honest dealers will refund the price of any book that is not what it is advertised to be.

There *are* questionable dealers who regularly make up imperfect copies with other imperfect copies and who supply odd bindings from a stock they keep for that purpose. They will generally justify such practices on the grounds that collectors do not want incomplete or disbound books. Some collectors do not, and they should be able to buy doctored copies if they want them. One would hope that dealers would represent honestly what they know to be the history of any book they offer for sale and allow customers to be the judges of what they want.

After a short time actively buying old books, a collector will learn which dealers are to be trusted and which are to be dealt with charily. Of course, desired books can appear for sale in unexpected and widely scattered places, and so no collector can hope to know the policies of every shop. You may be lucky enough to have a good, reliable bookseller in your home town, but in any case it is possible to build a relationship of mutual trust by mail or telephone with a number of the best booksellers worldwide.

Knowing the honesty of the seller of a book does not remove the responsibility of knowing about what you collect. As has been seen, the detection of fakes and forgeries requires accumulation of evidence of a number of different sorts—of general appearance, of type, of paper, of provenance and related circumstances, of bibliographical history—all of which combines to ring true or not. The knowledge that you are dealing with an honest bookseller is but one more piece of evidence that can give especial peace of mind.

Notes

1. In a bizarre development, the Wise forgeries have come to be of such interest to bibliographers that they themselves command good prices. Inevitably, the possibility of in turn forging the forgeries has been foreseen and written about in a recent detective novel, William H. Hallahan, *The Ross*

Forgery (Indianapolis: Bobbs-Merrill, 1974). It is of particular interest for its technical detail.

2. T. J. Wise, *The Ashley Library* (London: for private circulation, 1922–1926).

3. John Carter and Graham Pollard, *An Enquiry into the Nature of Certain Nineteenth Century Pamphlets* (London: Constable & Co.; New York: Charles Scribner's Sons, 1934).

4. Elizabeth Barrett Browning, *Works* (London: Chapman and Hall, 1850).

5. Fuller accounts of Wise's activities are to be found in: Wilfred George Partington, *Thomas J. Wise in the Original Cloth* (London: R. Hale, 1947); John Whitehead, *This Solemn Mockery* (London: Arlington Books, 1973), pp. 121–146; and Alan G. Thomas, *Great Books and Book Collectors* (London: Weidenfeld and Nicolson, 1975), pp. 237–245. Further evidence is presented in: John Carter and Graham Pollard, *The Firm of Charles Ottley, Landon & Co., Footnote to an Enquiry* (London: R. Hart-Davis; New York: Charles Scribner's Sons, 1948); William B. Todd, ed., *Thomas J. Wise: Centenary Studies* (Austin: University of Texas Press, 1959); and William B. Todd, *Suppressed Commentaries on the Wiseian Forgeries* (Austin, Texas: Humanities Research Center, 1969).

6. John Carter, *ABC for Book Collectors*, 5th ed. repr. (New York: Alfred A. Knopf, 1973), p. 132.

7. Jerome Kern, *The Library of Jerome Kern* (New York: Anderson Galleries, 1929), lot no. 511.

8. N. M. V. Rothschild, *The Rothschild Library* (Cambridge: privately printed at the University Press, 1954).

9. A lively account of the legal proceedings, including expert testimony of the bibliographic evidence and fascinating opinions on the American and English legal positions, is found in N. M. V. Rothschild, *The History of Tom Jones, a Changeling* (Cambridge: privately printed, 1951).

10. David Foxon, *Thomas J. Wise and the Pre-Restoration Drama; A Study in Theft and Sophistication* (London: Bibliographical Society, 1959).

11. Among the best are W. Pincus Jasper, W. Turner Berry, and A. F. Johnson, *The Encyclopedia of Type Faces*, 4th ed. (New York: Barnes & Noble, 1970); J. B. Lieberman, *Types of Type Faces* (New York: Sterling Publishing Co., 1967); and Alexander Lawson, *Primer of Type-Face Identification* (Arlington, Va.: National Composition Association, 1976).

12. See the account of this incident in Michigan University, William L. Clements Library, *Facsimiles & Forgeries: A Guide to a Timely Exhibition* (Ann Arbor, Mich.: The Ann Arbor Press, 1934).

13. One useful overview of binding history, with good illustrations, is Walters Art Gallery, *The History of Bookbinding, 525– 1950 A.D.* (Baltimore: Walters Art Gallery, 1957). Some forged bookbindings are discussed in Otto Kurz, *Fakes*, 2d ed. (New York: Dover, 1967), pp. 294–300.

14. The best single guide to book illustration is David Bland, *A History of Book Illustration*, 2d ed., 2d printing (Berkeley and Los Angeles: University of California Press, 1974). A splendid introduction to the recognition of graphic techniques is W. M. Ivins, Jr., *How Prints Look* (Boston: Beacon Press, 1958). For a discussion of counterfeit prints, see Kurz, *Fakes*, pp. 106–114.

8

Physical Care of Books and Manuscripts

Willman Spawn

F OR THE PURPOSE of this chapter, a distinction must be made between the collector who acquires books to preserve them for the future and the scholar who acquires them only in the study of a given subject. Those people who are passionately interested in a subject may well acquire books of value as they pursue their study, but they are unlikely to be interested in them as objects to preserve. As intelligent people they will not mistreat books; neither are they likely to give them the loving care of the true collector.

It is therefore to the true collector that the advice of this chapter is directed. The collector builds a collection of books (and related material) because of the desire and intention to preserve them for a future time. Whether this is because of the recognition of the value of books to the world of learning, because they are rare/beautiful/significant, because the person wants to be known as the owner of the biggest collection, because of the expectation someday to make a profit, all these reasons are immaterial to the advice and cautions that follow. No matter what the motive, the aim must be conservation, that is, the preservation of the collection for the future, including the needed or desired restoration of such individual items.

The Environment

The true collector's first rule for conservation deals with money: Get the most conservation for the most books with the funds on hand. It is only good sense *first* to provide the optimum environment for the entire collection and *second* to consider the special needs of individual items—unless the collector can afford to do both at once. Even in this plastic world, books are still composed mostly of organic materials that respond to heat, light, moisture, and chemicals in a great variety of ways, some of them contradictory to each other. Yet despite the seeming complexity of their requirements, the principles of this optimum environment can be reduced to a simple second rule: cool, damp (50 percent relative humidity), and dark.

"Cool" to most conservators means a *constant* temperature of 68° or less; some conservators would insist on 60 ± 5°. This requirement depends on a reliable and therefore expensive air-conditioning system and creates an atmosphere too cool for human comfort. A library can maintain such an atmosphere, at least in areas where books and people can be separated, but it poses a real problem for the collector whose books must coexist with people. The true collector has to choose between comfort and conservation, for it has long been proven that the deterioration of paper accelerates as the temperature rises.

"Damp" refers to the relative humidity (RH) of the environment, the amount of water vapor in the air expressed as a percentage of the total amount of vapor that the air could contain at a given temperature. The warmer the air, the more moisture it can hold. If the relative humidity reaches 100 percent, the air is saturated. For the collector, the important facts to remember about relative humidity are these: (1) the optimum RH should be maintained at 40–50 percent; (2) given the constant amount of water vapor in the air, the RH will decrease as the temperature rises, and increase as the temperature drops; and (3) paper is a hygroscopic material, that is, its fibers swell when damp and shrink when dry. This hygroscopic quality is what causes book boards to warp, framed manuscripts to pull loose from their mats, bookplates to wrinkle the endpapers they are pasted to, and much other less visible damage. When the relative humidity is excessive, above 70 percent, there is danger of mold growth, and when it sinks below 40 percent, paper tends to become brittle.

Although it is possible to keep an even temperature by means of an efficient air-conditioning system, it is rather more difficult to maintain a constant relative humidity. The air entering the system can vary widely in its moisture content, especially in those parts of the United States where the outdoor humidity can fluctuate from 15 percent to 75 percent with the seasons of the year. The collector must therefore invest in monitoring devices to measure the humidity in the particular environment (hygrothermographs and the like) as well as in an air-conditioning system that includes devices for altering the relative humidity and, ideally, filters for purifying the entering air. The importance of maintaining a *constant* temperature and relative humidity for the preservation of a book collection can hardly be overemphasized. R. D. Buck summarizes the point well: "By controlling the relative humidity of the . . . atmosphere, we indirectly control the moisture content of all the hygroscopic materials housed and retard their deterioration."[1]

The reference to mold growth may be amplified here. Mold (sometimes called mildew) is an airborne fungus that is always present in the environment. It thrives on moisture and such organic nutrients as paper, cloth, adhesives, sizing, and so on. Without any visible evidence of their presence, mold spores can exist for years on books and papers until conditions conducive to their growth occur. As long as a book collection is housed in an optimum environment, with careful attention to housekeeping and to the condition of new acquisitions, the collector has little to fear from mold but is wise to be on the watch. The explosive growth of mold associated with the aftermath of water damage or with the chance combination of very high relative humidity and temperature is treated in more detail elsewhere in this chapter.

"Dark" to the conservator means as little light as possible shining directly on the objects to be preserved. To the collector it must mean a minimum of exhibition time, either in frames or display cases, and protection from daylight and artificial light. As Anne Clapp comments, "All other factors being equal, paper seems to live best in darkness"; this is a primary reason for the good condition of books and papers found shut up in trunks and bureau drawers.[2] The fading or yellowing effect of light (depending on the makeup of the paper) is the obvious damage; the breakdown of the cellulose molecules is invisible, but the damage is occurring just the same.

There are three sources of light to consider: daylight, fluorescent light, and incandescent light. Although it is the ultraviolet (UV) end of the spectrum in daylight and fluorescent light that is more damaging to paper, the infrared radiation of incandescent bulbs can generate heat in the objects illuminated that will accelerate deterioration of the paper. The collector should keep in mind that the strength of ultraviolet radiation in daylight is twice as strong as an equivalent amount of fluorescent light, and that fluorescent light contains five times the ultraviolet radiation of incandescent light.

In point of fact, *any* long exposure to an uncontrolled light source is at least ill-advised. In museums, the UV damage is avoided by using shutters, shields, and filters on windows and fluorescent fixtures, and the danger from infrared radiation is reduced by locating the bulbs at safe distances from the objects illuminated and by using specially designed bulbs that generate less heat when used as spotlights. The collector who keeps a collection stored away safely most of the time need not worry about light damage or invest in such expensive devices. However, collectors will surely think twice about displaying their collections or any part of them under any but the optimum conditions of temperature, humidity, *and* light, no matter how flattering the offer to exhibit may be.

Storage

Once the collector has provided the best possible environment for the collection, the next consideration is the proper storage for it. Book storage is a relatively simple matter: shelves of sufficient height and depth, efficient and nondamaging bookends or supports, and provision for oversized or unusually shaped volumes. A shelf height of 12 inches and depth of 10 inches is suitable for most books, but collectors will find that the outsized if not the oversized book is more common than is first suspected. The best solution is to have shelves of varying heights, sections of 10-, 12-, and 14-inch heights being generally satisfactory.

The preferred method of storage is still the glass-fronted bookcase with sliding or windowed doors. Doors protect the books from dust, and they offer both a physical and psychological deterrent to too much handling. Additionally, the back of the bookcase offers some protection to the books if the bookcase is placed against an outside wall, where fluctuating external temperatures may cause condensation. In modern houses, where bookshelves are often built against or even into the walls, condensation is a definite risk; such shelves are unsatisfactory for books of any value whatsoever.

The collector who specializes in fields where oversized books are common has more difficult (and expensive) storage problems. Even if shelves of sufficient height can be provided, shelving oversized books vertically is poor practice; gravity causes the weight of the pages to pull at the sewing, putting too much stress on the spine. Shelving them horizontally one on another is also damaging, for two reasons: The shelf is almost always too narrow to support the entire side of the bottom book, and consulting any but the top book means shifting at least some of the others and thus subjecting them to unnecessary handling.

Oversized books must have horizontal shelving of a depth sufficient to support the whole width of a volume. This means a cabinet or bookcase with shelves set 6 to 8 inches apart and 12 to 14 inches deep, with correspondingly wider and deeper shelves for extra-oversized books. Equally important, the collector must also provide very near the storage cabinets or bookcases a flat, unencumbered surface, large enough to allow examination of the largest volume, open. This will obviate carrying the volume for a distance to find such a table or having to hold it while a table is cleared or having to support the book part way open because the table is too small—all sources of potential damage and annoying as well.

The most commonly used bookend or support is the metal angle, consisting of an upright and a tongue that slides beneath the books. These are inexpensive and space saving, but too often books are forced onto the upright by accident ("knifing"), which can damage the pages severely. A more visible bookend, large enough to support the entire side of the book next to it, is preferable for books of any value. If metal bookends *are* used, it is sensible to place a dummy block between it and the first book in the row, which will prevent "knifing" very nicely.

When shelving and bookends have been provided, the collector will think about protective containers for books and manuscripts. Fragile, mint condition, or easily damaged items certainly should have protection; so should important items in poor condition that must wait for restoration. This second category would once have been candidates for immediate rebinding, along with items that the collector sought to "improve." The urge to rebind for appearance's sake only has pretty well passed, thanks to the growing sophistication of collectors who recognize the value of the item in its original garb, whereas the high cost has often removed hand binding from consideration for books in poor condition. Two useful alternatives to rebinding have been developed: the "clam shell" box and the pamphlet folder (see Figures 1 and 2).

The "clam shell" box, custom-made to fit the individual book, has a number of advantages: It leaves the book in its original appearance; it supports the book efficiently, either closed or open for display; it keeps out dust and light; it is cheap in comparison to rebinding, and its exterior can be as simple or as lavish as its owner desires; and the box design can be modified within to provide pockets or partitions to house related documents, photographs, and similar material. This type of protective container is preferable to the slip case, because the book can be removed from the latter only by pulling on it. It is certainly preferable to the two-part Solander case in which the book slides down into the bottom half and the top half of the case is then fitted over the bottom half. As with the slip case, physical force is necessary to remove a book from a Solander case—occasionally quite a lot of force, if the Solander case has been made a snug fit. Any adaptation of the slip case or Solander case to prevent this stress on the book, such as an inner case

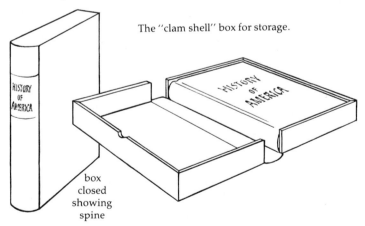

The "clam shell" box for storage.

HISTORY
OF
AMERICA

box
closed
showing
spine

FIGURE 1

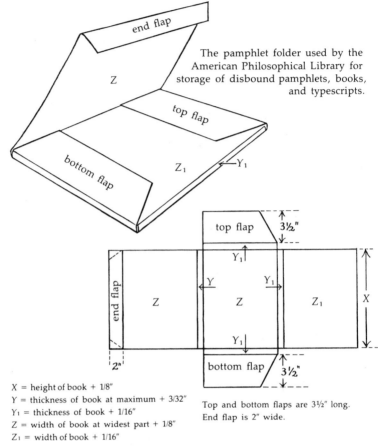

The pamphlet folder used by the American Philosophical Library for storage of disbound pamphlets, books, and typescripts.

X = height of book + 1/8"
Y = thickness of book at maximum + 3/32"
Y_1 = thickness of book + 1/16"
Z = width of book at widest part + 1/8"
Z_1 = width of book + 1/16"

Top and bottom flaps are 3½" long.
End flap is 2" wide.

The fractional additions are allowances for the thickness of the paper as the case folds over on itself.

FIGURE 2

or ribbons to pull on, only adds to the cost, which is high enough to begin with.

The second alternative method of storage, the pamphlet folder devised for disbound pamphlets at the American Philosophical Society (APS) Library in the 1950s, is now in use in a number of libraries and collections. The APS folder is made of a neutral, buffered folder stock (such as the Permatan handled by the Hollinger Corporation); the lightweight stock (.010 inch or 10 mil) is rigid enough to support a volume up to ⅜ inch wide, the heavier weight (.020 inch or 20 mil) will support a volume (or a pamphlet or set of leaves) up to 3 inches in thickness.[3] For example, the APS Library now uses these folders to store contemporary typescripts on 8½-by-11-inch paper. They are neat, efficient, and custom-sized. Collectors will find that with practice they can make these folders themselves, given the folder stock, equipment (mat knife, calipers, ruler, and square), and ample working surface. A pair of sharp scissors can even be substituted for the mat knife, if necessary. The most important requirement is careful measurement of the book to be enclosed, according to the formula shown with the illustration (see Figure 2). The folder shares most of the advantages of the "clam shell" box and adds a couple of its own—labels can be written or typed directly on the folder, and the folders are cheap enough to be discarded if they get dirty. And the "do it yourself" aspect appeals to many.

Although this guide is designed primarily for collectors of books, other items such as documents, autograph letters, loose prints, and maps often form part of a collection. The general principles for storing these flat items are simple: noninjurious containers, and horizontal rather than vertical shelving. The best container for a flat item is a folder of neutral, buffered paper, large enough to store the item unfolded, if possible, and rigid enough to support it when the folder is handled. These folders should be stored horizontally in a box just large enough to accommodate them, which will prevent their slipping back and forth within the box when it is moved. (Ideally, the box should be lidded, with a drop front for ease of access.) The box should then be stored horizontally. This storage method is quite flexible and is preferable to the vertical file, where the item must always rest on one of its edges, and where the folders sometimes become bent because they are allowed to slip and slide.

The Library of Congress is experimenting with a phased preservation program called "encapsulation" for flat items on paper. Each flat item is enclosed in a folder or envelope made of polyester film, which is then sealed all around (usually) with a double-faced pressure-adhesive tape; sometimes one side is left open so that the item can "breathe." The advantages of this treatment are many; the item is visible and can be handled freely, while it is protected from dirt. When torn or fragmented items are encapsulated, the pieces will stay in place so that further damage from movement is avoided. Ideally, each item should be deacidified before it is encapsulated. Unlike lamination, encapsulation provides an easily removed storage container. If a truly inert, noninjurious polyester film is used, then "Polyester film can provide protection on a phased treatment basis, and also for permanent preservation. No other supporting material of which we have knowledge can preserve artifacts for an indefinite length of time, and yet provide complete accessibility."[4]

If the flat item has already been matted, it is a good idea to cover it with a folder to keep the mat clean. It is unnecessary to unmount the item for storage *provided* that the mat is made of noninjurious materials: mat, mounting tabs, paste, cover tissue, and so on. If there is any reason to doubt any of these, it is best to unmount the item and discard the mat, however, expensive or handsome, rather than to run the risk of acid contamination from poor-quality materials. This rule goes double for framed items, which are even more vulnerable to damage from contact with poor materials such as cardboard or wooden backs, masking tape, kraft paper, cheap and/or colored matboard. Work with mats or frames is really best done by a conservator or a reliable framer who can guarantee the quality of the materials used.

In every case, the collector must remember the following cardinal rule: Never, never allow valuable paper, be it book or other item, to come in contact with acidic material. This means that all book tags must be made of acid-free and buffered paper, that copies, photographs, and documents must be stored separate from the book or manuscript to which they relate, that a barrier of neutral, buffered paper must come between any flat item and a suspect support. Acidity is the enemy of paper, any paper, and paper worth preserving must be protected from contamination.

Some final words. The true collector must assume a habit of modesty, even if it goes against the grain. The collector with a new acquisition will want, understandably, to show it off. That impulse must be stifled as firmly as possible, or the display reserved for those who will truly share the excitement. One must forego the pleasure of hanging a framed letter of a favorite novelist above a collection of the novelist's works, the pleasure of handing round a treasured item at a party, the flattering offer to exhibit a collection, displayed at unnatural angles and exposed to bright lights and low humidity. One must also be prepared to spend money on prevention of damage and on restoration as well as on acquisition, to spend time caring for a collection and seeking out the best ways to preserve it as well as on reading catalogues and visiting dealers. If the collector cannot do without the pleasure of showing off and is not prepared to obtain the optimum environment and storage, then that collector is not really concerned for the conservation of the collection. In the words of Carolyn Horton, "I would judge that more than 90 per cent of the books and documents that come to my bindery for repair or restoration are in a condition that could have been avoided by regular and appropriate preventive care."[5]

Specific Topics

ACIDITY

"Acidity in paper is one of the principal reasons for its deterioration," as libraries and collectors around the world are learning from sad experience.[6] The best environment cannot wholly compensate for the poor quality of most of the paper used in books for the past 100 years. The acidity in paper, which weakens its structure and makes it brittle, results from pollutants in the air, from contact with acidic materials such as paste, cardboard, and unstable plastics, and from impurities in the paper itself. The last-named cause of acidity is by far the most difficult to deal with.

The most seriously affected papers are those manufactured since the mid-nineteenth century that contain unpurified wood pulp and alum-rosin sizing. Books made of such paper are easily identified today: Their pages are brown at the edges and crack and shatter at a touch, they cannot be opened fully without breaking whole sections loose from the sewing. In numbers, the library problem is immense and growing every day and is exacerbated by the library's responsibility to make this fragile material somehow available to readers. Libraries are therefore investigating, experimenting, coping as best they can with this crisis by means of microfilming programs, deacidification programs, and cooperative conservation plans. In contrast to libraries, collectors may have only a few books in need of help, but they cannot make use of the library's tentative or stopgap solutions. They want the book itself, not a microfilm copy, and they are most unlikely to relinquish their treasures to someone else who may have better storage facilities. Deacidification, which sounds like a panacea, involves many new problems all its own.

"Deacidification" is more accurately called "neutralization and buffering." It introduces an alkaline substance into the paper in order to neutralize the acid in it, leaving behind a buffering agent to protect the paper against future contamination, at least for a time. At its most effective, it renders the paper pliable again and lengthens its life appreciably, according to aging tests. However, despite 20 years of experiment and research, there is still no agreement over its efficacy and the best method for performing it.

Three principal methods of deacidification have been developed so far: aqueous, nonaqueous, and gaseous, each with its variations and proponents. In the aqueous method, a book is disbound and the signatures separated into leaves; these are dipped into a water solution of calcium bicarbonate or magnesium bicarbonate, dried, reassembled, and rebound. The treatment is necessarily slow, and it requires experienced handling of the fragile leaves and expert knowledge of binding, inks, and paper, as well as considerable equipment.

The nonaqueous method was developed to speed up the process, eliminate the need for equipment, and avoid the risks always present when paper is immersed in water. One variation is a spray-can procedure, using a solution of magnesium methoxide in methyl alcohol Freon. The worker slowly turns the pages of the book to be deacidified, spraying each opening with a sweeping motion. This seems simple enough, but the spray may not penetrate the fibres deeply or evenly enough, there may be a color change in the paper due to the presence of groundwood fibres (especially true of modern papers), and the evaporation of the solvent causes the nozzle of the spray can to clog repeatedly.

Other methods of deacidification are still in the experimental stages and are not available to the collector. Some employ toxic chemicals and laboratory facilities, and so they are the province of the trained conservator only. Even when one or more methods are finally agreed on, there will still be decisions to be made on which papers are most benefited by which method, decisions best left to the conservator with experience in this field. Still, the collector should know that deacidification does exist, that the aqueous method is in routine use by some library and museum conservators, and that there is no agreement as

yet on the best method or on whether the results are truly beneficial *and* worth the risk and expense. The collector interested in
a more extended and detailed account of deacidification might
consult the articles by John C. Williams and George B. Kelly, Jr.,
cited in the bibliography at the end of this chapter.

BINDING

The binding on a book, no matter how elaborately decorated, is still essentially a cover to protect the pages from wear.
Unless the collector is especially interested in the history of
bookbinding or in the various styles of decoration or "finish-
ing," it will be the book's construction or "forwarding" that
will be most important, for its structure plays a major part in its
preservation. Bindings can be divided usefully into two periods
and types: pre-1880, the bound book using hand sewing, paper
wrappers or leather, wooden boards or cardboard, and paste;
and post-1880, the cased book using machine sewing, cloth or
paper covering, sometimes combined with decorative bits of
leather, cardboard, and glue. The first is a man-made object, the
second increasingly machine-made; today a book may be
bound (or cased) almost without human participation in the
process.

In the simplest terms, the handbound book consisted of
folded signatures (leaves) sewn together through the folds. A
thin binding was often covered with a stiffened paper wrapper
that was sewn directly to the signatures. In a thicker book, the
signatures were generally sewn on cords, up to six to a spine,
which strengthened the structure. The ends of the cords were
usually laced into the boards (of thin wood or cardboard), the
leather covering was pasted around the outside of the boards
and turned in over their edges, and the endpapers were pasted
down to line the inside of the boards and conceal the cord ends
and the turn-ins (see Figure 3). Even if the leather covering deteriorated quite badly, the sewing, the boards, and the laced-in
cords formed a sturdy structure that continued to protect the
pages within.

The cased book is rather another matter. The nineteenth
century's compulsion to mechanize all manufacturing processes, the introduction of cloth for binding, and the growing demand for cheap books all joined to create the cased book.
Signatures were sewn by ranks of bindery women, until the
invention of the Smyth book-sewing machine in 1879, and cas-

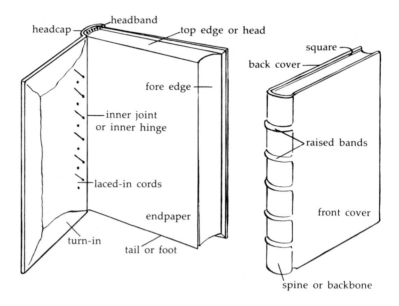

FIGURE 3

The handbound book.

es were made separately. To form the case, two pieces of cardboard were glued into the covering material of cloth or paper, forming the boards, and a piece of gauze of scrim was glued to the spine of the sewn signatures. The case was wrapped around the signatures, the scrim glued to the inside of the boards, and the endpapers glued to the boards over the scrim (see Figure 4). The machine-made signatures were married to the machine-made case, the whole structure held together only by glue. Casing lent itself marvelously well to mechanization; even cheap materials could be made to look slick and attractive—for a time. Alas, when the glue dried out or the cloth covering became brittle, the cased book had little structure to hold it together, with results familiar to all lovers of books.

In recent years, the ironically named "perfect binding" has proved to be the ultimate in the nonprotective binding. It consists of separate leaves, not signatures, glued together to a stiff paper cover. There really *is* no structure, not even sewing, only the adhesive; and when it fails or when the paper deteriorates, the book simply disintegrates. The same book that is manufactured without a human touch can be destroyed by the touch of a hand.

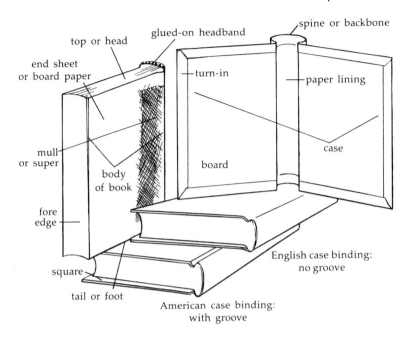

FIGURE 4

The cased book, American and English styles.

The handbound book can almost always be rebound, the cased book can often be restored but at considerable cost; the perfect binding cannot even be repaired. Therefore, the standard prescription for its preservation can only be a custom-made storage case of the type described previously, and as little handling as possible.

CLEANING

Cleaning of any type is potentially damaging to a collection. Although it may sound ridiculous, the old adage that "A good coat of dust preserves a book" can be true if altered to the past tense, for it indicates that the book has seldom been subjected to a vigorous cleaning. Even dusting can be damaging, no matter how soft the cloth or gentle the touch: corners may break off fragile paper covers, dirty fingerprints may be transferred to erstwhile pristine jackets, books may be dropped in handling.

If cleaning becomes essential, as happens in the best-regulated collections, then the owner is certainly the best-qualified person to perform it, for the owner knows the collection and cares for it as no one else can. Only the softest of cloths, kept clean so that the dust is not redistributed, should be used. Each book should be held firmly by its fore edge, not by its spine; this keeps the text block solidly together and prevents the dust from sifting inside. If a vacuum cleaner *must* be used, the shelves should first be checked for fragments that may already have become detached, and those fragments should be gathered up. Then the mouth of the nozzle should be covered with a piece of cheesecloth to cut down the suction and catch any other fragments that may come loose during the cleaning. The whole routine for a safe and effective cleaning is clearly outlined in Carolyn Horton, *Cleaning and Preserving Bindings and Related Materials*, a most useful guide for the collector (see the bibliography at the end of this chapter).

Once the books are clean, most leather bindings in good condition will benefit from a careful oiling. The dressing will improve their appearance and make the joints more supple; it will *not* prevent leather from deterioration by atmospheric pollutants or restore leather that has already begun to deteriorate. The oiling process, given in detail in Horton, can be summarized thus:

1. Provide an ample work surface, covered with layers of newsprint to be peeled off as they become soiled.
2. Make the dressing by warming an amount of anhydrous lanolin in a double boiler; add an equal amount of neat's-foot oil and mix well. These ingredients are available from chemical supply houses; the prepared dressing is available from such suppliers as TALAS (see Recommended Suppliers at the end of this chapter).
3. Select only as many books as can be accommodated on the work surface, dividing them into fullbound, halfbound, and quarterbound books.
4. Wrap a strip of brown paper the width of the pages around the text block so that it overlaps, and hold it in place by closing the covers; this will prevent the dressing from touching the pages.
5. Beginning with the quarterbound books, apply the dressing sparingly with the fingers of one hand, keeping the other hand clean for touching nonleather surfaces. Treat the halfbound and then the fullbound books in the same manner, keeping the second hand clean as long as possible.
6. Set the books aside for 48 hours, standing vertically but not touching.

7. Wipe them gently with a soft, dry cloth, turning it often and discarding it when it becomes greasy.
8. *Never* oil vellum or alum-tawed pigskin bindings, for disaster will result; these can be cleaned only by a professional conservator.

Smoke and soot damage from a fire are likely to need special treatment, especially if the smoke was greasy. The standard procedure calls for the use of a soft cloth moistened with naphtha or a commercial cleaning fluid. However, naphtha is flammable, and all solvents must be used in a well-ventilated work area. If the smoke damage is bad enough to call for the use of such solvents, the work had best be left to the professional conservator.

In connection with cleaning, the collector may find signs of insect infestation: droppings, larvae, little heaps of powdered paper or book covers. Even with good housekeeping and careful watch, insects can be brought into a collection on a new acquisition or on its wrapping; therefore, any new addition should be closely scrutinized before it is placed on the shelves. If insect life of any kind is suspected, preventing its spread is more sensible than getting rid of it later. The only equipment needed is a carton large enough to hold the new acquisition(s), a container for paradichlorobenzene crystals or naphthalene flakes, and polyethylene sheeting wrapped and sealed around the carton and its contents for two weeks. This procedure will kill both the insects and their larvae. For more general insect infestation, there is a whole range of pesticides to call on, as described in Clapp.[7] However, knowledge of pesticides and their short- and long-term effects is so constantly expanding that it would be wise to consult a professional exterminator for any other than a purely local infestation.

Dust Jackets

The dust jacket's original function was the protection of cloth bindings from fading and wear, while promoting the book in an inexpensive and eye-catching manner. Today's books are generally issued in dust jackets, some of marked artistic merit, so the collector understandably prefers to have a book in its original appearance. Unfortunately, if the book is handled at all, the jacket will suffer. There is really no way to maintain the jacket in mint condition except by removing it and storing it away like a print or broadside, substituting for it a plain jacket made of neutral, buffered paper.

It is no wonder then that collectors have expressed interest in the clear plastic covers currently in use in many libraries to protect dust jackets. There are two real disadvantages to these covers for the collector: they are commonly held in place by taping them to the inside of the book's covers, leaving a scar when the cover is removed, and there is no way to be sure that the plastic is stable and not harmful to the dust jacket or the book. It is true that inert, stable, nonharmful plastic sheeting is manufactured; Du Pont's polyester named Mylar is perhaps the best-known brand. But the plastic covers are a commercial item designed for short-term, throwaway use and are not manufactured to careful specifications for use in conservation. In the long run their use might do more harm than good. The collector is therefore advised to forego their use, as well as the use of food wrap, dry cleaner's bags, and similar plastic sheeting, and to purchase only the inert plastic products available from such firms as Hollinger and TALAS, which supply a full range of materials for conservators and the conservation-minded.

Exhibition

The exhibition of a collection is a clear sign that its owner has "arrived," together with other indicators such as the publication of a catalogue, citation in footnotes, bibliographies, and acknowledgments, and invitations to speak on his or her subject interest. Of all these, only the exhibition could be considered a threat to the collection, taking into account the possible harm from handling, transportation, exposure to light, dust, and low relative humidity, even possible theft. Therefore, a proposal to exhibit must be pondered with great care.

First, consider the source of the invitation. Does the institution offering to display the collection have a good reputation for the care of its own collections? If so, it may be good to someone else's collections. Does it change its exhibitions frequently? Three months, six at most, is the maximum time that material should be displayed if it is affected by light, heat, and humidity. Does it borrow from other reputable collections and institutions? If they trust it, perhaps it is worthy of trust.

Second, consider the collection. Does it include vellum bindings (likely to warp from lack of humidity), paper-covered pamphlets or books issued in parts (likely to fade under lights), dust jackets (ditto), stiff spines on books that will be opened for display (likely to split if the book is opened too far or for too long)? Have any of the items been exhibited before, often, or for long periods? If so, they may need time and seclusion to recuperate.

Third, consider the installer of the exhibition. Does he or she approach the material as an educator or as a designer? Is the installer interested in the exhibit's capacity to instruct others and in the preservation of the material, or is he or she more interested in the most effective presentation? Does the installer seem to know about the bad effects of acidity, ultraviolet and incandescent lights, fluctuation of temperature and relative humidity? Is the installer willing to guarantee the use of neutral, buffered paper as acid barriers, museum-quality mat board for framing, inert plastic, and acid-free paste and tissue paper where needed? Are the exhibit cases air conditioned and humidity controlled? Only when these questions are answered to the collector's full satisfaction should consideration be given to exhibiting all or any part of the collection.

FASHIONS

Fashions come and go in conservation as in other facets of culture. This is certainly true of manuscripts as well as of book collecting. For years, silking a manuscript with fine French fabric was considered the ultimate of preservation, until lamination came into being with the glamor of twentieth-century technology allied to inexpensive plastic. Unlike silking, lamination is an irreversible process, as its users learned to their sorrow when the plastic deteriorated. Pasting documents into albums was also once considered the thing to do, despite the fact that the documents sometimes got folded the wrong way when the pages were flipped too quickly. As long as good paste was used, the documents were fairly safe, but when the paste was exchanged for the new fashion of rubber cement (which oxidizes and discolors both the document and its backing), a good deal of harm was done before its injurious properties were realized. Then came the fashion for storing and displaying manuscripts in clear plastic folders. A potential for damage existed in the plastic's attraction to dust and the paper's hygroscopic ability to hold moisture, which occasionally resulted in mold growth; a more serious problem (known in at least one instance) was created when the chemical reaction of the plastic folder with the ink of the manuscript caused the writing to disappear entirely.

Fashions in book conservation have not been so varied or extreme. In earlier centuries the fashionable collection was the one rebound to a distinctive style, regardless of how many original bindings were destroyed in the doing. Sometimes, an otherwise acceptable binding was destroyed so that the signatures could be washed and/or bleached to remove stains, dirt, and foxing, and thus return the paper to its proper whiteness. (In addition, washing occasionally helped to conceal the fact that the book was a made-up copy.) In rebinding, it was often necessary to trim the edges in order to gild them, during which margins, marginalia, running heads, even text fell away under the binder's knife. True lovers of books can only be grateful for the apparent death of this particular fashion and can pray that it never be resuscitated.

GADGETS

Gadgets can be described as those useful devices promoted by ingenious designers and manufacturers to make life simpler. Where would we be without paper clips, elastic bands, pressure-sensitive plastic tape, masking tape, epoxy, staples, ballpoint pens, and marking pens? Useful as they are, do they have any place in contact with a collection worth preservation? The answer must be an unequivocal "No."

The best course for the collector is to steer clear of all gadgets that are touted as "cure-alls" for his or her problem, be they ever so highly recommended. A single example may serve as sufficient warning. Some years ago, a small company advertised an inexpensive substitute for rebinding, in the form of a coating that could be colored to match the bindings in need of repair. This was to be brushed on spines, joints, any places that needed help, and was supposed to hold the binding together, improve its appearance, and save the owner lots of money. Its use was accepted enthusiastically by quite a number of people, who very soon damned it with equal vigor—for when the temperature in the environment dropped somewhat, the coating cracked and peeled away, taking with it whatever had remained of the binding beneath.

ASSISTANCE

Help for the collector comes in a number of forms: guides such as this one, articles and books written for the librarian, archivist, or curator, seminars and conferences, and the employment of trained conservators. The last-named help has been the most difficult type to find. Collectors will be grateful to know that the Preservation Office of the Library of Congress has offered to help with technical questions and the location of competent conservators. The Library of Congress is also publishing a series of leaflets on conservation topics. Three titles are currently available: *Selected References in the Literature of Conservation; Environmental Protection of Books and Related Materials;* and *Preserving Leather Bookbindings.* For information and for copies of the leaflets (available without charge), the collector should write to the Assistant Director for Preservation, Administrative Department, Library of Congress, Washington, D.C. 20540.

Sometimes, help is needed instantly, and the most familiar example of such a crisis is water damage. No matter whether the source of the water is a flood, a leak, or a fire, the consequences can be beyond calculation. Again, the Library of Congress stands prepared to help with advice on steps to be taken and, if need be, to serve as a coordinating agency for emergency salvage efforts. In the meantime, all collectors should prepare themselves by obtaining a copy of the free booklet *Procedures for Salvage of Water-Damaged Library Materials,* prepared by Peter Waters, Restoration Officer of the Library of Congress. In 30 pages, he describes the problem of water damage and the physical factors affecting it, outlines the salvage operations, advises on evaluation of loss, and offers sources of assistance and supplies, equipment and services. The following lines from the preface will serve to indicate the catastrophic results of water damage to any collection of books and manuscripts:

> The complete restoration of water-soaked documents, particularly items in bound form, can be a costly process even under favorable conditions. In the majority of cases, the high costs involved do not justify the salvage and restoration of books which are in print and/or replaceable.[8]

Can there be any doubt that in conservation, an ounce of prevention is worth pounds of cure?

Recommended Suppliers

The Hollinger Corporation sells archival storage supplies (neutral buffered paper, boxes, envelopes, folders, tissue paper, plastic sheeting, museum mounting board) to libraries and other institutions and will sell in small lots to conservation-minded individuals. TALAS carries the Hollinger line, selling single items and by lots, and also supplies tools, equipment, and books for binders, papermakers, and calligraphers. Catalogues are available from both firms; the TALAS catalogue costs $1: The Hollinger Corporation, Box 6185, 3810 South Four Mile Run Drive, Arlington, Va. 22206 (703–671–6600) and TALAS, Technical Library Service, 104 Fifth Avenue, New York, N.Y. 10011 (212–675–0718).

Notes

1. R. D. Buck, "A Specification for Museum Airconditioning," Part I, Technical Supplement no. 6, *Museum News* 43, no. 4 (1964): 54.
2. Anne F. Clapp, *Curatorial Care of Works of Art on Paper*, rev. ed. (Oberlin, Ohio: Intermuseum Conservation Association, 1973), p. 23.
3. See Recommended Suppliers at the end of this chapter.
4. "Advances in Conservation Technology for Library Materials" (a lecture by Peter Waters and Robert E. McComb of the Library of Congress at the AIC Second Annual Meeting, May 30–June 1, 1974).
5. Carolyn Horton, *Cleaning and Preserving Bindings and Related Materials* (Chicago: American Library Association, 1967), p. xvii.
6. Clapp, *Curatorial Care of Works of Art on Paper*, p. 15.
7. Ibid., pp. 30–34.
8. Peter Waters, *Procedures for Salvage of Water-Damaged Library Materials* (Washington, D.C.: Library of Congress, 1975), p. iii.

Bibliography

Banks, Paul N. "Environmental Standards for Storage of Books and Manuscripts," *Library Journal* 99: (February 1, 1974): 339–341.

Useful summary of standards projected for new bookstack at Newberry Library by its conservator, with bibliography of technical sources not commonly cited.

"Books in Peril: A Mini-Symposium on the Preservation of Library Materials." *Library Journal* 101 (November 15, 1976): 2341–2351.
Papers by Pamela W. Darling and Paul N. Banks designed to stimulate the librarian into rational, immediate action on behalf of his or her collections.

Clapp, Anne F. *Curatorial Care of Works of Art on Paper*, rev. ed. Oberlin, Ohio: Intermuseum Conservation Association, 1973. 105 pp.
Clear, reliable, carefully compiled guide for the curator, of considerable value to the serious collector; highly recommended.

Horton, Carolyn. *Cleaning and Preserving Bindings and Related Materials*. Illus. by Aldren A. Watson. Chicago: American Library Association, 1967. 76 pp. (2nd ed., 1969).
No. 12 in Library Technology Program Series on Conservation of Library Materials, with concise, simple directions for reconditioning a library; invaluable to the collector.

Kelly, George B., Jr. "Practical Aspects of Deacidification." *Bulletin of the American Institute for Conservation* 13, no. 1 (1972): 16–28.
Technical summary of efficiency of various methods of deacidification by chemist in Research and Testing Office at the Library of Congress.

Ostroff, Eugene. *Conserving and Restoring Photographic Collections*. Washington, D.C.: American Association of Museums, 1976. 16 pp.
Revised version of technical reports first published in *Museum News* in 1974, in which the Smithsonian's Curator of Photography discusses environment, effects of residual chemicals, restoration, and storage.

Spawn, Willman. "After the Water Comes." *Pennsylvania Library Association Bulletin* 28, no. 6 (November 1973): 243–251.
Examples of water damage described by conservator with much experience in freeze-dry method of salvage.

Waters, Peter. *Procedures for Salvage of Water-Damaged Library Materials*. Washington, D.C.: Library of Congress, 1975. 30 pp.
  The indispensable pamphlet to own *before* the water comes.

Williams, John C. "Chemistry of the Deacidification of Paper," *Bulletin of the American Group-IIC* 12, no. 1 (October 1971): 16–32.
  Technical paper on deterioration and various methods of deacidification by Research Officer at Library of Congress.

9

Organizing a Collection

Jean Peters

From the moment you begin to form a library, you must pay some attention to its physical arrangement. Perhaps at the beginning you employ the most casual arrangement, simply placing together books on similar subjects or by the same author. And for a while this will do. But as the collection grows, you probably will need better control over your books.

You will need to be able to know at once, for example, whether or not you have a particular book or specific edition of a book. Or you may find that you need to have more than one approach to the contents of your books, or that you want to bring out various other important features about them, for instance, illustrators or binders. This can be best achieved by a careful shelf arrangement together with a written record or catalog (either on cards or in list form) describing and indexing the books, manuscripts, and other materials in your collection.

Classification—a systematic scheme for arranging books on the shelves according to subject—is a system used in public and institutional libraries, which must organize their books to meet the needs of many users. A very formal subject arrangement is not generally necessary for private collections, though some collectors (particularly those with many books covering a variety of subjects) may find that they do need to classify their books. Whatever order is decided upon, logical arrangement of some sort is vital, for a library becomes useful only after it has been organized. Gabriel Naudé, the creator of the great library of Cardinal Mazarin, listed "order and arrangement" as the seventh point in his *Advice on Establishing a Library*:

> Without . . . order and arrangement a collection of books of whatever size, were it fifty thousand volumes, would no more merit the name of a library than . . . a great heap of stones and building materials the name of a house large or small till they be properly put together to make a finished structure.[1]

Shelf Arrangement and Classification

Whether a private collection is arranged by author, press, publisher, illustrator, date of printing, style of binding, or any other feature depends entirely on the nature of the collection. The classification scheme that establishes a logical order and allows books to be located quickly and easily is the one that should be adopted. Collectors will usually find pleasure in organizing their books and will discover that a well-organized collection is a source of great satisfaction.

There is no end to the inventive ways of organizing one's books. In a recent article in the *New York Times*, a number of writers were asked to describe how they organize their private libraries. One of the more arresting arrangements was that of Alistair Cooke, who assembles his collection of books on America as a map of the United States, with books on New England in the upper right-hand corner, California at the lower left, and Illinois right in the middle. Nora Sayre arranges her library like an imaginery cocktail party, putting together only congenial authors, such as Henry James and Edith Wharton.[2] Most library arrangements, however, are not so fanciful as these; and many of us, exasperated and exhausted by trying to sort our books into a coherent arrangement, are probably often tempted to follow the course of the poet James Dickey, who has his 20,000-volume library arranged in a strictly alphabetical order by author. His reason for disregarding subjects is simply that "too many subjects overlap."[3]

Nevertheless, for most private collections some sort of subject arrangement is desirable. A logical way for a collector to arrive at a subject arrangement is to consider how a particular book is to be used. Works of reference, for instance—of which there are some in nearly every collection—are best separated from other kinds of books and further subdivided by subject. All English-language dictionaries and other word books will therefore be grouped together, as will foreign-language dictionaries, and literary and other types of reference books. Books that are not a part of the main collection can also be logically separated according to subject. Every personal library contains books that have been useful or important to us in the past and that we wish to keep, but that are no longer relevant to our main interests now. These books can be arranged by author or title within each subject classification, whichever is preferable. This simple and logical arrangement will enable the collector to locate such books with ease, and a written record of them with location numbers is usually not necessary.

A good way to begin organizing the collection of main interest is to acquire a new bookcase for it with shelves of adequate height and depth (as will be discussed later) and with glass doors or sliding glass panels to protect the books. The new shelving may cover only a small area at first if the collection is small, but can be added to later on as the need arises. This kind of "fresh start" for the housing of the collection can put the collector into the right psychological frame of mind for a careful and total reorganization of his or her books.

Most modern-day collectors tend to specialize rather than collect in a number of broad subject areas. A private collection in a single subject area can be easily and logically divided into useful subsections. Collectors will do this automatically, finding an arrangement that is most helpful to their purposes. A subject that can usefully serve as an example because of its interest to almost anyone who collects books is "books about books." Although such a collection might be limited to certain kinds of books about books, such as those about book collecting itself, it is more likely that anyone truly interested in books will acquire a miscellaneous collection in this area in addition to the collection of main interest. (Of course a collection of books about books can be—and often is—itself the collection of main interest.) The shelf arrangement of such a collection might start with general surveys and comprehensive treatments of the history of the book from earliest times to present day and proceed in a logically organized sequence through the subjects of bibliography, book collecting, the history of papermaking, of printing, of publishing, of bookselling, of book design, and of illustration, to name a few of the more general subjects that might be included in such a collection. Books within the sections on bibliography, book collecting, and the general histories of printing, publishing, bookselling, and bookmaking would probably be best arranged alphabetically by author. But histories of *individual* printers, typographers, publishers, booksellers, illustrators, and so on (which on the shelves would logically follow general books on the subject), would probably be most usefully arranged in an alphabetical sequence by the name of the person *about* whom they are written. In such a simplified arrangement, location numbers would hardly be necessary, although the collector might wish to draw up a list of the broad headings and subheadings used for location, which could be filed at the beginning of the card catalog of the collection.

Another arrangement is sometimes used for a subject collection: the order in which titles are arranged in a standard bibliography on that subject. In using this arrangement, titles acquired for the collection can be conveniently noted in the margins of the bibliography. This method of arrangement will be discussed more fully in the following paragraphs on the arrangement of collections of literature, in which the practice is probably more commonly used.

A literature collection, in which there is usually greater interest in literary value than in subject content, is best arranged simply by author. This is not to say, of course, that collections of literature are never built on the basis of subject content, but just that these kinds of collections are less usual than collections built because of an interest in a particular author. Quite interesting collections can be built around fictional treatments of subjects, such as books with war as the central theme (this could include such important works of literature as *War and Peace, All Quiet on the Western Front, The Red Badge of Courage*, and *A Farewell to Arms*, among many others), and a useful arrangement could be chronological by the specific war rather than by the more conventional author arrangement.

If a strict author arrangement is adopted, literature in all forms (novels, poetry, drama, essays, and so on) and from all countries (determined by language or nationality of the author) might stand together. An alternative arrangement, often preferable for larger collections, is either by country or by form, and then arranged by author within these categories.

A literature collection, while often ranging over the entire area of a given literature with certain high-spot titles (English literature or American literature, and so forth) will most frequently emphasize the works of one or more authors. It is here that arrangement according to a published author bibliography can be especially useful. The value of descriptive author bibliographies as an aid in collecting is discussed in Terry Belanger's chapter, "Descriptive Bibliography," and again in G. T. Tanselle's chapter, "The Literature of Book Collecting." In the organization of a collection, author bibliographies can serve a further purpose as a guide for the arrangement of books on the shelves.

In this arrangement, all the works of one author will stand together chronologically by date of publication rather than alphabetically by title, as they probably would in a less extensive collection. An author bibliography has its own system of notation, an alphabetical and numerical symbol representing each title. These notations are frequently cited in book dealers' catalogues to verify the descriptions of books listed in the catalogues and are symbols with which collectors become quickly familiar. Books in author collections arranged by the order of books in the bibliography take the notation, or symbol, of a title as it is listed in the bibliography. Thus, using this approach in a Virginia Woolf collection, the first book on the shelf, arranged according to *A Bibliography of Virginia Woolf*, by B. J. Kirkpatrick (London: Rupert Hart-Davis, 1967), would be *The Voyage Out*, Virginia Woolf's first book, published in 1915. It is listed with the notation A1a in Kirkpatrick. The next book on the shelf would be determined by the scope of the collection. One might collect only the true first editions of Virginia Woolf. Such a collector would not be interested in acquiring A1b, the first American edition of *The Voyage Out*, nor A1c, the first American edition—English issue, and so forth, but would want to move on to the second title listed in Kirkpatrick, containing the notation A2a, then on to A3a, and so on, through the end of the so-called "A" section of the bibliography, the section that identifies the separate book and pamphlet publications of an author. Of course the scope of a collection can include all the items in the "A" section of the bibliography, but the shelf arrangement might be in a sequence that differs from the arrangement of the bibliography. A frequently used shelf arrangement is grouping all the first editions (to use the same example) of Virginia Woolf together in one sequence, followed by all the first American editions in a second sequence, and so on.

Although the "A" section of any bibliography is generally regarded as the most important section, the remaining sections serve as a guide to identifying other kinds of publications of an author. For anyone collecting such publications, these later sections will serve as a guide not only to their identity, but also to their arrangement in a collection. In Kirkpatrick, for example, there are sections covering: "Contributions to Books" ("B"); "Contributions to Periodicals" ("C"); "Translations" ("D"); "Foreign Editions" ("E"); "Books and Articles Containing Single Letters or Extracts from Letters" ("F"); and "Manuscripts and Autograph Letters" ("G"). Some descriptive author bibliographies will also include sections on works *about* an author, and collectors who acquire material of this kind will be able to use this section as a guide to identification and shelf arrangement for these books. However, whether an author bibliography contains such a section or not, most collectors do acquire some books, either biographical or critical, about the authors they collect. Most collections contain some of each, and they are usually arranged in alphabetical sequence by author, following the works *by* the collected author.

Author collections are not the only kind that can be organized using a standard bibliography. Books collected because they have been issued from a particular press or by a particular publishing house are not collected for their subject content but because of interest in their printer or publisher. This kind of collection can also be best arranged according to the order of the standard bibliography. Should there be no bibliography, as is frequently the case with books of a particular publisher, then the best arrangement is probably chronological by date of publication, just as it would be if there were a bibliography. In these cases, the collector has an opportunity to make his or her own contribution to scholarship by using the books in the collection to produce a descriptive bibliography.

One problem area in organizing a collection is the ephemeral material, such as pamphlets or newspaper or magazine clippings, that relate to particular books in the collection. How can these be arranged for long-term preservation and easy location without being injurious to the more important books to which they relate? Pamphlets that are too small to be placed separately on the shelves, and that have no special significance other than their subject content, can be grouped together at the end of a subject in pamphlet files or boxes available from such commercial library supply houses as Gaylord Bros., Demco, or Bro-Dart. For extra protection, each pamphlet can be put into a folder of buffered paper. A type of file that is especially useful is the so-called "Princeton File," usually constructed of metal and open at the top as well as at the back. The open top allows for quick and easy identification of pamphlets that are too small to have their title and author printed on the spine by means of a strip of acid-free paper inserted into each pamphlet and extending several inches beyond the top, on which the author and title of each can be written. The location of these pamphlets can be indicated in the place on the shelf where they would normally appear by inserting a "dummy" in the form of a large card on which is written the name of the author and the title, with reference to the actual (out-of-order) location.

Of course, if a pamphlet is rare or important, it will merit special individual protection, in either a "clam shell" box or pamphlet folder, as described by Willman Spawn in the chapter on "Physical Care of Books and Manuscripts." Newspaper clippings must never be inserted into a book because the high acid content of newsprint will discolor book papers in a very short time. In addition, when a number of clippings are filed in a book, they distort its shape. Instead, newspaper and magazine clippings can be grouped together in a manila folder next to the book or sections of books, to which they refer. A collector might find it also helpful in maintaining ephemeral materials of this sort, as well as for keeping general records relating to the collection (as will be discussed later in the chapter), to purchase a two- or three-drawer file cabinet in which a series of folders could be arranged by subject.

A formal classification scheme should not be dismissed entirely as a means of organization in the larger and more diversified collection. A collector who has put together a sizable library of several thousand volumes on a number of subjects may wish to classify and arrange it according to classification numbers. However, because most classification systems were designed for the needs of public libraries, the private collector would be wise to consider the differences in the two kinds of libraries before deciding to classify. Private collections differ from public ones in the following ways: (1) they are generally used by the collector alone, who has the option to organize in the way that is most useful to his or her own needs and does not have to be concerned with the potential needs of any other user; (2) they are easier to organize than public ones because they tend to be more specialized in subject or types of books collected than are public libraries, which contain books in a broad range of subjects, requiring a complex system of division and further subdivision on many levels; and (3) they are usually smaller and therefore more easily managed than public ones. And so to be of value in a private library, a classification scheme must be adapted and simplified.

With this in mind, D. J. Foskett has written an interesting and helpful series of articles aimed at the private collector, "Classification for Private Libraries," in various numbers of the journal *The Private Library* from August 1959 through October 1961. Acknowledging the differences in purpose of private collections and the public ones for which these classification systems were designed, Foskett writes in the first article of the series: "We cannot therefore accept without question all the axioms of classification as professional librarians study it but, bearing this in mind, a study of classification methods can be very rewarding, both as an intellectual stimulus and as a means to the more effective use of one's own books."[4]

The classification systems covered are as follows: in the first article, the Dewey Decimal Classification, the forerunner of modern classification systems; in the second, the Universal Decimal Classification, the Library of Congress Classification, and a British scheme, the Subject Classification of J. D. Brown;[5] and in the third article, the Bliss Classification and the Colon Classification.[6] The fourth article examines abridged editions of the larger general schemes discussed in the previous articles and their advantages for use in a private library.[7] In the fifth and last article in this series, Foskett outlines a technique that private collectors might use to devise classification systems for their own particular needs.[8] These and other classification systems are discussed at greater length by Foskett in his essay on classification in the *Handbook of Special Librarianship and Information Work*.[9]

The above references, together with the excellent bibliography at the end of Foskett's essay in the Aslib *Handbook*, will serve as a good beginning for any collector who wishes to explore the possibility of classifying his or her collection either according to an established system or by devising one of his or her own. The classification schedules of the various systems are listed with their publisher and price in *Subject Guide to Books in Print* (New York: Bowker, issued annually).

In considering shelf arrangement, it is necessary to pay heed to the shelves themselves. The type of shelving best suited to ensure the proper physical care of books is discussed by Willman Spawn in his chapter on the "Physical Care of Books and Manuscripts." The aspect of shelving that becomes important when an organized shelf arrangement is being considered is size, and the collector will want to be sure that bookshelves are of an adequate height and depth so that all the books in the collection—with the exception of the oversized books—can be arranged in their correct order. There is nothing more frustrating when one is trying to arrange books in some organized fashion than to discover that the shelves in the bookcase are of different heights, with some too small for the books. Although conservationists rightly deplore the fact that a book might be sacrificed to a preconceived shelf or classification arrangement, no sacrifice need be made, either to arrangement or to preservation, if shelving for books is planned with knowledge and foresight. Shelves 12 inches high and 10 inches deep should be adequate for most books. Collectors should always be sure to have a section of shelving for oversized books also. Usually, 15–16 inches in height and depth should prove sufficient unless the collection is of a special nature, of illustrated books, for instance, for which taller and deeper shelving may be necessary, or, more preferably, horizontal shelving, as described by Willman Spawn.

Arrangement strictly by size of book is not a usual one, nor is it particularly useful in a present-day collection, but it is not unheard of. It is an arrangement that might be considered if one is short on space for shelving. According to a survey made by Willman Spawn, one shelf is gained for every ten where books are arranged by size. For preservation purposes, this is probably the best of all arrangements. Books of similar size will give each other support, keeping the taller books from warping and sagging, and the smaller ones from injury by their larger neighbors. In addition, there is less wear and tear on books if they are not constantly being shifted to make room for the latest acquisition. This arrangement goes back to that of the early libraries in which books had a fixed location by size and date of acquisition. A newly acquired book, instead of being interfiled within an author or subject arrangement, would simply be placed on the shelf next to the last book acquired of a similar size. In this arrangement shelves *would* be of different sizes—of perhaps only 5 or 6 inches for the smallest books, reaching all the way up to 16 inches or more for the folios. For collections containing over-sized books, horizontal shelving would be desirable. In such an arrangement, where books are not readily retrievable by means of the arrangement itself, a catalog listing by author and title and some form of notation or location number are absolutely essential. Where an approach to the content of the books is desired, some subject cataloging becomes necessary.

In arriving at some form of notation for such an arrangement, the simplest form might be used, merely labeling the bookcases by Roman numerals, the shelves by letter of the alphabet, and then numbering the books in sequence. Shelves holding the smallest books, and starting at the top of the first bookcase, might be labeled I.A, and the first book on that shelf numbered 1, so that the notation for that book would be I.A1; for the second book on that shelf, I.A2, and so on. The next larger shelving would be labeled I.B, with the same number sequence for the books themselves; and so on, until all the sizes of books are arranged on the appropriately labeled shelves and are numbered in sequence. The notation I.A1, or I.B25, or II.C14, and so on, would be added to the written entry for each book in the catalog. Notation numbers, of course, must never be written on, or affixed to, the books, but may be written on a strip of acid-free paper and inserted in each book, extending about an inch above the top of the book, so that the notation can be quickly read without having to remove the book from the shelf.

Photographs of rooms containing bookcases have a fascinating appeal to most collectors, who seem to be always in search of new ideas for shelving their own books. Finding additional room for bookshelves, especially in a small apartment, can become a very real problem for a collector. An interesting and unusual book that deals with this problem is Rita Reif's *Living with Books* (New York: Quadrangle, 1973). In commentary, photographs, and architectural designs, the author explores the choice and use of bookshelves in actual private libraries. Describing the scope of her book, she says in the Introduction:

Threaded through the pages of this book are some of the reasons why people collect books and how they live with them. There are the rooms that invite reading and those dedicated to work. . . . There are foyers and hallways, dining rooms and bedrooms stuffed with books and there are other areas more modestly stocked.

Solutions to book storage problems exist in abundance. Where books can be stored—covering all or part of a wall, framing windows, doorways, and mantels or filling room dividers—depends on the individual's desires and needs.[10]

One way to make space available again in a crowded bookcase is through the process of "weeding," or eliminating those books that are not relevant to the main collection. Weeding is not always easy. Often it involves getting rid of books that one may have become fond of over the years, even though they are outside the scope of the collection. Yet the weeding process is directly beneficial to the growth of the collection, for it leads to a tighter focus. Once the nongermane books have been removed from the shelves, the theme of the collection becomes visually apparent. The collection may then become even more sharply focused by filling the new space with books that relate directly to the collection. In this way, the weeding process becomes an important adjunct to good organization.

For the private collector, the best advice that can be given on arrangement and classification is simply to arrange or classify in a manner that is most logical, useful, and convenient. Arrange your books in a way that will best bring out the aspects of your collection that you consider the most important, while always keeping in mind their care and preservation. For the private collection, there are no rules of arrangement or classification that must be followed. The examples offered here are simply ways in which certain types of collections have been usefully arranged. You know your collection best, and you know the purposes for which it was formed and the uses that you intend to make of it.

The Catalog

Whether or not you catalog your collection is a personal choice, but there are good reasons for doing so. Keeping a written record of your books, which both describes them and indexes their contents, or brings out other important features about them, can be useful in a number of ways.

To start with, a written record reduces the possibility of buying the same book twice. This may occur more frequently than you would think as the collection grows. In a large collection, even the most careful shelf arrangement can sometimes get out of order, or a book can be misplaced and forgotten. Later, on seeing another copy listed in a book dealer's catalogue and not finding one on your shelf in the place you would expect to find it, you purchase a second copy. If discovery of the duplication is made early enough, within a few days of purchase, most dealers will allow you to return it and will refund the full purchase price. However, if the discovery does not occur until some time later, you will find yourself the owner of two copies of the same book. Had you kept a written record of your books and consulted your catalog before making the purchase, this double buying would probably not have occurred.

Secondly, cataloging allows for any number of aspects of a book to be brought out. A book can be shelved in only one place, but there may be a number of interesting facts about it that add to its importance and value and that its owner may wish to record. For example, a collector of the works of the English author Sylvia Townsend Warner would surely wish to own a small volume of her poetry, *Boxwood*, published in 1957 by the Monotype Corporation Ltd. On acquiring the book and examining it, the collector would find that this small volume was interesting in many ways. The unusual wording on the title page would probably be noticed first of all: "Boxwood; Sixteen Engravings by Reynolds Stone Illustrated in Verse by Sylvia Townsend Warner." The collector might infer from this that perhaps the most important aspect of this book, or the chief reason for its publication, was the engravings of Reynolds Stone. Thus in this book, the normal order followed in publishing had been reversed: Instead of selecting an artist to illustrate the words of an author, the author had been chosen to illustrate the engravings of an artist. Turning over to the verso of the title page, the collector would see that the book was the first to be printed in a new type design by Giovanni Mardersteig, that it was limited to 500 copies, and that it had been designed by the well-known book designer Ruari McLean. Reading on in the book, the collector would find in a Foreword by the distinguished writer and authority on typography Beatrice Warde an explanation of this unusual publishing situation, in which the author was chosen to illustrate the work of the artist, and would learn also that this was the first appearance in book form both of Mr. Stone's engravings and Miss Warner's poems. Thus, already seven interesting and unusual facts have surfaced about this book, all unrelated to the collector's original reason for purchasing it. And finally, if the collector is lucky enough to have found in the copy a slip with the heading "A Note about This Book," he or she will learn that this is the original printing of an edition that had been rejected by the publisher because of uneven printing and later reprinted in a small page size. Some time afterward, copies of the original edition were discovered intact in packages in the publisher's office and were distributed at that time. At this point the Sylvia Townsend Warner collector would doubtless realize that this book must be so desirable to collectors interested in the graphic arts that he or she would feel extremely lucky to have located a copy for an author collection and would value it all the more. The collector would certainly want to bring out all the special aspects of this book in the catalog.

In the same way, books covering several subjects can be cataloged to bring out these subjects, with a card or listing made for each.

A third reason for cataloging is to have a record of your books should an appraisal be required for insurance or tax purposes. The complex subject of appraisals is treated in detail by Katharine Kyes Leab and Daniel J. Leab in their chapter titled "Appraisal." For the purposes of this chapter, it is necessary only to point out that an appraisal will be required if a valuable collection is to be insured, or if it is to be sold or donated to an institution, or if a collector's estate is being valued for estate tax purposes. An appraisal must contain a written record of each book in the collection, complete with full bibliographic description. If this has not already been done by the collector, it must be done at the time of the appraisal—and at some expense if it is done by the appraiser.

Once you have made the decision to catalog your collection, you must then determine the following: (1) the form your catalog will take—whether it will be on cards or in list form; (2) whether you will do the cataloging yourself, transcribing information from the title page onto your cards or list, and if so, what bibliographic form you will follow and how much information you will include about each book; (3) whether you will purchase commercially printed cards for your books, such as those available from the Library of Congress.

In considering card versus list form, it is more practical, at least while you are in the process of cataloging the books, to use three-by-five-inch cards or slips of paper. Once the catalog is complete, you may wish to type it in list form, or at least to abbreviate each entry in a list form so that it will be convenient to carry with you when you go book hunting. The disadvantage of a catalog in list form is that later acquisitions cannot be inserted, or new information added about books already listed.

In considering commercially printed catalog cards versus cards you prepare yourself, the collector must be aware of certain realities concerning commercially printed cards. First, they are not available from as many sources as they once were. The printed cards most widely used now in institutional libraries by professional librarians are probably the Library of Congress catalog cards. Second, these cards are expensive for a private collector. The Library of Congress charges 45¢ for a set of eight cards if the cards are ordered by the Library of Congress number (which usually appears in the book itself on the copyright page). If cards are ordered by author and title only, that is, if the number is not printed in the book and the collector does not have access to a bibliographical source that will identify the Library of Congress numbers, such as the *Cumulative Book Index* (New York: Wilson, issued annually) or *Books in Print* (New York: Bowker, issued annually), the charge for each set of cards is $1.05. Catalog cards come only in sets of eight identical cards. The purpose of these seven extra cards is so that entries can be available in the catalog not only for author (or main entry) but also for title and subjects, as well as for any other feature that might best be brought out about a book. These additional entries are simply typed as headings on the printed card, thus eliminating the need to prepare a complete new card for each additional entry in the catalog. It is not possible to buy only one card for each book and then type any additional cards you may need yourself. An example of a Library of Congress printed catalog card appears in Figure 1.

As indicated by the so called "tracings" running across the bottom of the card, additional entries are to be made for the subject "English literature—19th century" and for "Dodgson, Charles Lutwidge, 1832–1898." Although these headings are appropriate for an institutional library, they may not be the

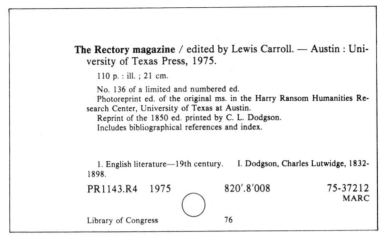

The Rectory magazine / edited by Lewis Carroll. — Austin : University of Texas Press, 1975.

    110 p. : ill. ; 21 cm.

    No. 136 of a limited and numbered ed.
    Photoreprint ed. of the original ms. in the Harry Ransom Humanities Research Center, University of Texas at Austin.
    Reprint of the 1850 ed. printed by C. L. Dodgson.
    Includes bibliographical references and index.

    1. English literature—19th century.   I. Dodgson, Charles Lutwidge, 1832-1898.

PR1143.R4   1975   820'.8'008   75-37212
                                                          MARC

    Library of Congress   76

FIGURE 1

ones a private collector would choose to use in his or her catalog. This brings us to the third reality concerning commercially printed catalog cards. These cards have been made for specific copies of books in one of the largest libraries in the world. Therefore, many of the subject headings would not be applicable to the private library, and there are bound to be certain adjustments that private collectors would have to make on these cards to reflect the interests of their own collection and the exact description of their own particular books.

The advantage of purchasing Library of Congress cards is in the time that it will save in preparing the original card and in typing all the cards. Some collectors might prefer to make the necessary adjustments and additions to the commercially printed cards and to discard any extras, rather than undertake the cataloging job themselves. Cards are available for most books, and the cataloging has been done by professional librarians.

Private collectors can establish an account with the Cataloging Distribution Service division at the Library of Congress and be billed monthly for the cards they order by completing the "New Account Application" included in the booklet *Catalog Cards: Price and Ordering Information*, available from the Library of Congress, Cataloging Distribution Service, Building 159, Navy Yard Annex, Washington, D.C. 20541.

In the short space of this chapter it is not possible to go into the complexities of cataloging in any depth, but the kind of cataloging done by the Library of Congress is not generally necessary for the private collection. A simpler form will suffice, and for this kind of cataloging, guidelines can be offered and some examples given.

The most important elements in a bibliographic description, and those that would be included in a basic catalog entry are the following: author, title, publisher or printer, place and date of publication, number of pages, size, and illustrations. All but the last three of these basic elements can in most books be found on the title page or its verso.

A book is generally entered on the catalog card under the last name of the author, if an author is indicated. This card is known as the author card; it is usually also the *main card*, or *main entry*, the card on which is recorded all the information necessary to identify a book. Some collectors may want to keep only this one card for each book, but others will find it useful to make subject cards, added entries, and title cards for their books.

In addition to the basic bibliographic description, the collector would add certain other information to the main card. This would include a description of the condition of the book, whether or not it has a dust jacket and its condition, the date the book was purchased, the seller, and the price paid. If there were an inscription or the author's signature in the book, or any notes or corrections made in the author's hand, this too would be noted on the main card. Thus, the main card for a book that is bibliographically uncomplicated, such as Ernest Hemingway's *A Farewell to Arms*, would appear as in Figure 2.

If a book is issued in a limited edition, this is also noted. Thus, the catalog card for the signed limited edition of *A Farewell to Arms*, which was issued simultaneously with the first regular edition listed above, would appear as in Figure 3.

For both of these editions of *A Farewell to Arms* there would most likely be at the most only two cards in the catalog—one under author (the main card) and the other under title, although some collectors might wish to eliminate the title card and keep a record only by author. However, if a collector were interested in the publications of Charles Scribner, that collector would be likely to make an additional card (an added entry) under the name of the publisher. It would then be possible to tell simply by looking into the catalog which books in the collection were

```
Hemingway, Ernest.
     A farewell to arms.     New York, Scribner's,
1929.
     355 p.   7 3/8 x 5 3/16 in.


                         First edition. Fine copy.
                         Dust wrapper slightly worn.
                         House of Books Ltd.,
                         6/2/74, $--
```

FIGURE 2

```
Hemingway, Ernest.
     A farewell to arms.     New York, Scribner's,
1929.
     355 p.   9 1/16 x 6 1/16 in.

     Number --- of an edition of 510 copies signed by
the author.

                         Limited edition. Fine in
                         slipcase. House of Books
                         Ltd., 4/1/73, $---
```

FIGURE 3

published by Charles Scribner, even though on the shelf they might be arranged by author or in some other fashion.

As noted earlier, one of the advantages of cataloging is that any aspect of a book can be brought out. To return for a moment to *Boxwood*, let us consider how it might be cataloged in a graphic arts collection. Using author as main entry, the catalog card might be prepared as in Figures 4a and 4b.

Warner, Sylvia Townsend.
    Boxwood; sixteen engravings by Reynolds Stone
illustrated in verse by Sylvia Townsend Warner.
London, The Monotype Corp. Ltd., 1957.
    37 p.   8 1/2 x 5 5/8 in.   illus.

    Printed in an edition of 500 copies in a new
type designed by Giovanni Mardersteig.
    Book designed by Ruari McLean.
    Foreword by Beatrice Warde.
                                   (Con't. on Card 2)

FIGURE 4a

                                                Card 2

Warner, Sylvia Townsend.
    Boxwood.

                    Fine copy. Chiswick Book
                    Shop, 9/20/75, $--

    I.Stone, Reynolds. II.Mardersteig, Giovanni.
III.McLean, Ruari. IV.Warde, Beatrice. V.Title.

FIGURE 4b

Thus, as indicated by the tracings at the bottom of the main card, five additional cards would be made for this book—for the illustrator, the type designer, the designer of the book, the person who wrote the Foreword, and for the title. All would be important in a graphic arts collection.

When making cards for title, subject, or other added entries, it is not necessary to repeat on each card the full bibliographic record of the main card. An abbreviated form, containing only author, title, publisher, and date of publication is all that is needed on these additional cards, as indicated in Figure 5.

The examples shown in this chapter represent basic and quite simplified cataloging. As a private collector you can make your catalog as simple or as complex as you choose according to the kind of description you feel will be most appropriate for your books and will best serve your own needs. For help in cataloging rare books, Paul Shaner Dunkin's *How to Catalog a Rare Book* (Chicago: American Library Association, 1973) is recommended. Another helpful source is *Simplified Cataloguing Rules for General Use in Private Libraries; Author and Title Entries*, which was published by the Private Libraries Association in 1959. This pamphlet is now unfortunately out of print, but may be reprinted in the near future in an issue of *The Private Library*. Further aid in cataloging can be found in a number of sources directed to the needs of public and institutional libraries but that can be helpful also to the private collector. Among them are *Aker's Simple Library Cataloging*, revised by Arthur Curley and Jana Varlejs (Metuchen, N.J.: Scarecrow, 1977), and *Commonsense Cataloging*, by Esther J. Piercy, revised by Marian Sanner (New York: Wilson, 1974).

Catalog cards (for the books you catalog yourself) and compact card catalog cabinets are available from such commercial library supply houses as Bro-Dart, Demco, and Gaylord Bros. (For their addresses, see the Appendix.) Attractive cabinets can

```
    Stone, Reynolds.
Warner, Sylvia Townsend.
    Boxwood.    The Monotype Corp. Ltd., 1957.




                    (   )
```

FIGURE 5

be purchased in a choice of woods or in steel (which some collectors prefer for protection against fire) in sizes as small as two-
drawers or as large as you need. Most drawers will accommodate approximately 1,300 to 1,500 cards.

Although cataloging is usually not a subject to which much
attention is given in books about book collecting, it is a part of
collecting that has its own pleasures and rewards for collectors
who love their books and become knowledgeable about them.
In a more public sense, contributions to scholarship have been
made as a result of well-cataloged private collections. Descriptive bibliographies have been compiled from private collections, among them the Adrian Goldstein and John Payne
bibliography of John Steinbeck and the Robert Wilson bibliography of Gertrude Stein. Even the catalogs of some private collections have been published, and some have become
important bibliographical tools used by collectors, dealers, and
bibliographers. Some of these are discussed by G. T. Tanselle
in his chapter on "The Literature of Book Collecting."

Other Records

A catalog of the collection is just one of several records that
collectors may keep. Although the most complete description of
each book is kept on the main card, or entry, in the catalog,
other records can be helpful. These include annotations in the
standard bibliography, lists of books already acquired, invoices
for books purchased, and carbon copies of orders for books not
yet received. Want lists, or desiderata, lists of books not already
owned but wanted, are also kept by most collectors.

If a standard bibliography exists for the author, press, publisher, or subject you collect, you can note in the margins next
to the entries for the books you have already acquired, the date
you purchased the book, the price you paid, and from whom
you bought it. This record is usually portable enough to carry
with you when you go book hunting. It can also serve as an
interim record of your books until your card catalog is complete.

If no standard bibliography exists for your collection, it is
often helpful to keep (in addition to your card catalog) a list of
the books you already own. In such a list the entries can be
brief, consisting in many cases of just author, title, press or
publisher, and date of publication. A list of entries even in such

an abbreviated form can prevent you from buying the same book twice, and it will be something you can give to your regular book dealer in lieu of a want list. For, if there is no standard bibliography for your collection, you can't be certain of all the books that have been issued on your subject or by your author or press, and therefore you probably will not be able to compile an accurate want list.

All invoices for books purchased should be kept. These can simply be filed in manila folders according to date and stored in a file cabinet or desk drawer. (Date of purchase could be discovered quickly if needed by checking the catalog card.) Should you ever wish to sell any of your more valuable books, the invoice would serve as proof of purchase. Or, if an insured book were stolen or destroyed in a fire, the invoice would serve as a record of the amount you paid for the book.

Collectors who order many books by mail, especially those who order new books directly from the publisher (who does not respond as quickly to an order as a book dealer does) may find it helpful to keep carbon copies of their orders until the books arrive and can be recorded in the catalog. If the book is a long time in arriving, this can be another way to prevent a double purchase.

Many collectors keep want lists. Such lists can be short, consisting only of the several books most desired for the collection, the ones that the collector has had difficulty in locating in bookstores or dealers' catalogues. These lists can be sent out with discretion, one at a time, to various book dealers who carry books in one's collecting field. Or, want lists can be longer, consisting of—in cases where the precise scope of the collection has already been established through a standard bibliography—all the titles that are yet to be acquired for the collection. These lists are especially useful as a record for collectors to keep for themselves (to carry in wallet or purse at all times) and can be left with one's regular book dealer. The caution with which the general distribution of such lists should be treated is discussed by Robin G. Halwas in his chapter on "Buying Books from Dealers."

Bookplates

A personal bookplate (a label placed in a book for identification of ownership) is used by many serious collectors. It is generally printed with the owner's name together with an illustration or an inscription. Often bookplates are inscribed with the term *Ex Libris* (meaning "from the library" of). A *book label* is usually smaller and simpler in style than a bookplate, consisting merely of the owner's name.

The writing of one's name in a book is considered sacrilege by most collectors, and the use of commercially designed, store-bought bookplates is regarded with equal distaste. The ideal bookplate is one that is personally designed by an artist and printed by a craftsman and will add the collector's own individual touch by projecting some of his or her own personality or interests into the book.

Mark Severin and Anthony Reid give some of the reasons for acquiring a personal bookplate in a chapter titled "Commissioning a Bookplate" in their *Engraved Bookplates; European Ex Libris 1950–70*:

> Anyone owning books should consider acquiring a bookplate. . . . Such a plate serves as a distinctive mark of ownership and transforms any volume, similar to thousands of others, into an unique copy with a pedigree. Random books acquire unity and become a library. Moreover, if volumes are later dispersed, an ex libris may greatly enhance the worth of a book, confirming it to have been the personal copy of an owner with association interest.
>
> Perhaps the greatest satisfaction, however, is the privilege it confers of making one a patron. . . . It is possible for us, and not prohibitively expensive, to commission from a living artist a personal bookplate, exactly to our dictated wishes.[11]

The variety of bookplates is endless. They come in various sizes and designs. The one general rule is that the dimension of the plate should relate to the size of the book in which it will be placed. For books of ordinary size, a rectangular plate three inches high by two inches wide will be sufficient. Smaller plates are more appropriate for tinier books. The shape of the plate can vary also—square, round, and diamond-shaped are some of the shapes that collectors have chosen for their bookplates.

A bookplate should be placed in the center of the inside front cover of a book (the pasted-down endpaper) and should be attached with plain library starch paste. Rubber cement, which may stain the book paper, should not be used. Nor is a gummed backing on the bookplate advisable, as it may also discolor the paper and sometimes cause it to disintegrate.

For subject, some collectors may choose a family or heraldic plate; others may choose plates reflecting their own interest or the theme of their collection. Many ideas for possible subjects are suggested in Severin and Reid's *Engraved Bookplates*, and many illustrations of bookplates are included.

The matter of choosing the right artist is sometimes difficult. Visits to graphic-arts exhibitions may be helpful, as may a search through illustrated books. If a calligraphic plate or label is desired, there are many books that illustrate the work of contemporary calligraphers. The American Society of Book Plate Collectors and Designers, as well as the Society of Scribes and the Society of Scribes and Illuminators may be helpful.

A collector should not be deterred from acquiring a bookplate by the phrase so often seen in book dealers' catalogues: "Bookplate of former owner on front endpaper, otherwise a fine copy." John Carter observed in his *ABC for Book Collectors*:

> Book-plates may be of artistic interest . . . or they may help to establish the book's PROVENANCE by identifying an earlier owner. Even when they have no apparent interest, it is absurd to regard them as a blemish . . . unless the work of art is so ugly as to qualify as a blemish in its own right.[12]

An anecdote will serve as a final word on the effectiveness of a good bookplate and the intrigue of a book's provenance as made known through a bookplate. While examining books at Sotheby Parke Bernet prior to an auction, a collector opened a book in which she saw a small bookplate identical to one in a book from her own collection. She was extremely fond of both book and bookplate. The plate, measuring one and one-half inches square and bearing only the initials of the former owner and a graceful figure with an open book, was immediately recognizable as a Rockwell Kent design. The collector was so startled and delighted to see the bookplate again, and so pleased to think that the owner of the plate she liked so well had her own taste in collecting, that she momentarily fantasized that she might re-create the original collection, buying copies of the books she wanted for her own collection only if they carried this bookplate. Although she has not seen the bookplate again, she still searches for it, and the idea that this earlier collector might have had a collection similar to her own and that she might be able to reassemble it piece by piece adds a further dimension to her own collection.

The use of a personal bookplate can be one of the unifying factors of a collection of books. Good arrangement and careful cataloging help collectors make better use of their books and can emphasize the focus of a collection. In these and other ways, organization and record keeping help collectors maintain control over their collections and, in general, make their lives easier and their collections more meaningful. In the words of A. W. Pollard, "Practically all collecting is good if it have a definite aim, which leads the collector to rescue books from destruction, and add to knowledge by classifying and cataloguing them."[13]

Notes

1. Gabriel Naudé, *Advice on Establishing a Library* (Berkeley: University of California Press, 1950), p. 63. This book was first published in 1627 under the title *Avis pour dresser une bibliothèque*.
2. Nan Robertson, "How Writers Navigate Their Sea of Books," *New York Times*, December 12, 1976, p. C10.
3. Ibid.
4. D. J. Foskett, "Classification for Private Libraries I," *The Private Library* 2 (August 1959): 76–77.
5. D. J. Foskett, "Classification for Private Libraries II," *The Private Library* 2 (October 1959): 89–91.
6. D. J. Foskett, "Classification for Private Libraries III," *The Private Library* 3 (July 1960): 26–28.
7. D. J. Foskett, "Classification for Private Libraries IV," *The Private Library* 3 (January 1961): 64–66.
8. D. J. Foskett, "Classification for Private Libraries V," *The Private Library* 3 (October 1961): 119–121.
9. D. J. Foskett, "Classification," in *Handbook of Special Librarianship and Information Work,* ed. by W. E. Batten (London: Aslib, 1975), pp. 153–197.
10. Rita Reif, *Living with Books* (New York: Quadrangle, 1973), p. 5.
11. Mark Severin and Anthony Reid, *Engraved Bookplates; European Ex Libris 1950–70* (Pinner, Private Libraries Association, 1972), p. 13.
12. John Carter, *ABC for Book Collectors* (London: Rupert Hart-Davis, 1974), p. 46.
13. A. W. Pollard, *Books in the House* (Indianapolis: Bobbs-Merrill, 1904), p. 73.

10

Appraisal

Katharine Kyes Leab and Daniel J. Leab

T HE BUSINESS OF THIS CHAPTER is to guide the collector, or in-
heritor of a collection, who is faced with the task of defining
books or manuscripts in monetary terms. There comes a point
in the life of every significant literary property when this property must be subjected to the tender ministrations of an appraiser, whether for insurance, sale, donation, or estate
purposes. It may be a happy time—your collection has become
important enough to warrant insuring, or you have decided to
reap the rewards of a lifetime of judicious collecting and gain a
certain sort of immortality through sale at public auction or donation to an institution. It may be a sad time—the expenses of
ill health force you to sell your beloved books, or Aunt Harriet,
whose collection had never interested you, dies and leaves you
with a bunch of books on your hands that you know virtually
nothing about.

Whatever the precise circumstances, appraisal is usually
called for at an *important* time in one's life. Thus it is essential
to know something about what to look for in an appraisal—and
in an appraiser. Should, say, an insurance company or the Internal Revenue Service (IRS) explode an appraisal, it is the owner, not the appraiser, who will be left sitting stunned amid the
rubble. This sort of shell shock is unnecessary and eminently
avoidable if a modicum of attention is paid to a few basic appraisal principles and procedures.

Kinds of Value

On a practical level the owner of a literary property should know about two kinds of value: replacement value (buyer's retail cost of a duplicate or substitute within a reasonable time) and fair market value (the price at which a property would change hands between a willing buyer and a willing seller, neither being under any compulsion to buy or sell and both having reasonable knowledge of the relevant facts). The first applies to insurance appraisals; the second, to any appraisal that may be examined by the IRS, be it for donation or estate purposes.

There are other kinds of appraisable value, such as cost price and wholesale price, but these do not usually pertain to the collector. Auction price may be identical to fair market value when literary properties from an estate are sold at auction, and more will be said on that subject later in the chapter. And, finally, there is something called forced-sale value, which means precisely what it says and which we hope the collector will never have to learn about. Time was when forced-sale value was often used in appraisals made for estate tax purposes. In practice it tended to mean: What would be the value of this literary property if sold at auction in Guam at midnight during a transportation strike and a violent snowstorm in a sale presided over by an auctioneer who spoke only Natick? It is easy to see why the tax authorities learned to throw thunderbolts at this kind of appraisal, often responding to the phrase "For Estate Purposes Only" on an appraisal by at least doubling the amount stated. These days, forced-sale value has no validity in law. The IRS recognizes fair market value only.[1]

To Insure or Not to Insure

Should the same literary property be evaluated for both insurance purposes and for tax purposes, the insurance figures will almost inevitably be higher. This is partly because insurance appraisal is based on the cost of securing a replacement in the retail market within a short period of time and partly because a bit of room for inflation is often built into an insurance appraisal so that a partial reappraisal will not be necessary within months. The danger here is that the figures for insurance can climb to dizzying heights, resulting in temporary euphoria on the part of the collector as the increased value of the collection is contemplated—and in the possibility of a pain-

ful tumble later on. Too high an insurance valuation may prej-
udice a future estate tax case: The IRS might well wonder why a
book insured for $2,000 is given a value of $500 in an estate. At
the very least, an overoptimistic valuation may result in unnecessary expense and perhaps a challenge to your claim if loss or
damage does occur.

One of the best short statements on replacement value and
insurance appraisal was made by perhaps the foremost appraiser of literary properties in the mid-twentieth century, the late
Robert Metzdorf:

> The value set has to be set as of the date of the appraisal, and in
> effect is the "fair market value" of the material at the time the
> appraisal is signed and the policy issued. (This is always subject
> to the possibility, of course, that a reasonable replacement is
> available in the market at the time of the appraisal—in the case of
> unique material the problem becomes more complex.) If loss oc-
> curs later, settlement is adjusted according to the replacement fig-
> ure at the time of the appraisal, not necessarily at an accrued
> valuation which time and a rising market may have affected. That
> is why it is important to have frequent and informed review of
> appraisal schedules, particularly when values are changing rapid-
> ly.²

These days it is expensive to insure literary or artistic properties, particularly in cities. In early 1977, it cost a minimum of
$1,500 a year to insure a $500,000 collection of literary properties
located in Manhattan in a vault or a private residence. You may
be required to provide for the protection of some articles either
through an alarm system or by placing them in a vault or safety
deposit box. An additional expense is the partial reappraisal of
a collection from time to time as values change.

Because prices have risen so steeply in recent years, many
collectors feel they cannot afford to insure their collections. If
such is the case, you might want to talk with your insurance
representative about holding fire insurance only.

In deciding whether or not to insure, several other factors
should be weighed. If you choose not to insure and decide instead to take a tax deduction in case of loss by fire or theft,
remember that your deduction is limited to either the adjusted
basis of the property (that is, what you paid for it or what it was
worth when you inherited it) or the fair market value, whichever is *lower*. Should this situation arise, you will have been
wise to have saved your sales slips so that you can document

your claim. Because of the limitation on deductions, if you paid $2,000 in 1970 for a set of Edward S. Curtis' *The North American Indian*, that sum is all you can deduct if the set is destroyed in a fire. That the going price is around $60,000 simply doesn't matter. Should a fully insured Curtis be incinerated, the insurance proceeds must be used to purchase similar literary properties within two years. If you just kept the money, you would be faced with a taxable gain of $58,000.

If you are ever so slightly paranoid about theft and insurance company records, or if you are a potential tax evader, you probably won't want to insure your literary properties. Otherwise, in these increasingly chancy and inflationary times, it probably is wise to insure your collection if you can afford to do so.

Choosing an Expert

Assuming that you have decided to insure your collection, how do you proceed to get an appraisal? Is the procedure the same for estates and charitable contributions? Who should appraise the collection? How do you know whether he or she is making a solid and proper appraisal of your property? How much should an appraisal cost? A host of such questions demand answers.

You are looking for an expert whose opinion will prevail if the appraisal value is questioned by an insurance company or the IRS. The ideal appraiser possesses certain qualities similar to those which A. E. Housman hoped to find in textual critics: "Knowledge is good, method is good, but one thing beyond all others is necessary; and that is to have a head, not a pumpkin, on your shoulders, and brains, not pudding, in your head."[3] The appraiser you want is, first of all, an expert in literary properties. Unless your collection has little value, a firm of household appraisers is not for you. We were dismayed to learn that some of these firms simply add 50 percent to recent auction prices and call the resulting document an appraisal. Auction price is probably the single most important index to the value of literary properties, but expert interpretation is essential. In the words of the IRS: "The principal method for determining the value of books, manuscripts, autographs, and related items is by selecting comparable sales and adjusting such price according to the differences between the comparatives and the items being evaluated. This is a complex and technical task that, except for a collection of small value, should be left to the expert appraiser.''[4]

The expert appraiser may be an auction-house representative, a dealer, or a specialist librarian. Some of the best appraisers have gone on to be appraisal consultants after gaining experience in one or all of these areas. He or she must be *au courant* with the fast-paced price changes throughout the world. For the expert appraiser to remain expert, living in a major city—New York, London, Paris—is not essential, but visiting libraries and collections, attending auctions and book fairs, talking with scholars and dealers, reading and examining as many pertinent books, scholarly journals, and dealers' catalogues as possible are indeed essential.

If you have a fairly general collection, you probably are better off with an auction-house appraisal, but a highly specialized collection may be more properly the province of a specialist dealer. For dealers, membership in the Antiquarian Booksellers Association of America (ABAA) often is a clear indication of expertise, and you may wish to write to the ABAA for a list of specialist book dealers in your area. However, to quote *IRS Publication 561* again, "membership in appraisal organizations will not automatically establish the appraiser's competency. Nor will the absence of certificates, memberships, and the like automatically detract from competency that otherwise exists" (p. 6). Consult librarians, collectors, and insurance people in your area to see which dealers and appraisers they recommend.

In each generation, a few experts are almost beyond challenge and thus are used as bench marks by younger appraisers. But, for reasons of geography and time, not all of us can have an appraisal made by one of the handful of dealers of truly international caliber. How then do we know whether or not the appraiser we have chosen is doing an acceptable job? A person who is paying between $150 and $400 per day for appraisal services certainly deserves a good piece of work in return.

Producing the Written Appraisal

First of all, the appraiser should see and handle the literary property piece by piece. Many appraisals are made each year on the basis of written lists alone; such appraisals are open to question from the start. "The appraiser's opinion is never more important than the facts upon which it is based," says IRS, and

"No, I've never actually seen the collection" does not sound very convincing in court or to the agent of the IRS or an insurance company.[5]

Although appraisals cannot be based on written lists alone, the collector who has taken the time and trouble to keep a card catalogue of literary properties will have a clear advantage when appraisal or reappraisal time comes around. A well-known Johnsonian from Colorado keeps a notebook in which each item in his collection is fully described, including physical description, provenance, and cost. This catalogue saves him money at appraisal time, for the appraiser does not have to undertake the time-consuming cataloguing work that often is associated with appraisal. The sources of a collector's books also provide clues to items that may need special attention: Mr. X sells books in prime condition, carefully noting any flaws in condition or completeness, while Mr. Y's wares are often imperfect. In short, any aids that you can provide the appraiser to shorten his or her task will save you money, and good record keeping is the biggest money saver of all.

Second, after briefly surveying the collection, the appraiser should estimate the cost of the appraisal. One of two fee structures will be used: either a *per diem* ranging from about $150 to about $400 plus expenses or a percentage of the total value of the collection. Most of the major auction houses charge between 1 percent and 1½ percent of the value of a collection to produce a written appraisal; this fee is usually refundable if the collection is sold through that house within a year. In the case of a very large or a very small collection a flat fee may be set. When an appraiser works on a *per diem* basis, the time taken will vary with the difficulty of the material and the expertise of the appraiser. A master appraiser can cover a great deal of territory in a single day, particularly in an insurance appraisal and most particularly if you have provided an inventory or catalogue. Remember also that if the appraisal is being made to determine the amount of an income tax deduction, the appraisal fee is deductible.

After you have come to an agreement about price, the appraiser will set to work. At the conclusion of the job the appraiser should produce a written and signed statement of appraisal. The format of this statement is of some importance. A signed document reading "2,000 art books with an average value of $200" is worse than useless. A good model for format is that required by the IRS for appraisal reports on items deducted as charitable contributions:

> In general, an appraisal report should contain at least the following:
> 1) A summary of the appraiser's qualifications to appraise this particular property;
> 2) A statement of the value and the appraiser's definition of how that value was obtained;
> 3) A full and complete description of the article to be valued;
> 4) The bases upon which the appraisal was made, including any restrictions, understandings, or covenants limiting the use or disposition of the property;
> 5) The date the property was valued;
> 6) The signature of the appraiser and the date the appraisal was made.[6]

Fullness of description should vary directly with the value of the property. As aids to description, the camera and the copier may be used to good effect. Generally speaking, an appraisal should be as detailed as a seller's offering to a potential buyer. As in auction or dealers' catalogues, descriptions will vary in length, with unique or expensive items usually boasting longer descriptions or specific references to entries in bibliographies. Works of very little value may be lotted up by subject or author: "20 books on the American Civil War with an average value of $10" is acceptable as an entry. For some unknown reason, Section 20.2031-6(d) of the Estate Tax Regulations specifically states that "books in sets by standard authors should be listed in separate groups," so make certain that is done if the appraisal is for estate purposes.

Below is an example of a page from an insurance appraisal done by Sotheby Parke Bernet in New York in 1971 (provenances have been omitted to ensure the collector's privacy). Note the attention paid to completeness ("With the half-title . . .") and to condition ("Very fine" or "some margins closely trimmed affecting some letters"). And such bibliographic references as "Rothschild 1028 variant 3" or to "the possible 96 points of a prime *Pickwick*" provide a short form of reference as well as reflecting the expertise of the appraiser.[7]

DE QUINCEY, THOMAS
Confessions of an English Opium-Eater.
London, 1822

First edition. With the half-title and the advertisement leaf. Original boards, uncut, portion of printed label preserved; most of spine chipped away. Morocco case $400.00

DEFOE, DANIEL
The Life and Strange Surprizing Adventures of Robinson Crusoe, 1719. *Serious Reflections*, 1720. London, 1719–20
First editions. 3 vols. Frontispiece and folding map. Contemporary calf, third volume disparate. Morocco case. Fine $12,500.00

DICKENS, CHARLES
Martin Chuzzlewit. London, 1843–44
First edition in the original 19/20 parts. Original printed wrappers, part VII with the rare inset slip; some backstrips repaired. Morocco case $200.00

DICKENS, CHARLES
Pickwick Papers. London, 1836–37
First edition in the original 19/20 parts. With 84 of the possible 96 points of a "prime" *Pickwick*. Original printed wrappers. Cloth case. Very fine $5,000.00

DODGSON, CHARLES LUTWIDGE
Alice's Adventures in Wonderland. London, 1866
First published English edition. Original red cloth. Morocco case. Exceptionally fine $2,000.00

GOETHE, JOHANN WOLFGANG VON
Faust. Tubingen, 1808
First edition. Contemporary green morocco gilt; library release stamp on endpaper, some margins closely trimmed affecting some letters $200.00

GOLDSMITH, OLIVER
The Vicar of Wakefield. Salisbury, 1766
First edition. 2 vols. Contemporary calf. Rothschild 1028 variant 3 $1,500.00

Charitable Contributions

To this point we have discussed the appraisal of literary properties in general terms. Now let us take a look at several specific areas, beginning with charitable contributions of books and manuscripts.

First, an IRS caveat: "Sometimes an appraisal will be given less weight if the appraiser is associated with either the donor or the charitable organization."[8] For this reason, many libraries ask that donors secure their own appraisals before giving a gift to the library. Others, like the Library of Congress, have set up elaborate procedures for evaluation by committee of expensive gifts. If the Library of Congress accepts your proffered donation, it will provide you with an advisory evaluation free of charge, should you request one. Generally speaking, if you are contributing valuable literary properties to a charitable organization, check with your lawyer first to learn about such matters as the status of the charitable organization (50 percent or 20 percent), the related use rule, and the possibility of giving fractional interest in the property.

If you wish to donate a book or group of books worth less than $200, you may not need an appraisal. If you have owned a book for less than nine months (a year, if the donation is made in 1978 or thereafter), your charitable deduction is limited to what you paid for it. And *IRS Publication 561* directs you to *American Book Prices Current* and other reference material to aid you in determining fair market value "if the collection you are donating is of modest value, not requiring a formal written appraisal. . . ."[9]

Autographs and Manuscripts

The monster in the new tax law lurks in the region of autographs and manuscripts. Holding up a sign reading "self-created value," the monster will prevent you from taking a deduction on "any letters, memorandums or similar property donated by the person who created them or the person for whom they were created. . . ."[10] Washington's own collection of Dr. Frankensteins created this monster as a guard against people who were claiming outrageous deductions for donated papers or manuscripts. And the monster's creation did result in one or two notorious tax cases, mainly involving the misdating of appraisals to avoid the provisions of the new law. But, like all Frankenstein monsters, this newly created guard is a destroyer, a death-dealer. In the long run the cultural history of America will suffer. Original manuscripts and letters, business records, and other primary sources for scholars that might have been donated to libraries will instead be discarded because the donor could not take a tax deduction. Preservation and monetary value tend to go hand in hand in our society. And can we not afford the poet at least a deduction beyond the cost of pencils and paper in recognition of his or her achievement so that we can preserve the manuscript?

Here, to paraphrase Dickens, the law really is an ass, for the same manuscript or letter can have no tax value one moment and be worth thousands the next. For example, if Ernest Hemingway wrote you a series of letters about his life and work, in your hands these letters do not qualify as capital assets. If you give them to a library, you get no deduction, and if you sell them the proceeds are ordinary income. But if you die, the tax value of these letters in your estate is their fair market value.[11] This instant transformation into capital assets may provide some comfort to your heirs, but it does not reflect sensible thinking by our nation's lawmakers.

While we're on the subject of manuscripts and papers, how are they appraised for insurance purposes? Corporate papers usually are appraised using a combination of sampling techniques and an index based on dimensions or, say, the cost of copying the records on acid-free paper. The insuring of unique and thus irreplaceable manuscripts and letters requires discussion with your insurance agent and appraisal by a specialist.

Estate and Tax Planning

If your literary property forms a significant part of your estate, a bit of planning is a necessity. Otherwise, valuable books or manuscripts may be lost, discarded, or sold for a fraction of their value. Consider the recent sale at auction of the Henry Hubbard Middlecoff copy of Herman Melville's *The Whale* (the first edition of *Moby Dick*). This three-volume set was presented by Melville to Middlecoff's ancestor Henry Hubbard in 1853, and it had remained in the family until the Middlecoff heirs offered it to their lawyer as a gift in the mid-1970s. The lawyer, a supremely honest man, refused the gift, for he recognized the unique value of this particular copy and what its sale at auction could mean to the Middlecoff heirs. Melville had inscribed this book to "his old shipmate and watchmate" on the *Acushnet*. Moreover, the characters Pip and Stubbs are identified in Hubbard's hand. The lawyer secured no fewer than three local appraisals before approaching the major auction houses about selling the book. The final result: The Henry Hubbard Middlecoff copy of *The Whale* sold at Sotheby Parke Bernet on January 26, 1977, for $53,000. But for the lawyer, its value might have gone unrecognized.[12]

Another special situation is appraisal to determine retroactive fair market value for tax purposes. Auction houses are the logical and certainly the most experienced appraisers here. They have been faced with the task of, say, reconstructing a market model of the year 1965 and determining what a collection of manuscripts or books would have been worth then, and they know how to do this sort of appraisal properly.

Appraisal for Sale

Finally, we come to the matter of appraisal for sale. If the collection is your own, chances are that you have developed a good working relationship with one or more dealers. Then the matter of selling is simple and informal. The more specialized the collection, the more likely you may be to sell it through a specialist dealer. If the collection is large and expensive, you may wish to call in dealers, auction-house experts, or perhaps even an appraisal consultant to help you determine whether to sell to a dealer, a collector, a historical society, or a library or whether or where to sell by auction.

As for the executor of a will, when faced with the disposal of somebody else's valuable and diversified collection, he or she normally will turn to the auction house. It is often the safest course, for Revenue Procedure 65–19, 1965–2C.B. 1002 permits estate tax return values to equal the price paid at public auction if the sale is within a reasonable time and market conditions have not changed substantially. Many executors simply submit the sale catalogue and price list as the estate tax appraisal.

Very often the heirs to an estate end up with literary properties that they know little about—and they are content not to know about these properties. What do you do with Aunt Harriet's books on arms and armor or your congressman grandfather's correspondence files? If selling them is your aim, a good place to begin is with the ABAA membership listings, for each dealer's specialty is given under his or her name. Let us suppose that you locate a nearby dealer whose interests include works on arms and armor and American political autographs. The dealer drops by and casts an eye over the collections. If they are virtually worthless, you will be told so without charge. In this instance, they are not, and so the standard ABAA procedure is followed as set forth in the association's flier "When Books Are Offered for Sale or Appraisal." First the dealer will determine whether or not you want to sell the books, that is, whether he is appraising for tax or insurance purposes or as a potential buyer. He will then explain the fee schedule to you, be it on a percentage or a *per diem* basis (some dealers will waive the fee if a sale is consummated). The dealer will provide you with a written and signed appraisal. If he does not feel that the nature of the collection falls within his area of competence, he will refer you to another dealer. And he will also refer you to another dealer should he not be interested in buying the collection.

However, not everybody lives near an antiquarian book dealer, auction house, or appraisal consultant. In this situation, you begin by picking up your pen and making an inventory of your collection, listing for each book the following information: author; title; place, publisher, and date of publication; size and number of pages; number of illustrations; and remarks on the condition of the book and what its binding looks like. Next, you go to the library and check through *American Book Prices Current*, *Bookman's Price Index*, *The Book Collector's Handbook of Values*, and any other pricing guides your librarian might recommend. List any of the books from your collection that you find included in these publications and send that shorter list to dealers. If you think that some of the remaining books are valuable, ask the librarian about them. Do not emulate the fellow who wrote to our predecessor Edward Lazare, then editor and publisher of *American Book Prices Current*, asking about the value of a book and enclosing the title page for identification purposes, thereby removing the value along with the title page. If a dealer is interested in your list, he or she will write and arrange to see the books. In the case of autograph material, you may wish to copy or photograph some of it. Do not expect to be offered anything like the amounts you see listed in *American*

Book Prices Current or *Bookman's Price Index* for your books or autographs. The latter lists dealer's asking prices, which are retail sales prices and sometimes unrealistically high ones at that. And *American Book Prices Current* lists actual prices fetched at public auction sales. At auctions at the major houses, the dealers often are working on a 10 percent commission only, and they are flying the flag in public. Moreover, the dealers are in competition with their peers and other interested parties in an open market. When you sell to a dealer, you are selling into a wholesale situation. Whether or not you have immediate need for the proceeds will also be a factor in your decision to sell to a dealer or through an auction house. You often will get more for a book at auction, but you will have to wait for several months from the time of consignment to cash in hand; dealers may pay less, but they pay cash.

The appraisal of literary properties partakes of both art and science. If you take reasonable care in securing an appraisal, you then can face the tax agent, the insurance agent, the battling heirs to an estate, or any other possible adversary with the cheerful confidence of the well fortressed.

Notes

1. The technically minded may refer to Section 20.2031 of Estate Tax Regulations, Section 25.2512-I of Gift Tax Regulations, or Section 1.170A of Income Tax Regulations before discussing all this with their lawyers.
2. Robert Metzdorf, "The Appraisal of Literary Properties," *1965 AB Bookman's Yearbook*, pt. II, p. 315.
3. A. E. Housman, "The Application of Thought to Textual Criticism," *Proceedings of the Classical Association* XVIII (1922): 84.
4. *IRS Publication 561*, 1976 Edition, p. 8.
5. Ibid., p. 6.
6. Ibid., p. 6. See also IRS Revenue Procedure 66–49, Section 3.02.
7. Our thanks is due Anthony Fair of Sotheby Parke Bernet in New York for making available this material.
8. *IRS Publication 561*, p. 6.
9. Ibid., p. 8.
10. Ibid., p. 4. These are considered "ordinary income property, and the deduction is limited to the fair market value

reduced by the amount of appreciation over cost or other adjusted basis [the result of this subtraction problem generally is zero]."

11. What happens if you give the letters to a member of your family is unclear at this writing because of recent changes in the tax law and new regulations that are being written. Consult your lawyer before taking action.

12. Also, if a collection might have to be sold after your death, be certain that your lawyer has drafted your will in such a manner as to ensure that expenses like commissions to an auction house will be deductible as necessary expenses. This is a difficult area, as the Streeter, Smith, and Park cases have shown, and needs careful attention.

11

The Book Collector in the World of Scholarship

Susan O. Thompson

GIVEN THE HUMAN INSTINCT for classification and order, not to mention acquisitiveness, it is hardly surprising that the tribe of book collectors is virtually as old as books themselves. A library of clay tablets from the third millennium B.C. has been excavated at Ur in Mesopotamia.[1] When books became so plentiful that private collections proliferated, the bibliophile's bad press also began, with the virulent writings of Seneca and Lucian: "One who opens his eyes with an hideous stare at an old book; and after turning over the pages, chiefly admires the date of its publication."[2] Over 1,000 years later, *The Ship of Fools* put into classic form Western culture's concept of the book-fool:

> Style am I busy bokes assemblynge,
> For to have plenty it is a pleasant thynge
> In my conceyt, and to have them ay in my honde:
> But what they mene do I nat understounde.[3]

Yet our civilization's debt to the lover of books is enormous; Raymond Irwin has pointed out that the personal libraries criticized by Lucian, not the Roman public libraries, transmitted our Latin heritage to the early monasteries.[4] This kind of contribution, actual books passing from the private domain to the public, continues throughout the history of book collecting. One has only to look at the origins of national libraries or the titles of university rare book collections to see the evidence.

Huntington, Folger, and Morgan are names known to every book collector.

Beyond this well-documented relationship to the larger world there lies a more subtle one—the role of the collector in the organization of knowledge itself, a major aspect of which is his or her affinity with learned societies. Here the genealogy stretches back farther than books. The forming of groups devoted to knowledge must be almost as ancient as humankind itself. Even before the development of writing, medicine men had their lodges, taboo to the uninitiated. A millennium after the invention of writing, Plato's Academy, sometimes referred to as the first university, was formed. The greatest library of antiquity, in Alexandria, had its circle of resident scholars. The early Middle Ages were illumined by the monastic scriptoria; the High Middle Ages saw the emergence of universities as we know them.

But it was not until the printed word and the ensuing increase, first in the dissemination of knowledge, then in its accumulation, that learned societies as such emerged. Cosimo de' Medici's Accademia Platonica is said to be a forerunner. Cosimo died in 1464, at the very time Sweynheym and Pannartz were setting up the first Italian printing press at Subiaco. Just over a century after Caxton introduced printing to England, the Assembly of Antiquaries was founded around 1586 by Sir Robert Cotton, William Camden, John Stow, and others.[5]

The turbulent seventeenth century gave birth to modern science and scientific academies, which published their transactions. The Royal Society of London for Improving Natural Knowledge, as it was first called, was incorporated in 1662. Book collecting was increasing to the point that the practice of book auctions was imported from Holland to England. According to Frank Mumby, after William Cooper's pioneer English sale of this kind, in 1676, the popularity of the new method in its own turn fostered the love of reading.[6]

In the eighteenth century there were manifest both a strong antiquarianism and the beginnings of romantic bibliophily. The newly discovered ruins of Pompeii brought antiquity into the present as never before, while the forebear of Gothic Revival could be seen at Horace Walpole's Strawberry Hill. With Baskerville, England's typographical prestige spread to the continent for the first time. Very old books were becoming noticeably scarce and therefore desirable. Continuing in the spirit of the earlier Assembly, the Society of Antiquaries, including Humphry Wanley, John Bagford, and John Talman, held meetings at which both manuscripts and printing were discussed, although, after its incorporation in 1751, interest shifted from literary to archaeological research. The Society of Dilettanti, composed of traveled gentlemen led by the notorious Sir Francis Dashwood, was another eighteenth-century body primarily concerned with archaeology but also, according to Harold Williams in *Book Clubs & Printing Societies of Great Britain and Ireland*, the first organization to print and publish books at its own expense, thus anticipating a principal activity of modern learned societies.[7]

Eighteenth-century gentlemen collected private libraries on a large scale. One of the greatest of these collections, which had belonged to the late third duke of Roxburghe, came to the auction block in 1812. The sale of the Valdarfer *Decameron* for £2,260 was an event so sensational that it precipitated the formation of the first purely bibliophile society, the Roxburghe Club, with Earl Spencer as president and the Reverend Thomas Frognall Dibdin as vice-president.

Largely aristocratic in composition, restricting its publications in the early days to members, given to elaborate dinners, the Roxburghe Club was nevertheless a major influence on the image of book collecting in the eyes of the world. This was to be not just a hobby among hobbies but the most serious of them all. Dibdin, as potent an influence as the Roxburghe itself, called it a madness in his *Bibliomania* (1809). The "Advertisement" says: "In laying before the public the following brief and superficial account of a disease, which, till it arrested the attention of Dr. Ferriar, had entirely escaped the sagacity of all ancient and modern physicians, it has been my object to touch chiefly on its leading characteristics, and to present the reader (in the language of my old friend Francis Quarles) with an 'honest pennyworth' of information, which may, in the end, either suppress or soften the ravages of so destructive a malady."[8]

In America things were simpler and more republican. Adolf Growoll, the authority on early American book clubs, believes that they started with The Junto of 1726, organized by Benjamin Franklin as a debating society but active eventually in the sphere of book collecting when in 1731 what is now the Library Company of Philadelphia was formed.[9] The simple love of reading and educated conversation, in a land where both were in short supply, lies at the origin of American scholarly organization.

The frenzied enthusiasm of the Dibdin era in England did spread to the United States, at least in an attenuated form. There was buying and selling of rare books in the mid-nineteenth century and the establishment of book clubs as well as learned societies, but only after the Civil War did American bibliophily reach its first Golden Age. The landmark here is the founding of the Grolier Club of New York in 1884, now the oldest and most prestigious of American bibliophilic societies.

In a sense, the last quarter of the twentieth century is light years away from 1884. The technology of bookmaking, then in the midst of mechanization, now may be on the verge of utter transformation. We find ourselves disoriented amidst an inundation of printed paper and other forms of communication, the so-called "information explosion." Has the role of the book collector also changed? I think not: Changes in technology only mean *different* things to collect, increased communication, *more* things. What *is* new about our century is that the pioneer efforts at organization of scholarship and of bibliophily just described have evolved into a vast network of specialist societies. The collector today is not likely to be an isolated figure but a member of several often interlocking and overlapping groups.

First of all, there are the clubs for collectors of rare books. The Grolier Club of New York owns a clubhouse with an outstanding library on every aspect of the history of the book, and this collection is open to the qualified researcher. It voted in 1976 to admit women to membership, a precedent-breaking step. Exhibitions, program meetings, publishing, receptions, dinners, and organized tours form the pattern of activities, followed in a similar or lesser degree by the other collector societies.

Publications of the Grolier Club, including exhibition catalogues and books about books, have been printed by the finest craftsmen of the time. Lawrence C. Wroth's *Colonial Printer*, printed for the Grolier Club by the Merrymount Press in 1931, is an example that also, as an accepted classic, shows the importance of many of the texts. The founding fathers intended the Grolier Club's books to set a physical standard for other publishers; such an influence cannot be documented, but it is safe to say that the Grolier Club played a not inconsiderable part in the so-called "revival of fine printing," not only in the field of design and craftsmanship but also in the general interest in printing as an art.

In 1937, Ruth Shepard Granniss, then librarian at the Grolier Club, summed up the ideal results:

> (1) The publication of books which the general publisher refuses or is unable to undertake, be it a reprint of a rare or unique work, or an original contribution to the literature of the book.
>
> (2) The elevation of popular taste in the technique of bookmaking by demanding the best in design and workmanship, the demand itself giving an impetus to book workers—printers, illustrators, binders, etc.
>
> (3) The provision of libraries on the arts of the book and exhibitions illustrative of those arts, where they may be freely studied, not only by workers but by the general public.
>
> (4) The sharing of mutual pleasures in such a way that fine enthusiasm is kindled and the contagion spread until all choice spirits know the joy of the book hunter and the satisfaction of the preserver of books.[10]

The Club of Odd Volumes in Boston goes back to the same decade as the Grolier Club, 1886. Its name recalls Ye Sette of Odd Volumes, founded in London in 1878. Surviving from the 1890s are the Rowfant Club of Cleveland and the Caxton Club of Chicago. California, one of the states where bookish interests have centered, has the Zamorano Club in Los Angeles (Agustin Vicente Zamorano was the state's first printer) and the Book Club of California and the Roxburghe Club in San Francisco. Other American regional clubs exist, such as the Baltimore Bibliophiles, the Philobiblon Club of Philadelphia, and the Yale Bibliophiles.[11] Still another club has another orientation. Because women have been excluded from many of these societies, the Hroswitha Club was founded in 1944 as an exclusive home for them. The name comes from the tenth-century nun of Gandersheim who wrote epic poems and plays. As H. Richard Archer said in a July 1958 *Library Journal* article, the history of twentieth-century American book-collector clubs would make an interesting topic for a broad survey.[12]

The Private Libraries Association is aimed directly at the individual collector, whether of rare books or more modest volumes. It has a large international membership and an active program. The list of publications includes a quarterly journal, a newsletter, an exchange list, an annual bibliography of private press books, and an annual gift book for its members. There are meetings in London and visits to places of special interest.

Closely allied to clubs composed of book collectors are the printing societies. Their membership is made up not only of practitioners of the book arts—printers, book designers, type designers, illustrators, calligraphers, binders—but also of collectors, librarians, publishers, and anyone else interested in the art of the book. The Boston Society of Printers, itself a product of the revival of fine printing in 1905, is at one end of the country, the Rounce and Coffin Club of Los Angeles at the other. New York City has the Typophiles, and London, the Double Crown Club. The Columbiad Club of Connecticut is centered in Hartford.

History, as well as current practice, is naturally a concern of these clubs but there are two Anglo-American bodies that emphasize the historical aspect: the Printing Historical Society in Great Britain and the American Printing History Association. The latter, founded in 1974, has a large membership already, with local chapters getting under way.

Another subspecies of printing society is the sort devoted to the memory of one great printer, whether from the incunable period (Wynkyn de Worde in England) or recent times (Goudy in the United States). The William Morris Society is active in both countries and is composed not only of printing enthusiasts but also of those interested in Morris' writings, political theories, or design in fields other than books.

Related to the printing societies are organizations for other kinds of book art, such as the Society of Scribes and Illuminators and the Guild of Book Workers, most of whose members are handbinders. These bodies tend to be made up of actual practitioners but most of them admit collectors and other sympathetic souls.

For those interested in graphic art as a whole there is the American Institute of Graphic Arts. More limited interests are covered by such bodies as the American Society of Bookplate Collectors and Designers, the Playing Card Collectors' Association, or the International Postcard Collectors Association.

Bridging the gap between bibliophile groups and the rest of the scholarly world are the bibliographical societies composed of scholars, librarians, collectors, and dealers. From the work of scholars like A. W. Pollard, W. W. Greg, and R. B. McKerrow stems modern analytical bibliography, another natural focus point for those interested in rare books. London, Cambridge, and Oxford all have bibliographical societies. In the United States there is a national one that meets each year in New York and one at the University of Virginia (see the Appendix for their addresses).

A similar bridge is provided by professional organizations. The Association of College and Research Libraries, part of the American Library Association (ALA), has a Rare Books and Manuscripts Section which regularly holds a summer conference just before the annual ALA meeting. Collectors and dealers, as well as librarians, are welcome at these three-day sessions. A collector of music might wish to join the Music Library Association, and a collector of old documents, the Society of American Archivists. (There is also the Manuscript Society, with interests in all kinds of handwritten materials, especially in the field of American history.)

Moving to the traditional type of learned society, there are general ones of prime interest to the collector of Americana. The oldest in the country is the American Philosophical Society, founded in 1743 in Philadelphia. It has around 600 members, elected for scholarly distinction. The American Antiquarian Society in Worcester, Massachusetts, has the preeminent collection of American newspapers and early American printing. It publishes a journal as well as monographs and bibliographies.

Much more numerous are societies aimed toward subject specialists. The subjects can be as broad as whole disciplines: the American Historical Association or the Modern Language Association. They can be as narrow as one individual: the Dickens Fellowship or the Johnsonians. They can be concerned with periods of history: the Medieval Academy of America or the Victorian Society. They can be oriented toward place: the New-York Historical Society or the Historical Society of Pennsylvania. Book collectors need to know the subject content as well as the bibliography of their field, whether it is the history of optometry, French Romantic illustration, or first editions of Samuel Beckett. The days are gone when wealthy collectors, under the guidance of dealers, picked up one high spot after another. We are now in a more creative period of finding new collectibles. Perseverance, imagination, and scholarship are needed as much as money.

Still another type of society is an extension of one of the collector's own motives—the preservation of texts. The Early English Text Society, among many others, has reproduced old documents surviving in fragile form. From another angle, now that we are so concerned with the deterioration of modern paper, the collector might want to participate in the American Institute for Conservation of Historic and Artistic Works.

Libraries are yet another way of preserving books. The private collector's age-long generosity to libraries for public use has already been mentioned. Now, in this survey of the contemporary scene, "friends of the library" groups are a major class among organizations important to collectors. Activities generally include exhibitions, publishing programs, social occasions, public relations, and fund raising. All sorts of libraries have such groups. The Friends of the Huntington Library were organized in 1939. Boston University Libraries has one of the most active groups in the country. The Detroit Public Library has been a leader in the field. Whether the title chosen is "friends," "associates," or "fellows," across the country the total of work done by bibliophiles to aid libraries is enormous. One has only to scan the brochure for the Independent Research Libraries Association, the body made up of libraries without other institutional connections, to see how essential the "friends" are.

A final type of organization that book collectors may join consists of the commercially run societies publishing finely printed books issued at regular intervals. Many of these operations are dubious ones, shunned by the discriminating bibliophile. The Limited Editions Club, however, under George and Helen Macy produced books that are still much in demand among collectors. The Macy idea was to select a standard text of enduring value, have it edited by a scholar, illustrated, printed, and bound by the finest artists and craftsmen, and distributed monthly at a standard price to the list of 1,500 subscribers.[13]

We have seen the book collector as a preserver and transmitter of the literature and as a participant in societies dedicated to the organization and dissemination of knowledge. Book collectors are often even more directly engaged in the organization of knowledge by creating bibliographies themselves. Sir Geoffrey Keynes has done notable work of this sort. The collector is also in a position to add to knowledge itself by writing books about books. (The literature of bibliophily is vast, one of the most charming items being John Hill Burton's *The Book-Hunter*, in which he describes his subject's functions **under the rubrics of "The Hobby," "The Desultory Reader or**

Bohemian of Literature," "The Collector and the Scholar," "The Gleaner and His Harvest," "Pretenders," "His Achievements in the Creation of Libraries," "The Preservation of Literature," "Librarians," "Bibliographies.")[14] Collectors may write on other subjects using their own collection, or they may allow other scholars to use their libraries. Sir Thomas Phillipps, the world's greatest collector of manuscripts, took delight in putting up visiting scholars at Middle Hill. As A. N. L. Munby says at the end of *Portrait of an Obsession*: "We can picture him leading his guest along airless and encumbered passages, threading their way, like Mr. Boffin among his dustheaps, through box-lined rooms, amid stacked crates and vast accumulations of charters, rolls and codices in their dedicated search for knowledge, until, when the day is far spent, Sir Thomas provides by way of relaxation one of those 'desserts of manuscripts' of which he never wearied."[15]

The collector may wish to attend one of the series of bibliographical lectures that can be found at the Universities of Oxford, Cambridge, Pennsylvania, Texas, and California. Theodore Besterman was a Shoemaker lecturer at Rutgers, Gordon N. Ray, a Zeitlin-Ver Brugge lecturer at UCLA. Andrew H. Horn has described the purposes of the latter as the encouragement of bibliographical study and of "a closer association among scholars, collectors, and bibliophiles of the University and its surrounding community."[16]

These speeches are part of the educational process, in which collectors may find themselves involved in other ways. They may receive groups of interested people in their libraries for an exhibition of its treasures. They may participate in a lecture course for the general public, for an undergraduate group, or for a group of budding collectors. George Parker Winship, the Widener librarian, used to give a course on the history of the book to Harvard students, who, according to George H. Sargent in the March 21, 1925, *Publishers' Weekly*, were also encouraged by instructors to seek out old editions of their texts at the Dunster House Bookshop, while Yale and Princeton students went to the Brick Row Book Shops.[17] More recently, Karl Kup taught such a course at Princeton, where there is also an undergraduate bibliophile club, the Colophon Society. College libraries, as one of their promotion devices, and sometimes local collectors, have given prizes for the best undergraduate book collection.

For their own research, as opposed to educating others, can collectors find a welcome in rare book libraries? The answer is generally yes, with qualifications. The Pierpont Morgan Library requires a letter of recommendation, The New York Public Library does not. The latter will not admit undergraduates to its special collections, the former prefers doctoral-level research. Columbia University does not have a restriction as to level but wants a satisfactory explanation of need. No survey has been done of practices in American rare book libraries, but a similar variation is doubtless true nationwide. In general, serious collectors will find themselves welcomed as visiting scholars, but they should go armed with credentials and, if possible, having requested aid in advance, especially in these days when libraries are understaffed and severely limited in funds.

The relationship between private collectors and rare book libraries is a symbiotic one, but the balance is in favor of the former. Collectors can live without libraries, although they may find them useful, while the libraries would not have been born if collectors had not existed. As A. W. Pollard has said: "it is by the zeal of collectors that books which otherwise would have perished from neglect are discovered, cared for and preserved, and those who achieve these results certainly deserve well of the community."[18]

More recently, Louis B. Wright, in his essay in *Book Collecting and Scholarship*, described the American scene: "The United States owes a vast debt to book collectors, a debt far greater than the average citizen realizes. For the devoted book collectors of our country have contributed enormously to the cultural development of the nation and they have made possible scholarship and learning which we could not have had without their libraries. They deserve to rank with the founders of colleges and universities as public benefactors."[19]

Notes

1. Sidney L. Jackson, *Libraries and Librarianship in the West: A Brief History* (New York: McGraw-Hill, 1974), pp. 3–4.
2. Lucian, quoted in Thomas Frognall Dibdin, *Bibliomania; or Book-Madness; A Bibliographical Romance*, new and improved ed. (London: Chatto & Windus, 1876), p. 486.
3. Sebastian Brandt, quoted in Holbrook Jackson, *The Anatomy of Bibliomania* (New York: Farrar, Straus, 1950), p. 513.

4. "There is . . . little doubt that the main traditions of Latin literature were passed down through the grammarians and schoolteachers and the private collections of individual scholars, rather than through the public libraries . . . in Rome, which had no true university of its own, and where none of the public libraries was associated with a long tradition of teaching, the private library was developed on a far wider scale than it ever had been at Athens or Alexandria, spreading as time went by wherever Roman civilization penetrated . . . and becoming thereby the true vehicle of the Latin literary tradition." Raymond Irwin, *The English Library: Sources and History* (London: George Allen & Unwin, 1966), p. 79.

5. Arthur Brown, "The Growth of Literary Societies," in *Librarianship and Literature: Essays in Honour of Jack Pafford*, ed. by A. T. Milne (London: University of London Athlone Press, 1970), pp. 84–85.

6. Frank Arthur Mumby, *Publishing and Bookselling* (London: Jonathan Cape, 1934), pp. 164–167.

7. Harold Williams, *Book Clubs & Printing Societies of Great Britain and Ireland* (London: First Editions Club, 1929), p. 15.

8. Thomas Frognall Dibdin, *The Bibliomania; or Book-Madness; Containing Some Account of the History, Symptoms, and Cure of this Fatal Disease* (London: Longman, Hurst, Rees, and Orme, 1809), p. iii.

9. Adolf Growoll, *American Book Clubs: Their Beginnings and History, and a Bibliography of Their Publications* (New York: Dodd, Mead, 1897), pp. 4–5.

10. Ruth Shepard Granniss, *The Work of a Book Club: An Address Prepared for the Washington Square College Book Club of New York University* (New York: New York University, 1937), p. 35. Also valuable are the same author's "American Book Collecting and the Growth of Libraries," in Hellmut Lehmann-Haupt, *The Book in America: A History of the Making, the Selling, and the Collecting of Books in the United States* (New York: Bowker, 1939), pp. 295–381, and "What Bibliography Owes to Private Book Clubs," *Papers of the Bibliographical Society of America* 24 (1930):14–33.

11. For lists containing still other names see "Private Book Clubs," in *American Book Trade Directory*, 22nd ed. (New York: Bowker, 1975), pp. 494–495; and "Societies of Interest to Book Collectors," in *International Directory of Book Collec-*

tors 1976/77, comp. by Roger and Judith Sheppard (Beckenham, Kent: Trigon Press, 1976), pp. 199–223.

12. H. Richard Archer, "Bookmen's Clubs for All," *Library Journal* 83 (July 1958): 1994–1999.

13. For another broad survey of organizations having to do with books, see Lois Rather, *Books and Societies* (Oakland, Calif.: Rather Press, 1971); for a discussion of their social side, see Colin Steele, "Food for Thought," *Antiquarian Book Monthly Review* 3 (January 1976):16–21.

14. John Hill Burton, *The Book-Hunter: A New Edition with a Memoir of the Author* (Edinburgh: Blackwood, 1882), p. ix.

15. A. N. L. Munby, *Portrait of an Obsession: The Life of Sir Thomas Phillipps, the World's Greatest Book Collector* (New York: Putnam, 1967), p. 269.

16. Andrew H. Horn, *A Decade of Lectures in Bibliography in the Library Schools of the University of California 1961–1970* (Los Angeles: Plantin Press, n.d.), unpaged leaflet.

17. George H. Sargent, "Making the New Book Collectors," *Publishers' Weekly* 107 (March 21, 1925): 1111–1115.

18. *Encyclopaedia Britannica*, 11th ed., s.v. "Book-Collecting," p. 222.

19. Louis B. Wright, "American Book Collectors," in *Book Collecting and Scholarship* (Minneapolis: University of Minnesota Press, 1954), p. 51.

12

The Literature of Book Collecting

G. Thomas Tanselle

Collectors of all kinds of objects have occasion to consult the books written about their fields; but because books are themselves the objects that the book collector is interested in, it is not surprising that the urge to put bookish information into books has been particularly strong and that a vast literature of book collecting exists. Book collectors are in the unique position of being able to have working reference libraries that are at the same time integral parts of their collections. There are few book collectors, in fact, who do not collect books about books to some extent, and for many of them such a collection is not merely an adjunct but is itself the main collection; for dealers, bibliographical collections are a necessity, and dealers can in part satisfy their own collecting instincts by assembling the books that are professionally useful to them.

All book collectors, however, whether or not they are professionally concerned with books, find that they cannot progress very far without reference to what has been written on their subjects. Of the education of the collector, John Carter has observed: "Probably few collectors are so methodical as to put themselves through any formal education for what is, after all, a fairly sophisticated pursuit. Few, on the other hand, even of the most happy-go-lucky, have not discovered at some point in their career the advantage they have gained from some sort of informal education, and perhaps wished they had had more of it earlier." Some beginning collectors—depending on their temperaments—are inclined, as Carter puts it, not to complicate "simple pleasures with abstruse bibliographical technicalities." But as they learn that they cannot do without reference books, they also come to recognize that the pleasures and rewards of collecting are greater when one is conscious of utilizing and building upon the accomplishments of the past.

The literature of book collecting has no easily defined limits, for it constantly overlaps the fields of historical, analytical, and descriptive bibliography: The collector must understand something of the history of printing and publishing, must be able to analyze the physical evidence present in books, and must know how to read technical descriptions of books. Indeed, the basic bibliographical literature of all fields of endeavor is part of the literature of book collecting as well, because it contains information about books and therefore contributes to the total stock of knowledge about them. A short survey cannot pretend to do more than sketch the contours of this large and continually expanding body of work. The following pages attempt simply to characterize and offer an introductory guide to this literature, which can be grouped into nine classes: general introductions and manuals; historical studies and memoirs; periodicals; bibliographies and checklists; catalogues; price records and guides; directories of dealers and collectors; the related fields of conservation, bookplates, and manuscripts; and guides to further reading.

Some of the titles to be mentioned are works indispensable for current reference; others serve the less practical but equally important function of exhibiting aspects of the heritage shared by all book collectors of the English-speaking world. Books that are no longer useful for reference, or volumes of reminiscences and familiar essays never intended as reference books, remain of interest as repositories of the history and customs of bibliophily. Collectors who explore widely in this literature will gain an overview of bibliographical patterns and movements and thus a fuller sense of the context into which their own activities fall.

General Introductions and Manuals

Introductory handbooks play a basic role in any field, for they not only help to shape the attitudes and approaches of the

beginner but also provide—at least the best of them do—an illuminating distillation of a large body of material to which the
experienced person will repeatedly return. In the field of bibliophily there is no book that better fulfills this dual role than
John Carter's *Taste & Technique in Book-Collecting* (Cambridge
Univ. Pr., 1948).* It is based on his Sandars Lectures in Bibliography for 1947, and his preface specifically denies that it is "a
primer or a text-book or a manual for beginners." Nevertheless,
his subject is "the essential nature of book-collecting, the play
of cause and effect in its development, the evolution and also
the rationale of our present technical approach to it," and the
collector is fortunate whose introduction to collecting comes
through these thoughtful and humane pages. The alliterative
nouns in Carter's title show that his concern is both with the
choice of material to be collected and with the manner of con-
ducting the pursuit. The first half of the book, "Evolution," is
an astute analysis of the patterns of collecting from the mid-
nineteenth century to the mid-twentieth; the second, "Method," is full of penetrating observations on such matters as terminology, rarity, condition, and relations with dealers. What
the book as a whole accomplishes is to show how the collector
of any given time plays a role in a continuously developing tradition and influences the course of scholarship. Carter demonstrates—as much through his own learned and civilized
approach as through the content of his remarks—the importance of the collector as a preserver of a cultural heritage, a pioneer who recognizes neglected areas and assembles the
materials for studying them. Written with elegance and wit,
and buttressed by a remarkable range of allusion, this book
manages the difficult feat of conveying both the atmosphere
and the significance of the world of collecting. It is one of the
great classics in the field—and, as is true of classics, it is not
outdated except in trivial respects (a new printing, with an epi-
logue covering developments after 1948, was published by the
Private Libraries Association in 1970). For the reader who requires more detailed explanations of various terms used in it,
Carter himself has supplied the perfect companion piece—his

*Many of the books mentioned here are identified by the publisher (or city
and publisher) and year of their original publication; but in the interests of
economy this practice is not rigidly adhered to, particularly in cases where
books are cited allusively as examples or where some of the facts are made clear
by the context. No attempt is made to indicate which books are currently available from new-book dealers, for such information changes rapidly and can be
checked in *Books in Print* and *British Books in Print*.

ABC for Book Collectors (London: Hart-Davis, 1952), which appeared in a fifth (revised) edition in 1972. Arranged in glossary form, *ABC* offers definitions, and often extended discussions, of the basic terms in the bibliographical vocabulary, couched in Carter's characteristic turn of phrase and revealing the same critical intelligence as *Taste & Technique*; it is therefore no ordinary glossary but one that can be read straight through with pleasure, and anyone who does so will pick up much valuable instruction in the process. The two books complement one another and together form an ideal introduction for the collector (and one that will not be outgrown).

Carter—whose professional life was spent in the London office of Scribner's antiquarian department (1927–1953) and as an associate director of Sotheby's (1955–1972)—was at the center of a brilliant group of dealers and collectors who during the second quarter of the twentieth century were vocal in expressing the importance, for collecting, of a careful study of book production and a detailed analysis of the physical features of books. Of all the seminal books that issued from this group (sometimes called the "biblio boys" because of their concern with analytical and descriptive bibliography), perhaps the most representative is the landmark anthology that Carter edited, *New Paths in Book-Collecting* (London: Constable, 1934). In addition to Carter's pioneer essay on detective fiction, the volume contains discussions of such then unexplored subjects as "yellow-backs," serial fiction, transatlantic editions of English-language books, musical first editions, and late nineteenth-century book illustration, written by Thomas Balston, Percy H. Muir, C. B. Oldman, Graham Pollard, David A. Randall, Michael Sadleir, and John T. Winterich—names that frequently reappear in any account of twentieth-century collecting. The book may not technically be an introductory guide, but it presents a splendid series of examples of imaginative approaches to collecting. Other books by this group, too, taken as a whole, constitute a sort of large-scale manual, full of illustrations of the responsible handling of bibliographical problems. Sadleir, for instance, edited for his firm, Constable, a series of volumes collectively called "Bibliographia," with the revealing subtitle "Studies in Book History and Book Structure"; as Carter later pointed out, the volumes "were all marked by a scholarly appreciation of the importance of book-structure and publishing practice to the intelligent collector, whose acquiescence in this proposition was enlisted by being taken for granted." The series includes Sad-leir's *The Evolution of Publishers' Binding Styles, 1770–1900* (1930), R. W. Chapman's *Cancels* (1930), Muir's two volumes of *Points* (1931–1934), Carter's *Binding Variants in English Publishing, 1820–1900* (1932), Iolo A. Williams' *Points in Eighteenth-Century Verse* (1934), and I. R. Brussel's two volumes of *Anglo-American First Editions* (1935–1936). (Another Constable series, "Aspects of Book-Collecting," includes separate printings of some of the essays from *New Paths*, as well as pamphlets like Carter's *More Binding Variants* [1938].)

The most famous book to emerge from this group is Carter and Pollard's *An Enquiry into the Nature of Certain Nineteenth Century Pamphlets*, brought out by Constable in the same year as *New Paths* (1934). Proving that a number of "rare" pamphlets were actually fabrications, clearly perpetrated by Thomas J. Wise, one of the most respected bibliographers and collectors of the day, this book was bound to create excitement; but equally exciting was the demonstration of what could be achieved by the analysis of physical evidence, which was simply a more dramatic example of the work that was being undertaken in the "Bibliographia" series. Several members of the group did produce books intended as introductory manuals: Winterich's *A Primer of Book Collecting* (New York: Greenberg, 1927, 1935; revised by Randall in 1946 and 1966), supplemented by *Collector's Choice* (Greenberg, 1928); Williams' *The Elements of Book-Collecting* (London: Elkin Mathews & Marrot, 1927); and Muir's *Book-Collecting as a Hobby* (London: Gramol, 1944, 1945), with its sequel, *Book-Collecting: More Letters to Everyman* (London: Cassell, 1949). These books are very elementary but are generally engaging and sensible. All three writers advise collectors to choose their own subjects, but Williams is the most explicit in pointing out (on his opening page) that "the object of all collecting is the increase of the general sum of knowledge upon some particular subject." His book is the most bibliographically oriented of the lot, devoting much space to instructions for analyzing and describing books, and is salutary in its emphasis on the bibliographical value of every collection: "I defy any intelligent person," he says, "to look at all carefully over even a small collection without making bibliographical discoveries in quantities" (p. 133). Muir also provides some bibliographical instruction, including (in his 1945 revised edition) a short history of book production; and Winterich's earlier book, made considerably more substantial by Randall's additions, contains a fund of interesting examples of bibliographical points and fields of collecting. Many other valuable writings by members of this celebrated group remain uncollected in periodicals, although John Carter did gather a few of his miscellaneous essays into an appealing volume, *Books and Book-Collectors* (London: Hart-Davis, 1956).

Not long before Carter delivered his Sandars Lectures, Colton Storm and Howard Peckham offered a series of lectures on book collecting at the University of Michigan, lectures that were turned into a comprehensive book, *Invitation to Book Collecting* (New York: Bowker, 1947). This work stands above most of its rivals and is certainly one of the best of the general introductions. Aimed more directly at beginners than is Carter's book, and less polished in style, it nevertheless rests on the same fundamental assumptions about collecting. It, too, sketches the historical background and surveys traditional fields of collecting (including manuscripts, prints, and maps) before moving to the "techniques of acquisition and evaluation." And it stresses the connoisseurship of the true collector, the need to develop a "trained and discriminating judgment" (p. 39). "Anyone can gather books without intelligence," the authors say, "but there really seems to be little use in collecting books unless the mind is used" (p. 50). Storm and Peckham clearly savor the intellectual pleasures of collecting, and their book offers sound observations on the foundation of those pleasures.

Because book collecting and bibliography are so intertwined, any listing of the best general handbooks on book collecting must also include the best manuals on bibliography. R. B. McKerrow's *An Introduction to Bibliography for Literary Students* (Oxford: Clarendon, 1927) is the classic of analytical bibliography, lucidly explaining how the physical evidence present in books can reveal facts of their printing and publishing histories (and can thus also be relevant in settling textual problems); written by one of the men most responsible for the development of analytical bibliography in the early years of the century (the others are W. W. Greg and A. W. Pollard), the book conveys a sense of the excitement of discovery and the open-ended quality of the search for historical truth. Many developments have occurred in analytical bibliography since 1927, but for the most part these must be searched out in the periodicals.

Philip Gaskell's *A New Introduction to Bibliography* (Oxford: Clarendon, 1972) serves a somewhat different, but equally important, purpose: It provides a compact and workmanlike historical account of the materials (type, paper, binding) and the processes (composition, imposition, presswork, publication) connected with the production of printed books from 1500 to 1950. And Fredson Bowers' *Principles of Bibliographical Description* (Princeton Univ. Pr., 1949) is a masterly codification of the method that had been evolving over the previous half century for recording detailed physical descriptions of books. None of these books was written specifically for collectors, but collectors will find themselves returning to all three time after time. If one must restrict one's basic reference shelf to the barest minimum, McKerrow, Gaskell, and Bowers belong on it, along with Carter's *Taste & Technique* and his *ABC*.

A number of other introductory works, published over the last century or so, should be briefly mentioned. The earlier ones are of course outdated, but if they were responsible treatments in their time they probably still have something to offer; and because such works naturally concentrate on the books available to their readers and reflect contemporary fashions in collecting, they contain comments on many books not taken up in more recent manuals. One of the most widely read books on collecting in the nineteenth century was John Hill Burton's *The Book-Hunter* (Edinburgh: Blackwood, 1862). For the next generation Burton's successor was J. Herbert Slater, founder of *Book-Prices Current* in 1887, who published *Book Collecting: A Guide for Amateurs* (London: Sonnenschein, 1892) and the larger *How to Collect Books* (London: Bell, 1905), as well as other bookish essays, such as *The Romance of Book-Collecting* (London: Stock, 1898). During these years there were also John Power's *A Handy-Book about Books* (London: Wilson, 1870), Andrew Lang's *The Library* (London: Macmillan, 1881), Percy Fitzgerald's *The Book Fancier* (London: Low, 1886), W. T. Rogers' *A Manual of Bibliography* (London: Grevel, 1891), Arthur L. Humphreys' *The Private Library* (London: Strangeways, 1897), William Harris Arnold's *First Report of a Book-Collector* (New York: Dodd, Mead, 1898), Ainsworth Rand Spofford's *A Book for All Readers* (New York: Putnam, 1900), A. W. Pollard's *Books in the House* (Indianapolis: Bobbs-Merrill, 1904)—containing the sensible statement that "it is by following their own tastes that collectors are most likely to promote the cause of learning and literature" (p.

66)—and James Duff Brown's *A Manual of Practical Bibliography* (London: Routledge, 1906), along with the earlier bibliographical work of Thomas Hartwell Horne, *An Introduction to the Study of Bibliography* (London: Cadell & Davies, 1814). The late nineteenth century also saw the production of three important series of books, forerunners of Sadleir's "Bibliographia" in the quality and scholarly approach of their contributors. The largest and most widely known is "The Book Lover's Library" (1886–1902), 25 volumes published by Elliot Stock and edited by H. B. Wheatley, including books by W. C. Hazlitt and William Blades and the editor's own *How to Form a Library* (1886). Smaller, but more distinguished, were A. W. Pollard's "Books about Books" series (London: Kegan Paul, 1893–1894)—consisting of six valuable historical studies (on collecting, bookplates, manuscripts, early books, illustration, and binding) by E. Gordon Duff, Falconer Madan, Pollard, and others—and his "English Bookman's Library" (London: Kegan Paul, 1899–1902), three volumes on bindings, printing, and collectors, by C. J. H. Davenport, H. R. Plomer, and W. Y. Fletcher. Other series containing some books of interest to collectors, such as Richard Garnett's "The Library Series" (London: Allen, 1897–1899), appeared at this time, and information on all of them can be found in Ruth S. Granniss' "Series of Books about Books," *Colophon*, n.s., 1 (1935–1936): 549–564.

In the years between 1925 and the 1950s, several introductions besides those already named were published, but most of them, by comparison, seem either limited in content or superficial in attitude: Haslehurst Greaves' slight book, *The Personal Library* (London: Grafton, 1928); Richard Curle's often aptly phrased *Collecting American First Editions* (Indianapolis: Bobbs-Merrill, 1930); Guy A. Jackson's brief *A Primer of Rare Books and First Editions* (Boston, 1930), written for booksellers; Reginald Brewer's garrulous but fairly comprehensive *The Delightful Diversion* (New York: Macmillan, 1935), ending with a list of the points and values for 600 American books; Herbert Faulkner West's *Modern Book Collecting for the Impecunious Amateur* (Boston: Little, Brown, 1936), which, after three introductory chapters, describes the author's own enthusiasms and ends with a list of 100 "fine modern books"; and Robert L. Collison's *Book Collecting* (London: Benn, 1957)—which, like Arundell Esdaile's *A Student's Manual of Bibliography* (1931; 4th ed., revised by Roy Stokes, London: Allen & Unwin, 1967), is a handbook of historical bibliography inferior to McKerrow and Gaskell. More recent general surveys for collectors (of which there has been a considerable flurry in the 1970s, with half a dozen in 1976 alone) have tended to concentrate more on the various fields of collecting than on techniques and methods. One new development has been the appearance of several large-size books full of illustrations, many in color; they are not merely picture books, however, for they contain extensive, if generally casual, texts. In this category fall Eric Quayle's series based on his own collections—*The Collector's Book of Books* (London: Studio Vista, 1971), *The Collector's Book of Children's Books* (1971), *The Collector's Book of Detective Fiction* (1972), and *The Collector's Book of Boys' Stories* (1973)—and also Alan G. Thomas' *Great Books and Book Collectors* (London: Weidenfeld & Nicolson, 1975) and *The Country Life Book of Book Collecting*, edited by Richard Booth (Feltham: Hamlyn, 1976). These books can make pleasant enough reading, but they can also be rather haphazard, and only the first and last make any gesture toward formal instruction in the methodology of collecting. Of the more conventional recent manuals, all fail to reach the standard of the best of the earlier books, and some pay excessive attention to the question of books as investments: Seumas Stewart, *Book Collecting: A Beginner's Guide* (Newton Abbot, England: David & Charles, 1972); Maurice Dunbar, *Fundamentals of Book Collecting* (Los Altos, Calif.: Hermes, 1976); Salvatore J. Iacone, *The Pleasures of Book Collecting* (New York: Harper & Row, 1976); Jack Tannen, *How to Identify and Collect American First Editions: A Guide Book* (New York: Arco, 1976); and Jack Matthews, *Collecting Rare Books for Pleasure and Profit* (New York: Putnam, 1977). There have also recently been some illustrated books on specialized fields, such as A. W. Coysh's *Collecting Bookmarkers* (Newton Abbot, England: David & Charles, 1974) and John Lewis' *Collecting Printed Ephemera* (London: Studio Vista, 1976).

It is difficult in many cases to draw the line between introductory handbooks and anecdotal surveys, or between such surveys and personal reminiscences. The literature of book collecting abounds in volumes of genial gossip on bookish matters, and many of them can serve (and have often served in the past) as appealing introductions, convincing incipient collectors to join the ranks and informing them in the process of some of the traditions and concerns of the field. The most famous, and most prolific, nineteenth-century writer on book collecting was Thomas Frognall Dibdin, whose massive works inaugurated the tradition of anecdotal history and reminiscence in bibliophily; several generations drew their inspiration from his *Bibliomania* (London, 1811, 1842), *The Bibliographical Decameron* (1817), *A Bibliographical Antiquarian and Picturesque Tour* (1821, 1829), and other books carefully recorded in William A. Jackson's bibliography of Dibdin (Cambridge: Houghton Library, 1965). An equally famous writer in the twentieth century, who probably has no equal as an influential popularizer of book collecting, is A. Edward Newton; *The Amenities of Book-Collecting* (Boston: Atlantic Monthly Pr., 1918), *This Book-Collecting Game* (Boston: Little, Brown, 1928)—which ends with Newton's famous list of "One Hundred Good Novels"—and several more titles can, to the right person in the right mood, be ingratiating and seductive, and the person who enters collecting by this route will be equipped with a considerable mass of bibliographical lore. A few other well-known books representing varieties of this extensive category are Andrew Lang's *Books and Bookmen* (New York: Coombes, 1886), Eugene Field's *The Love Affairs of a Bibliomaniac* (New York: Scribner, 1896), William Loring Andrews' *Gossip about Book Collecting* (New York: Dodd, Mead, 1900) and numerous other titles, Austin Dobson's *De Libris* (London: Macmillan, 1908), P. B. M. Allan's *The Book-Hunter at Home* (London: Allan, 1920), Edmund Lester Pearson's *Books in Black or Red* (New York: Macmillan, 1923), Cyril Davenport's *Byways among English Books* (London: Methuen, 1927), Vincent Starrett's *Penny Wise and Book Foolish* (New York: Covici-Friede, 1929), and Barton Currie's *Fishers of Books* (Boston: Little, Brown, 1931). (Some readers are also attracted to novels, mysteries, and poetry on bookish themes, such as Christopher Morley's *The Haunted Bookshop* [Garden City, N.Y.: Doubleday, Doran, 1919], Julian Symons' *Bland Beginning* [London: Gollancz, 1949], or Howard S. Ruddy's collection of *Book Lovers' Verse* [Indianapolis: Bowen-Merrill, 1899].) This tradition is sometimes traced, by stretching a point, back to Richard de Bury's *Philobiblon* (finished in 1345), which is available in a number of modern editions; another early commentator is Gabriel Naudé, whose *Avis pour dresser une bibliothèque* (1644) was translated by John Evelyn in 1661 and by Archer Taylor, under the title *Advice on Establishing a Library*, in 1950 (Univ. of California Pr.). But however long the time during which comments about books have been made, very few of them can have escaped the net of Holbrook Jackson, who gathered thousands of passages and phrases according to topics and fitted them together in the vast mosaic of *The Anatomy of Bibliomania* (London: Soncino Pr., 1930, 1932).

Essays and other short pieces by various hands have sometimes been collected into agreeable anthologies. The best known are probably those compiled by William Targ, *Carousel for Bibliophiles* (New York: Duschnes, 1947), *Bouillabaisse for Bibliophiles* (Cleveland: World, 1955), and *Bibliophile in the Nursery* (Cleveland: World, 1957); a similar one devoted to typographical matters is Paul A. Bennett's *Books and Printing* (Cleveland: World, 1951, 1963). Several distinguished collections of original essays follow in the tradition of the epoch-making *New Paths* of 1934: first came *Book Collecting: Four Broadcast Talks* (Cambridge: Bowes & Bowes, 1950), with essays by John Carter, R. W. Chapman, John Hayward, and Michael Sadleir; then a volume that could serve as a general introduction more handsomely than most works specifically intended as such, *Talks on Book-Collecting*, edited by P. H. Muir (London: Cassell, 1952), with contributions by Carter, Ifan Kyrle Fletcher, E. P. Goldschmidt, Muir, Howard M. Nixon, Simon Nowell-Smith, and Ernest Weil; and finally the *ABA Annual 1952* and the 1953 annual, *Books and the Man* (London: Dawson), with essays by Sadleir, A. N. L. Munby, and others. American collections of lectures include *Book Collecting and Scholarship* (Univ. of Minnesota Pr., 1954), *Bowker Lectures on Book Publishing* (1957), and *Four Talks for Bibliophiles* (Free Library of Philadelphia, 1958). Several other important anthologies and *Festschriften* of generous proportions are American in origin: *Bibliographical Essays: A Tribute to Wilberforce Eames* (Cambridge, Mass.: Harvard Univ. Pr., 1924), Earl Schenck Miers and Richard Ellis' *Bookmaking & Kindred Amenities* (Rutgers Univ. Pr., 1942), *Bookmen's Holiday . . . in Tribute to Harry Miller Lydenberg* (New York Public Library, 1943), *To Doctor R.* (Philadelphia, 1946), and *Essays Honoring Lawrence C. Wroth* (Portland, Maine, 1951). Essays by some of the leading bibliographical writers have also been assembled into volumes—W. W. Greg's *Collected Papers* (Oxford: Clarendon, 1966), William A. Jackson's *Records of a Bibliographer* (Cambridge, Mass.: Belknap, Harvard Univ. Pr., 1967), Fredson Bowers' *Essays in Bibliography, Text, and Editing* (Bibliographical Society of the University of Virginia, 1975), A. N. L. Munby's *Essays and Papers* (London: Scolar, 1977)—but many significant articles remain uncollected in the journals. The *Encyclopaedia Britannica*, too, contains several excellent essays relating to books: One could not wish for a better brief introduction than William H. Bond's superb article on "Book Collecting" (1961), which surpasses A. W. Pollard's fine earlier piece (1910); Bond's skillfully constructed and gracefully written essay offers more sound observations than some of the book-length treatments of the subject are able to provide. Another important essay, analyzing with great insight the relations between collectors and scholars, is Gordon N. Ray's "The Private Collector and the Literary Scholar," in *The Private Collector and the Support of Scholarship* (Los Angeles: Clark Library, 1969).

Although John Carter's *ABC for Book Collectors* is the highwater mark of the compact glossaries, there are other dictionaries available with different aims. Geoffrey Glaister's largescale *Glossary of the Book* (London: Allen & Unwin, 1960), published in the United States as *An Encyclopedia of the Book*, offers well-illustrated and authoritative coverage of all aspects of book production. L. M. Harrod's *The Librarian's Glossary* (1938; 3rd ed., London: Deutsch, 1971) is also a hefty volume, including more terms from librarianship and providing fairly brief definitions. The fifth (and fiftieth-anniversary) edition of *The Bookman's Glossary* (New York: Bowker, 1975), edited by Jean Peters, covers the terminology of the book trade as a whole and is more compact in scale. (Margaret Haller's recent *The Book Collector's Fact-Book* [New York: Arco, 1976] is unsatisfactory and unnecessary.) Several glossaries assist the reader of catalogues in understanding bibliographical terms in other languages—notably Menno Hertzberger's *Dictionary of the Antiquarian Book Trade* (Paris: International League of Antiquarian Booksellers, 1956), Jerrold Orne's *The Language of the Foreign Book Trade* (Chicago: American Library Assn., 1949, 1976), and the most comprehensive, C. G. Allen's *A Manual of European Languages for Librarians* (New York: Bowker, 1976). One other category of collectors' reference books has for years consisted of a single entrant: Whereas several introductory works summarize briefly various publishers' practices in identifying first printings, only H. S. Boutell's 1929 book, *First Editions of To-Day and How to Tell Them*—now in its fourth edition (Berkeley, Calif.: Peacock Pr., 1965), revised by Wanda Underhill—has published a large number of statements (normally from the publishers themselves, though not always entirely trustworthy) describing the practices of British and American publishers. (Tannen's *How to Identify and Collect American First Editions*, mentioned earlier, contains a list, intended to supersede Boutell, recording the methods of 270 American firms. It can be helpful but, like Boutell, should be used with caution.)

Most introductory works for collectors say something about the history of book production, but the importance of such knowledge for an intelligent approach to collecting may well cause collectors to seek more detailed information in certain areas than can be found even in Gaskell's *A New Introduction to Bibliography*. For a basic survey of printing history, S. H. Steinberg's *Five Hundred Years of Printing* (1955; 3rd ed., Harmondsworth, England: Penguin Books, 1974) is to be preferred to Douglas McMurtrie's old standby, *The Book* (New York: Oxford Univ. Pr., 1943), and it might be supplemented by Norma Levarie's *The Art & History of Books* (New York: Heineman, 1968) and W. Turner Berry and H. Edmund Poole's *Annals of Printing* (London: Blandford, 1966). James Moran's history, *Printing Presses* (London: Faber & Faber, 1973), is now standard, and for technical processes there are L. A. Legros and J. C. Grant's classic *Typographical Printing Surfaces* (London: Longmans, Green, 1916) and Victor Strauss' more recent *The Printing Industry* (New York: Printing Industries and Bowker, 1967). Stanley Morison's *Type Designs of the Past and Present* (London: Fleuron, 1926) and A. F. Johnson's *Type Designs: Their History and Development* (1934; 3rd ed., London: Deutsch, 1966) can be highly recommended, along with Morison and Kenneth Day's *The Typographic Book, 1450–1935* (London: Benn, 1963) and Roderick Cave's *The Private Press* (London: Faber & Faber, 1971). Standard historical works in their fields are Dard Hunter's *Papermaking* (New York: Knopf, 1943, 1947); David Bland's *A History of Book Illustration* (London: Faber & Faber, 1958, 1969); and Edith Diehl's *Bookbinding: Its Background and Technique* (New York: Rinehart, 1946), plus Carter's and Sadleir's histories of publishers' binding, and *Bookbinding in America* (Portland, Maine: Southworth-Anthoensen, 1941), edited by Hellmut Lehmann-Haupt. To name more than these few basic titles would obviously be to embark on the enormous field of historical bibliography and cannot be undertaken here. A judicious guide to further reading along these lines is the essay entitled "Reference Bibliography" at the end of Gaskell's *New Introduction*; and a series of admirable essays summarizing the developments in bibliography in the first half of the twentieth century are gathered in *The Bibliographical Society, 1892–1942: Studies in Retrospect* (London: Bibliographical Society, 1945).

Historical Studies and Memoirs

Although the most penetrating discussion of the history of book collecting during the last century and a half is in John Carter's *Taste & Technique*, there are various other sources for more detailed narrative history and accounts of the great collectors of the past. Good compact surveys are Seymour De Ricci's *English Collectors of Books and Manuscripts (1530–1930) and Their Marks of Ownership* (Cambridge Univ. Pr., 1930) and Ruth S. Granniss' "American Book Collecting and the Growth of Libraries," in Hellmut Lehmann-Haupt et al., *The Book in America* (New York: Bowker, 1939), pp. 293–381. (The emphasis of the first of these works on marks of ownership indicates one of the important uses of book-collecting history: tracing the pedigrees of particular copies. The scholarly value of such knowledge is described in a pamphlet by Frederick B. Adams, Jr., *The Uses of Provenance* [Univ. of California, 1969].) Further details can be found in Charles I. and Mary A. Elton's *The Great Book-Collectors* (London: Kegan Paul, 1893), William Y. Fletcher's *English Book Collectors* (London: Kegan Paul, 1902), Carl L. Cannon's *American Book Collectors and Collecting* (New York: Wilson, 1941), and Edwin Wolf 2nd's "Great American Book Collectors to 1800," *Gazette of the Grolier Club*, n.s., no. 16 (June 1971), pp. 3–70. Many of the books that can be regarded as introductions to collecting (and are mentioned above) contain some commentary on collecting history, and Dibdin's works are basic sources in this regard. Other historical accounts by nineteenth-century figures are William Clarke's *Repertorium Bibliographicum* (London: Clarke, 1819), F. Somner Merryweather's *Bibliomania in the Middle Ages* (London: Merryweather, 1849), James Wynne's *Private Libraries of New York* (New York: French, 1860), Bernard Quaritch's *Contributions toward a Dictionary of English Book Collectors* (London, 1892–1921), and W. C. Hazlitt's *The Book-Collector* (London: Grant, 1904). (Hazlitt also compiled a list of some 17,000 names of British collectors from the fourteenth century onward in *A Roll of Honour* [London: Quaritch, 1908].) Good accounts of collecting in particular fields can be found in John L. Thornton's *Medical Books, Libraries and Collectors* (1949; 2nd ed.,

London: Deutsch, 1966), Thornton and R. I. J. Tully's *Scientific Books, Libraries and Collectors* (1954; 3rd ed., London: Library Assn., 1971), A. Hyatt King's *Some British Collectors of Music, c. 1600–1960* (Cambridge Univ. Pr., 1963), and R. A. Skelton's *Maps: A Historical Survey of Their Study and Collecting* (Univ. of Chicago Pr., 1972). Some historical investigation of the idea of rarity is reported in Ralph Franklin's "Conjectures on Rarity," *Library Quarterly* 44 (1974): 309–321, and M. S. Batts' "The Eighteenth-Century Concept of the Rare Book," *Book Collector* 24 (1975): 381–400.

The history of book collecting is inextricably bound with the history of manuscript collecting, and two of A. N. L. Munby's distinguished and readable contributions to collecting history are important in this field: *The Cult of the Autograph Letter in England* (London: Athlone, 1962) and *Connoisseurs and Medieval Miniatures, 1750–1850* (Oxford: Clarendon, 1972). An earlier more general history is M. R. James' *The Wanderings and Homes of Manuscripts* (London: SPCK, 1919). The history of institutional libraries is naturally another related area, both because such libraries are an element in the collecting scene and because private collections often become parts of institutions (see George Watson Cole, "Book-Collectors as Benefactors of Public Libraries," *Papers of the Bibliographical Society of America* 9 [1915]: 47–110; and Louis B. Wright, "The Book Collector as Public Benefactor," in *The Private Collector and the Support of Scholarship* [Los Angeles: Clark Library, 1969]). The many general works in this field range from Edward Edwards' *Memoirs of Libraries* (London: Trübner, 1859) and Ernest A. Savage's *The Story of Libraries and Book-Collecting* (London: Routledge, 1909) through the books of James Westfall Thompson on ancient and medieval libraries (1939–1940) down to Raymond Irwin's *The English Library* (London: Allen & Unwin, 1966) and Sidney L. Jackson's *Libraries and Librarianship in the West* (New York: McGraw-Hill, 1974). Still another source of information on the history of collecting is the material on the history of book clubs. The two greatest clubs in the English-speaking world have been accorded individual histories: Nicolas Barker's *The Publications of the Roxburghe Club, 1814–1962* (Cambridge, 1964) and John T. Winterich's *The Grolier Club, 1884–1967* (New York, 1967)—to which one should add *Grolier 75: A Biographical Retrospective* (1959), for its valuable biographical sketches of leading collectors. (Historical accounts of other clubs exist, such as Russell H. Anderson's of the Rowfant

Club of Cleveland [1955], Robert E. Spiller's of the Philobiblon Club of Philadelphia [1973], and a brief *Historical Sketch* of the Club of Odd Volumes of Boston [1950], as well as retrospective lists of publications, such as those in the yearbooks of the Caxton Club of Chicago or Duncan Olmstead and David Magee's for the Roxburghe Club of San Francisco [1968].) Broader surveys are Harold Williams' *Book Clubs & Printing Societies of Great Britain and Ireland* (London: First Edition Club, 1929) and, for American clubs, Lois Rather's *Books and Societies* (Oakland: Rather, 1971); the earlier, more extended treatments for the two countries are Abraham Hume's *The Learned Societies and Printing Clubs of the United Kingdom* (1847; 2nd ed. with supplement, London: Willis, 1853) and Adolf Growoll's *American Book Clubs* (New York: Dodd, Mead, 1897), supplemented by Florence M. Power, "American Private Book Clubs," *Bulletin of Bibliography* 20 (1950–1953): 216–220, 233–236. There is also historical information in Ruth S. Granniss' "What Bibliography Owes to Private Book Clubs," *Papers of the Bibliographical Society of America* 24 (1930): 14–33.

An understanding of book-collecting history cannot be divorced from a study of bookselling history. The collector and the seller are obviously interdependent, and their histories are perpetually intertwining. Furthermore, bookselling—whether of old or of new books—is a publishing activity, and its history cannot be separated from the history of publishing and book distribution in general (particularly for earlier times, when the roles of printer, publisher, and bookseller were less distinct). Besides, publishing history is naturally of concern to the collector—as Sadleir, Carter, and their circle effectively pointed out—because the physical features of a book can be most productively studied in the context of contemporary circumstances of publication. The standard one-volume survey of English publishing from its beginnings is Frank A. Mumby's *The Romance of Bookselling* (1910), more explicitly entitled *Publishing and Bookselling* in its later editions (5th ed., with Ian Norrie; London: Cape, 1974); it can be supplemented by Marjorie Plant's *The English Book Trade* (London: Allen & Unwin, 1939, 1974). There are also some excellent studies of particular periods, most notably Graham Pollard and Albert Ehrman's *The Distribution of Books by Catalogue from the Invention of Printing to A.D. 1800* (Cambridge, 1965), H. S. Bennett's three-volume *English Books & Readers* to 1640 (Cambridge Univ. Pr., 1952–1970), and W. W. Greg's *Some*

Aspects and Problems of London Publishing between 1550 and 1650 (Oxford: Clarendon, 1956), along with Richard D. Altick's *The English Common Reader* (Univ. of Chicago Pr., 1957) for the nineteenth century. The American book trade is covered by Hellmut Lehmann-Haupt, Lawrence C. Wroth, and Rollo G. Silver's *The Book in America*, 2nd rev. ed. (New York: Bowker, 1951) and by John Tebbel's *A History of Book Publishing in the United States* (New York: Bowker, 1972–); for reading tastes, there are Frank Luther Mott's *Golden Multitudes* (New York: Macmillan, 1947), James Hart's *The Popular Book* (New York: Oxford Univ. Pr., 1950), and Alice Payne Hackett and James H. Burke's *Eighty Years of Best Sellers, 1895–1975* (New York: Bowker, 1977).

A volume more strictly limited to bookselling is *Bookselling in America and the World*, edited by Charles B. Anderson (New York: Quadrangle, 1975), containing historical surveys by John Tebbel and Chandler Grannis (on American bookselling) and Sigfred Taubert (on bookselling throughout the world). And two books particularly appealing for their illustrations are Taubert's wide-ranging and handsomely produced two-volume *Bibliopola: Pictures and Text about the Book Trade* (Hamburg: Hausewedell, 1966) and Richard Brown and Stanley Brett's *The London Bookshop* (Pinner: Private Libraries Assn., 1971). Some earlier well-known English histories, full of interesting anecdotes if not entirely reliable, are Charles Knight's *Shadows of the Old Booksellers* (London: Bell & Daldy, 1865), Henry Curwen's *A History of Booksellers* (London: Chatto & Windus, 1873), William Roberts' *The Earlier History of English Bookselling* (London: Low, 1889) and *The Book-Hunter in London* (London: Stock, 1895), and Edward Marston's two-volume *Sketches* (London: Low, 1901, 1902). Valuable information on the history of selling by auction can be found in John Lawler's *Book Auctions in England in the Seventeenth Century* (London: Stock, 1898) and Clarence S. Brigham's "History of Book Auctions in America," in George L. McKay's *American Book Auction Catalogues, 1713–1934* (New York Public Library, 1937), pp. 1–37—along with the related books by William Roberts, *Rare Books and Their Prices* (London: Redway, 1895), and H. B. Wheatley, *Prices of Books* (London: Allen, 1898), the brief articles in the fiftieth volume of *American Book-Prices Current* (1944), A. N. L. Munby's lecture *The Libraries of English Men of Letters* (London: Library Assn., 1964), and the chapter titled "Bibliomania" in Wesley Towner's *The Elegant Auctioneers* (New York: Hill & Wang, 1970). Recent overviews of the current book trade are provided in two issues of *Library Trends*, one edited by Howard Peckham on "Rare Book Libraries and Collections" (April 1957) and one edited by Lehmann-Haupt on "Current Trends in Antiquarian Books" (April 1961), and in Part II of the 1965 *AB Bookman's Yearbook*. But the best way to gain a sense of current trends is to read Gordon N. Ray's two thorough and penetrating surveys, drawing on questionnaires sent to prominent figures, "The Changing World of Rare Books," *Papers of the Bibliographical Society of America* 59 (1965): 103–141, and "The World of Rare Books Re-examined," *Yale Univ. Library Gazette* 49 (1974–1975): 77–146.

The histories mentioned here, like all histories, contain many biographical sketches, and a major category of book-collecting literature consists of the biographies and reminiscences of collectors, dealers, and librarians. Wilmarth Lewis has made distinguished contributions to this literature in two ways: through his recollections of his own career, in *Collector's Progress* (New York: Knopf, 1951) and *One Man's Education* (Knopf, 1967), and through his scholarly account of another collector, in *Horace Walpole's Library* (Cambridge Univ. Pr., 1958). The work that is often regarded as the greatest scholarly account of a collector deals with the greatest of accumulators: A. N. L. Munby's five volumes on Sir Thomas Phillipps (*Phillipps Studies*, Cambridge Univ. Pr., 1951–1960), now adapted by Nicolas Barker into one volume, *Portrait of an Obsession* (London: Constable, 1967). Phillipps' collection was particularly renowned for its manuscripts, and another collection of manuscripts, those of Robert Harley, has also been investigated with distinction, by Cyril E. Wright in *Fontes Harleiani* (London: British Museum, 1971). An equally detailed and careful history of a remarkable collection of printed material, formed by two of the earls of Crawford and Balcarres, has recently been provided by Nicolas Barker, in *Bibliotheca Lindesiana* (London: Quaritch, 1977). And Anthony Hobson's impressive *Apollo and Pegasus: An Enquiry into the Formation and Dispersal of a Renaissance Library* (Amsterdam: van Heusden, 1975) undertakes the difficult task of identifying the owner of a collection known for its bindings (Giovanni Battista Grimaldi of Genoa is named). The collector whose activities have been examined the most thoroughly, however, is Thomas J. Wise, although the research, following from Carter and Pollard's *Enquiry*, has focused almost entirely on his forgeries rather than on the books that he acquired in the more usual way. Wise has become the subject of an extensive literature, of which the central items would include Wilfred Partington's *Forging Ahead* (New York: Putnam, 1939; revised and enlarged as *Thomas J. Wise in the Original Cloth* [London: Hale, 1946]), Fannie Ratchford's edition of the *Letters of Thomas J. Wise to John Henry Wrenn* (New York: Knopf, 1944), D. F. Foxon's *Thomas J. Wise and the Pre-Restoration Drama* (London: Bibliographical Society, 1959), and the *Thomas J. Wise Centenary Studies* by William B. Todd, Carter, and Pollard (Univ. of Texas Pr., 1959). Other substantial biographical studies are O. A. Bierstadt's *The Library of Robert Hoe* (New York: Duprat, 1895), Carl Sandburg's *Lincoln Collector* (New York: Harcourt, Brace, 1949) on Oliver R. Barrett, B. L. Reid's *The Man from New York* (New York: Oxford Univ. Pr., 1968) on John Quinn, David Buchanan's *The Treasure of Auchinleck* (New York: McGraw-Hill, 1974) on Ralph Isham's Boswell collection, and E. H. McCormick's *Alexander Turnbull* (Wellington: Turnbull Library, 1974). Briefer sketches of individual collectors appear frequently in the periodicals. The *Times Literary Supplement* ran a series on "Private Libraries" in the late 1930s and early 1940s, for instance, and the *Book Collector* at present maintains a series called "Portrait of a Bibliophile." Among the printed primary materials on which scholarly accounts of collectors draw are catalogues of the collectors' libraries (commented on below) and reminiscences by the collectors themselves. Some of the books that might be classed as introductions to, or historical surveys of, collecting (like Dibdin's, or Field's, or Newton's) could equally well be considered reminiscences; a few additional examples of reminiscences are W. C. Hazlitt's *The Confessions of a Collector* (London: Ward & Downey, 1897), A. H. Joline's *The Diversions of a Book-Lover* (New York: Harper, 1903), William Harris Arnold's *Ventures in Book Collecting* (New York: Scribner, 1923), Paul Lemperly's *Among My Books* (Cleveland: Rowfant Club, 1929) and *Books and I* (1938), Paul Jordan-Smith's *For the Love of Books* (New York: Oxford Univ. Pr., 1934), Frederick W. Skiff's *Adventures in Americana* (Portland, Oreg.: Metropolitan, 1935)—with its list of "Some Worthwhile First Editions"—and Edward A. Parsons' *The Wonder and the Glory* (New York: Thistle Pr., 1962). An important series of reminiscences by distinguished collectors, under the title "Contemporary Collectors," has appeared in the *Book Collector* from time to time since 1954.

One of the famous books about a nineteenth-century collector is Henry Stevens' *Recollections of Mr. James Lenox of New York* (London: Stevens, 1886), which is also a book dealer's reminiscence and calls attention to the great contribution that dealers have made to the biographical literature of collecting. Indeed, the memoirs of dealers, because they report on a variety of collectors and their activities, are in general more likely to present a broad view of the tastes and techniques of a period than are collectors' reminiscences. A. S. W. Rosenbach's *Books and Bidders* (Boston: Little, Brown, 1927) and *A Book Hunter's Holiday* (Boston: Houghton Mifflin, 1936), come readily to mind as summing up an era; and one can learn much about the Sadleir-Carter circle in P. H. Muir's *Minding My Own Business* (London: Chatto & Windus, 1956) and David A. Randall's *Dukedom Large Enough* (New York: Random House, 1969). E. Millicent Sowerby's reflections on her days with Wilfrid Michael Voynich, Sotheby's, and Rosenbach, *Rare People and Rare Books* (London: Constable, 1967), and David Magee's delightful *Infinite Riches* (New York: Eriksson, 1973) are among the more attractive recent additions to a list that goes back at least to the memoirs of James Lackington (1791, 1804) and William West (1830) and includes Walter T. Spencer's *Forty Years in My Bookshop* (London: Constable, 1923), Charles E. Goodspeed's *Yankee Bookseller* (Boston: Houghton Mifflin, 1937), Charles P. Everitt's *The Adventures of a Treasure Hunter* (Boston: Little, Brown, 1951), Maurice L. Ettinghausen's *Rare Books and Royal Collectors* (New York: Simon & Schuster, 1966), Harold C. Holmes' *Some Random Reminiscences* (Oakland, Calif.: Holmes, 1967), David Low's *'with all faults'* (Tehran: Amate Pr., 1973), Leona Rostenberg and Madeleine B. Stern's *Old & Rare* (New York: Schram, 1974), and John H. Jenkins' *Audubon and Other Capers* (Austin, Texas: Pemberton Pr., 1976). Two scholarly biographies of great bookmen of two generations are Wyman W. Parker's *Henry Stevens of Vermont: American Rare Book Dealer in London, 1845–1886* (Amsterdam: Israel, 1963) and the highly readable and detailed *Rosenbach* (Cleveland: World, 1960) by Edwin Wolf 2nd with John F. Fleming. Two more recent accounts take up two other well-known dealers: Donald E. Bower's *Fred Rosenstock: A Legend in Books and Art* (Flagstaff, Ariz.: Northland Pr., 1976) and D. B. Covington's *Ben Abramson and the Argus Book Shop: A Memoir* (West Cornwall, Conn.: Tarrydiddle Pr., 1977).

Margaret Maxwell's *Shaping a Library: William L. Clements as Collector* (Amsterdam: Israel, 1973) illustrates the close connection between biographies of collectors and histories of institutions. Such histories frequently offer revealing glimpses of the collecting world, as in Phyllis Dain's *The New York Public Library* (New York Public Library, 1972) and Edward Miller's *That Noble Cabinet: A History of the British Museum* (London: Deutsch, 1973); and the same holds true for rare-book librarians' memoirs, as in Clarence S. Brigham's *Fifty Years of Collecting Americana for the Library of the American Antiquarian Society* (Worcester, Mass., 1958) and Margaret B. Stillwell's *Librarians Are Human: Memories in and out of the Rare-Book World* (Boston, 1973). Some historical accounts of libraries occur in the *Encyclopedia of Library and Information Science* (New York: Dekker, 1968–   ); and further references on all aspects of the book trade (including studies of individual publishers) can be found in Robin Myers' *The British Book Trade* (London: Deutsch, 1973) and G. T. Tanselle's *Guide to the Study of United States Imprints* (Cambridge, Mass.: Belknap, Harvard Univ. Pr., 1971).

Periodicals

Book collecting and bibliography in the English-speaking world in the twentieth century have been well supplied with periodicals. As in most fields, journals are required reading for the person who wishes to keep abreast of the latest developments. It has been pointed out on more than one occasion that because contributions to bibliographical knowledge often consist of notes on particular copies of books, supplementing standard bibliographies or histories, periodicals form the natural medium of publication. Runs of journals contain both current news and a vast body of scholarship that only gradually becomes incorporated into book-length studies. What a book-collecting journal at its best can accomplish is illustrated by *The Book Collector*, the English quarterly that has been the leading publication in the field since its founding in 1952. Its high standards and urbane approach were set by John Hayward (whose editorial board included John Carter and P. H. Muir) and have been continued by Nicolas Barker, who became editor after Hayward's death in late 1965. Each number contains the editor's well-informed and skillfully written commentary on recent auctions, catalogues, exhibitions, meetings, deaths, and other events of bibliographical significance, and each one now also includes a learned and polished editorial essay on a topic of current (but not passing) interest. In addition, there are articles, responsibly prepared and wide-ranging in content, offering bibliographies of writers, accounts of particular collections or libraries, studies of bindings and presses, and the like; and at the end are sections of bibliographical notes and queries (an extremely useful medium for the exchange of information) and of book reviews (frequently thorough and detailed). The physical appearance of the journal, it may be added, matches the attractiveness of the contents.

Of the journals presently being published, the other basic ones for the collector are three sponsored by scholarly bibliographical societies. Although their focus is not directly on collecting, the concerns of the collector and the bibliographer overlap to such a degree that these periodicals are central to both. The one with the most distinguished history is *The Library* (1889–   ), a quarterly that since 1920 has been the organ of the Bibliographical Society in London (from 1893 through 1919 the Bibliographical Society published a series of *Transactions*; before 1920 *The Library*, though unaffiliated with the society, showed itself to be as interested in the new techniques of analytical bibliography as in matters of librarianship). Much of the history of twentieth-century bibliography is reflected in its pages, and many seminal pieces by the most influential scholars in the field have appeared there. Its American counterpart, the *Papers of the Bibliographical Society of America* [*PBSA*] (1904-   ), if it has not played so formative a role, has nevertheless published much excellent material. Both journals contain articles, notes, and reviews; *The Library* also includes a helpful record of the contents of other relevant periodicals, and *PBSA* prints many addenda to previously published bibliographies. The third of these journals, *Studies in Bibliography* (1948–   ), is sponsored by the Bibliographical Society of the University of Virginia and has been edited by Fredson Bowers since its inception. A distinguished annual volume of essays and notes (no reviews), it (like its editor) has become particularly known for pioneering articles on new developments in analytical bibliography and editorial theory. All these publications can touch on nearly any aspect of the history, analysis, and description of books and manuscripts as physical objects and on the editing of them; the subjects taken up and the conclusions reached are bound to have an effect, directly or indirectly, on the activities of every collector.

One should not turn from these journals without recalling several other illustrious ones, no longer published, that have achieved a permanent place in the literature of book collecting. One of the earliest is A. W. Pollard's *Bibliographica* (1895–1897), an extremely successful three-year experiment containing solid pieces by the leading bibliographers of the day. Then in the 1930s there were three important ventures, of which the American *Colophon* (1930–1940, followed by *New Colophon*, 1948–1950) was the longest-lived and the most elaborately produced. Each quarterly number is a separate hard-cover volume, and in the first series (1930–1935) each article represents the work of a different press; the contents are equally distinctive, both in the quality of the art work and in the readability and originality of the articles. Another impressively executed American publication was *The Dolphin* (1933–1941), issued at irregular intervals by the Limited Editions Club and containing an imaginative assemblage of material, with an emphasis on printing and book production (the third volume is the famous *A History of the Printed Book*, edited by Lawrence C. Wroth). In England at this time Desmond Flower and A. J. A. Symons' *Book Collector's Quarterly* (1930–1935), the organ of the First Edition Club, contained articles, reviews, and annotated checklists by a distinguished roster of bibliographically informed persons. (Many of the same people also turned up in the succeeding years in P. H. Muir's *Bibliographical Notes and Queries* [1935–1939], the forerunner of the department of that name in *The Book Collector*. Useful pieces also appeared from time to time in the *Bookman's Journal and Print Collector* [1919–1931], Charles F. Heartman's *American Collector* [1925–1928] and *American Book Collector* [1932–1935], the *Book Collector's Packet* [1932–1946], *Book Handbook* [1947–1952], and *Book Collecting & Library Monthly* [1968–1973]. Well-informed contributors appeared in earlier years in Paul Leicester Ford's *Bibliographer* [1902–1903] and in the *Bibliographical Register* [1905–1907]. Among the yet earlier journals of bibliophily still worth dipping into are *Philobiblion* [1861–1863], *Bibliomane* [later *Bibliophile* and *Book-Worm*; 1861–1870], *Bibliographer* [later *Book-Lore* and *Bookworm*; 1881–1894], and *Book Lovers' Almanac* [1893–1897].)

At the present time, there are many periodicals, other than the basic ones already mentioned, that collectors should be acquainted with. Some book-collecting clubs or associations publish journals, such as the Private Library Association's attractive quarterly *Private Library* (1957–   ), the Grolier Club's *Gazette* (from 1921, preceded by its *Transactions*, 1884–1919), the

Book Club of California's *Quarterly News Letter* (1933–), the Zamorano Club's *Hoja Volante* (1934–), and the *Actes* (1961–) and bulletin (1963–) of the Association internationale de bibliophilie. There are other bibliographical societies with journals of interest, too, although their contents are likely to be somewhat more restricted to materials associated in some way with a particular area or subject: examples are the publications of the bibliographical societies of Edinburgh (1890–), Oxford (1922–); Cambridge (1949–), Canada (1962–), and Australia and New Zealand (1970–), and the *Journal of the Society for the Bibliography of Natural History* (1936–). Similarly, the Gutenberg Gesellschaft's *Gutenberg Jahrbuch* (1926–) contains some articles of value in English, and the Library Association's Scottish Group publishes *The Bibliotheck* (1956–) on Scottish bibliography. Several new bibliographical journals have begun to appear, such as *Proof* (1971–) and *Analytical and Enumerative Bibliography* (1977–). There has always been a place also for less scholarly, more journalistic, magazines on book collecting, which can provide a convenient means of keeping up with current news and trends. Three representatives of this tradition at the moment may be named, the oldest being the *American Book Collector* (1950–); it has now been joined by the English *Antiquarian Book Monthly Review* (1974–) and the American *Book Collector's Market* (which began in 1975 as *Bibliognost*). All three are uneven in quality, but the last two in particular contain some incisive reviews, and *ABMR* has several informative and opinionated regular columns; all provide auction news and lists of dealers' catalogues. Several related magazines are devoted to special fields of collecting, such as newspapers, comic books, "dime novels," and children's series; often amateurish, they nevertheless record bibliographical data available nowhere else (two of the better ones are *Dime Novel Round-Up* and *Baum Bugle*).

Because book collectors' interests naturally impinge on those of other students of the book, there are periodicals in several related fields that the collector should not neglect. In the library field, for instance, the American *Journal of Library History* (1966–) and the English *Library History* (1967–) contain material on the history of collecting, and the *Library Quarterly* (1931–) regularly reviews books of bibliographical interest. Many libraries, particularly those with organized groups of "friends" or "associates," publish magazines dealing with rare books, special collections, or individual collectors, and these include some of the most appealing, attractive, and worthwhile of the journals for collectors—such as the *Yale University Library Gazette* (1926–   ), *Bodleian Library Record* (1938–   ), *Princeton University Library Chronicle* (1939–   ), *Harvard Library Bulletin* (1947–   ), and *British Library Journal* (1975–   ). In the field of typography and printing, there is the distinguished *Journal of the Printing Historical Society* (1965–   )—as well as several earlier publications of permanent value, notably Oliver Simon and Stanley Morison's great *Fleuron* (1923–1930), but also *Ars Typographica* (1918–1934), *Signature* (1935–1954), and *Printing and Graphic Arts* (1953–1965), among others. For the field of publishing there is now Michael Turner's *Publishing History* (1977–   ); and in the field of paper Hercules Chemical Company's *Paper Maker* (1932–   ) offers many historical articles. Trade publications in these fields, and other journals without a basically historical emphasis, may of course be relevant at times to the collector's interests—*Publishers Weekly* (1872–   ), *Inland Printer* (1883–   ), *British Printer* (1888–   ), *Penrose Annual* (1895–   ), *Printing Art* (1903–1941), and *Direct Advertising* (1912–   ), to name only a few.

Two further categories of periodicals—which for many collectors will be among the most useful of all—remain to be mentioned. First are the newsletters, which have proliferated in the 1970s. Their function is to convey current information about the world of books more efficiently than is possible in the quarterlies or monthlies. Two of the most helpful are Terry Belanger's lively and trenchant *Bibliography Newsletter* (1973–   ), with its lists of remaindered books, comments on new books, and reports of meetings and lectures; and Sandra Kirshenbaum's *Fine Print* (1975–   ), which concentrates on announcing and reviewing the work of private presses. Other readable newsletters are put out by organizations (such as the Private Libraries Association, the Printing Historical Society, and the American Printing History Association) and by libraries' "friends" groups. A related class consists of the newsletters (or more elaborately produced journals) concerned with single figures. For collectors of individual authors, these publications, often largely bibliographical in nature, are essential; determining whether one exists for a given writer can be accomplished easily by checking Margaret C. Patterson's "V.I.P. Publications: An International Bibliography of 300 Newsletters, Journals, and Miscellanea," *Bulletin of Bibliography* 30 (1973): 156–169.

A second kind of utilitarian journal is that devoted to listing books wanted and for sale. The most familiar one to American collectors—and indeed one which has no exact counterpart in England—is *AB Bookman's Weekly* (formerly called *Antiquarian Bookman* and still referred to as "*AB*"), which began in 1948 as an outgrowth of a book-exchange section in *Publishers' Weekly*. The bulk of each issue consists of dealers' advertisements for books wanted, with a smaller appended section of books for sale. But the opening pages, edited for years by Sol M. Malkin and now by Jacob L. Chernofsky, contain succinct reports of current news presented in a highly personal style (with occasional articles by others); *AB* is therefore subscribed to not only by dealers but also by many collectors and librarians, who find it a pleasant and convenient way to keep in touch with current happenings. In England, the long-established weekly listing of books wanted is *The Clique* (1890–   ), which, like the same firm's *The Book Market* (now incorporated into *The Clique*), can be subscribed to only by dealers. The present highly successful rival weekly, *Bookdealer* (1972–   ), contains lists of books wanted and for sale by dealers and can be subscribed to by anyone; its publisher also issues the monthly *Book Exchange* (1948–   ), which contains more editorial matter and permits listings by individuals. (Excellent coverage of current bibliographical news and books was provided in former years by the back page of the London *Times Literary Supplement*, but unfortunately such material appears now with less frequency in the *TLS*.)

The periodicals named here are only examples of the main categories. For a fuller listing, accompanied by information about the indexing of these journals, see G. T. Tanselle, "The Periodical Literature of English and American Bibliography," *Studies in Bibliography* 26 (1973): 167–191. The most comprehensive list of periodicals in this field, now somewhat out of date, is Carolyn F. Ulrich and Karl Küp's *Books and Printing: A Selected List of Periodicals, 1800–1942* (New York Public Library, 1943).

Bibliographies and Checklists

The most fundamental of all reference works to collectors and dealers are the bibliographies and lists that record the existence of particular books. They serve both as guides to what material there is to be collected and as tools for identifying what has already been located. Whether one is collecting a subject, an author, or an imprint, one will find it helpful to know what the field consists of and what relation any given book bears to others in that field and to other editions of the same title. Books do not always convey accurately such basic facts about their own histories as place and date of publication; and to find out whether or not a book is accurate in these respects, and to learn other important facts that help to classify it as a physical object, one must turn to outside sources and either consult reference books, primarily bibliographies, or undertake the research oneself, looking into publishers' records and other copies of the book in question. When a relevant bibliography exists, it can obviously be of great help, but it can also be obsolete or incompetent, and collectors may find that they soon know more about their own fields of interest than the bibliographers whose works they have been using. Collectors are then in a position to publish bibliographies themselves, or at least to supply bibliographical journals with some addenda and corrigenda. (See G. T. Tanselle, "A Proposal for Recording Additions to Bibliographies," *Papers of the Bibliographical Society of America* 62 [1968]: 227–236.) Bibliographical scholarship is constantly advancing through this cooperative process, for imaginative collectors are always expanding the boundaries of what is known. Collectors should be grateful for the many bibliographies that are available, but they should not choose a field for collecting merely because a bibliography of it exists, and they should not feel that a bibliography has said the last word on the subject. Approached in this critical spirit, bibliographies are at the heart of what book collecting as an intellectual pursuit is all about.

Records of books vary enormously in form and thoroughness, ranging from full-fledged descriptive bibliographies, which provide detailed physical descriptions of books, to checklists or handlists, which offer a considerably—often drastically—abbreviated style of entry. In the nineteenth century it was still possible for bibliographers to undertake comprehensive works attempting to list all "collectible" books, or all from a particular country. The mainstays of this tradition are Jacques Charles Brunet's *Manuel du libraire et de l'amateur de livres* (Paris, 1810; 5th ed. and supps., 8 vols., Paris, 1860–1880), Robert Watt's *Bibliotheca Britannica* (4 vols.; Edinburgh, 1824), William T. Lowndes' *The Bibliographer's Manual of English Literature* (11 vols.; London, 1834; revised by Henry G. Bohn, 1857–1864), J. G. T. Grässe's *Trésor de livres rares et précieux* (7 vols.; Dresden,

1859–1869), and W. Carew Hazlitt's *Hand-Book to the Popular, Poetical, and Dramatic Literature of Great Britain* (London, 1867) and his series of *Bibliographical Collections and Notes* (1876–1903). These works can still be useful at times, but they have naturally been superseded in most respects by hundreds of more specialized bibliographies and lists. It is now necessary, therefore, to consult bibliographies of bibliographies in order to ascertain what reference books there may be in a given field. The basic listing of reference books—formerly called "Mudge," then "Winchell," and now "Sheehy"—is the American Library Association's *Guide to Reference Books*, 9th ed., edited by Eugene P. Sheehy (Chicago: ALA, 1976); and the largest listing of separately published bibliographies in all fields is Theodore Besterman's *A World Bibliography of Bibliographies*, 4th ed. (Lausanne: Societas Bibliographica, 1965–1966), supplemented by the *Bibliographic Index* [1937–   ] (New York: Wilson, 1938–   ), which records bibliographies occurring in periodicals as well as those published separately.

Perhaps the present-day counterpart of the nineteenth-century "universal bibliographies" is the *National Union Catalog* (pre-1956 imprints—London: Mansell, 1968–   ; post-1955 imprints—Washington: Library of Congress, 1956–   ), which is the most comprehensive compilation of books of all kinds ever assembled (the pre-1956 section running to some 600 large volumes); it can answer many questions and is of immense usefulness; but its entries (arranged by author) are of course dependent on the holdings and the cataloguing practices of the participating American and Canadian libraries, and *NUC* cannot be expected to be as thorough or as bibliographically sophisticated as a scholarly bibliography of a smaller field. The number of such bibliographies is so large that it is obviously not feasible here to do more than provide a sketch of the various approaches that have been taken to the recording of books, with a few prominent examples of each. In general, bibliographies and lists fall into four classes, according to whether they are organized by place of printing, by subject, by author, or by printer or publisher. Because a book may be of interest from any or all of these points of view, it may reappear in several kinds of bibliographies, and one may sometimes need to use a little ingenuity to locate the most recent and complete description of a book. A collector of works on a particular subject, for instance, may often have to look beyond the standard bibliogra-

phy of that subject: One book in the field may have been written by a prominent author who has been supplied with a
bibliography more recently, and another may have been printed by a famous press that has been the subject of a more detailed bibliography.

ARRANGEMENT BY PLACE OF PRINTING

The geographical approach—the attempt to record everything printed within a certain country or area during a specified
time—is the most encompassing of the four and is in some
ways the most basic; certainly the large bibliographies of this
kind are among the most often cited, because they fit a book
into the context of all the other printed matter of its time and
place. One of the best, recording books printed in Europe before 1501, is the great *Gesamtkatalog der Wiegendrucke* (Leipzig:
Hiersemann, 1925–   ), which after a long interruption (1940–
1968) is now in progress again. (An earlier bibliography of incunabula, still frequently cited, is Ludwig Hain's *Repertorium
Bibliographicum* [Stuttgart, 1826–1838], supplemented by Walter
A. Copinger [London: Sotheran, 1895–1902]. Frederick R. Goff's
Incunabula in American Libraries [New York: Bibliographical Society of America, 1964, 1972] is a convenient listing of a large
number of titles, and Goff numbers are regularly mentioned in
catalogue entries for incunabula.) Another of the deservedly famous bibliographies of this class is A. W. Pollard and G. R.
Redgrave's *A Short-Title Catalogue of Books Printed in England,
Scotland, and Ireland, and of English Books Printed Abroad, 1475–
1640* (London: Bibliographical Society, 1926), generally known
as the "*STC*"; for years the work of revising this bibliography
(which is arranged alphabetically by author) was carried out by
W. A. Jackson and F. S. Ferguson, and it is now being admirably completed by Katharine F. Pantzer (one volume having appeared in 1976). For the next period there is Donald G. Wing's
Short-Title Catalogue . . . 1641–1700 (New York: Index Society,
1945–1951), a revision of which is also being published currently. At present there is no *STC* for English eighteenth-century books, but a project for producing one is under discussion.
American books from 1639 through 1800 are listed in
Charles Evans' chronological *American Bibliography*, completed
by Clifford K. Shipton (Chicago: Privately printed, 1903–1934;
Worcester, Mass.: American Antiquarian Society, 1955), sup-

plemented by Roger P. Bristol (Charlottesville: Univ. Pr. of Virginia, 1970) and by Shipton and James E. Mooney's alphabetical *National Index of American Imprints through 1800* (Worcester, Mass., and Barre, Mass.: American Antiquarian Society and Barre Publishers, 1969). A start has been made on nineteenth-century American books with Ralph R. Shaw and Richard H. Shoemaker, *American Bibliography* for 1801–1819 (New York: Scarecrow, 1958–1966), and Shoemaker et al., *A Checklist of American Imprints for 1820* [–1829] (1964–1973), now being continued into the 1830s by Gayle Cooper and others (1972–   ). Coverage farther into the nineteenth century (and in some cases more detailed coverage for earlier years) can be found in some of the numerous works listing American imprints for more restricted areas (states or cities); they are recorded in G. T. Tanselle's *Guide to the Study of United States Imprints*. English provincial imprints have been less thoroughly chronicled than American, but the bibliographies that exist are named in T. H. Howard-Hill's *Bibliography of British Literary Bibliographies* (Oxford: Clarendon, 1969), supplemented by the last half of his *Shakespearian Bibliography and Textual Criticism: A Bibliography* (1971). The books of more recent years (after 1800 in England and after 1876 in the United States) have been listed in compilations for the use of the book trade, especially *The English Catalogue of Books* [1801–   ], *The American Catalogue* [1876–1910], and the *Cumulative Book Index* [1898–   ], along with that remarkable assemblage of American publishers' catalogues, *The Publishers' Trade List Annual* [1873–   ]. Although these works are not the products of scholarly research and are dependent on information supplied by publishers, they can be of great value, if they are approached with a proper skepticism. The *Catalogue of Copyright Entries* [1906–   ] and related lists form another important source of current data on American books. Additional national bibliographies (for these and other countries) can be located through Sheehy.

ARRANGEMENT BY SUBJECT

A second class of bibliographies and checklists—those arranged by subject—is even more numerous. And because one of the commonest ways to approach the assembling of books is by subject, these reference works are frequently consulted by collectors and cited in dealers' catalogues. One can locate the bibliographies for particular fields in Besterman and Sheehy and, for English and American books, in Howard-Hill and Tanselle. In addition, both *The New Cambridge Bibliography of English Literature* [*NCBEL*] (Cambridge Univ. Pr., 1969–1974) and the *Bibliography* volume of *The Literary History of the United States* [*LHUS*] (New York: Macmillan, 1948)—with Richard M. Ludwig's Supplement (1959, 1972)—take "literature" in a broad sense and include references to subject bibliographies other than those dealing strictly with *belles lettres*. A number of more condensed guides, such as Richard D. Altick and Andrew Wright's *Selective Bibliography for the Study of English and American Literature*, 5th ed. (New York: Macmillan, 1975), and Margaret C. Patterson's *Literary Research Guide* (Detroit: Gale, 1975), are available. Of all the hundreds of subject bibliographies that are named in these various sources, only a few can be mentioned here as examples. In the field of literature—defined, more narrowly, as imaginative writing—the "subjects" are likely to be literary genres. The greatest of the bibliographies conceived along these lines are W. W. Greg's *A Bibliography of the English Printed Drama to the Restoration* (London: Bibliographical Society, 1939–1959) and D. F. Foxon's *English Verse, 1701–1750: A Catalogue* (Cambridge Univ. Pr., 1975), both of which pay considerable attention to the physical structure of the books recorded; the most notable American bibliography of a literary genre, offering less detailed entries, is Lyle Wright's *American Fiction* [1774–1900] (San Marino, Calif.: Huntington Library, 1939–1969).

A related field—encompassing both literature and history—is Americana (or Canadiana, Australiana, or any other body of material relating to a country or area). The most comprehensive (and often detailed) bibliography of Americana is Joseph Sabin et al., *Bibliotheca Americana* (29 vols.; New York: Sabin et al., 1868–1936); and a concise one-volume selection of important items of Americana is Wright Howes, *U.S.-iana* (New York: Bowker, 1954, 1962). For some other areas, see José Toribio Medina, *Biblioteca hispano-americana (1493–1810)* (Santiago: Medina, 1898–1907); Rubens Borba de Moraes, *Bibliographia Brasiliana* (Amsterdam, Rio de Janeiro: Colibris Editora, 1958); Valerian Lada-Mocarski, *Bibliography of Books on Alaska Published before 1868* (New Haven, Conn.: Yale Univ. Pr., 1969); C. R. H.

Taylor, *A Pacific Bibliography*, 2nd ed. (Oxford: Clarendon, 1965); and Henri Cordier, *Bibliotheca Sinica*, 2nd ed. (Paris: Guilmoto et al., 1904–1908, 1922–1924).

Books illustrating the history of the sciences and technology have been intensely collected in recent decades, and a sampling of relevant bibliographies that one often sees cited in catalogues follows:

> Louis Agassiz. *Bibliographia Zoologiae et Geologiae.* London: Ray Society, 1848–1854.
>
> Georg A. Pritzel. *Thesaurus Literaturae Botanicae.* Leipzig: Brockhaus, 1872–1877. Supplement by Benjamin D. Jackson, 1881.
>
> Henry C. Bolton. *A Select Bibliography of Chemistry, 1492–[1902].* Washington: Smithsonian, 1893–1904.
>
> Paul Brockett. *Bibliography of Aeronautics.* Washington: Smithsonian, 1910. Supplement, 1921–1936.
>
> Albert L. Caillet. *Manuel bibliographique des sciences psychiques ou occultes.* Paris: Dorbon, 1912–1913.
>
> Ludwig Choulant. *History and Bibliography of Anatomic Illustration.* Translated and edited by Mortimer Frank. Univ. of Chicago Pr., 1920. Revised, 1945.
>
> Gordon Dunthorne. *Flower and Fruit Prints of the Eighteenth and Early Nineteenth Centuries.* Washington, 1938.
>
> Fielding H. Garrison and Leslie T. Morton. *A Medical Bibliography.* London: Grafton, 1943. 3rd ed., 1970.
>
> Claus Nissen. *Die botanische Buchillustration.* Stuttgart: Hiersemann, 1951–1952. Supplement, 1966.
>
> Sacheverell Sitwell, Handasyde Buchanan, and James Fisher. *Fine Bird Books, 1700–1900.* London: Collins, 1953.
>
> Sacheverell Sitwell and Wilfrid Blunt. *Great Flower Books, 1700–1900.* London: Collins, 1956.
>
> Claus Nissen. *Die zoologische Buchillustration.* Stuttgart: Hiersemann, 1966–   .
>
> Eugene S. Ferguson. *Bibliography of the History of Technology.* Cambridge, Mass.: MIT Pr., 1968.

Some excellent bibliographies of this kind devoted to single countries exist, like Ronald V. Tooley's *English Books with Coloured Plates, 1790 to 1860*, 2nd ed. (London: Batsford, 1954), and Blanche Henrey's *British Botanical and Horticultural Literature before 1800* (London: Oxford Univ. Pr., 1975). Biographical works with extensive lists of books are also frequently cited: J. C. Poggendorff's *Biographisch-literarisches Handwörterbuch zur Geschichte der exakten Wissenschaften* (Leipzig: Barth et al., 1863–1904, 1925–

1940, 1955–), for example, or the *Dictionary of Scientific Biography*, edited by Charles C. Gillispie (New York: Scribner's, 1970–1976). A few other examples of subject bibliographies, suggesting the range of subjects treated, are Benjamin Rand's *Bibliography of Philosophy, Psychology and Cognate Subjects* (New York: Macmillan, 1905), René Colas' *Bibliographie générale du costume et de la mode* (Paris: Colas, 1933), R. Toole Stott's *Circus and Allied Arts* (Derby: Harpur, 1958–1971), and—of special interest to book collectors—E. C. Bigmore and C. W. H. Wyman's *A Bibliography of Printing* (London: Quaritch, 1880–1886). (Many other well-known lists of books on particular subjects are in fact catalogues of collections and are commented on later.)

ARRANGEMENT BY AUTHOR

A third approach to the recording of books is to focus on the authors. (For assistance in determining the authorship of unsigned works, Samuel Halkett and John Laing's *Dictionary of Anonymous and Pseudonymous English Literature*, 2nd ed. [Edinburgh: Oliver & Boyd, 1926–1962], is indispensable, as is the *National Union Catalog*.) Bibliographies of this kind are particularly associated with the field of literature, where author collecting is probably the dominant form of collecting; but collectors in other fields sometimes specialize in individual writers, and author bibliographies do exist, if in lesser numbers, for writers in those fields. Bibliographies and checklists of English writers are listed in Howard-Hill and those of American writers in Tanselle; both works cite reviews of the items listed, and Tanselle has also provided critical surveys of two areas in "The Descriptive Bibliography of American Authors," *Studies in Bibliography* 21 (1968): 1–24, and "The Descriptive Bibliography of Eighteenth-Century Books," in *Eighteenth-Century English Books* (Chicago: Assn. of College and Research Libraries, 1976), pp. 22–33. Bibliographies are constantly being supplemented by notes of addenda in various journals (and even by footnotes in articles not otherwise bibliographical); one can keep up with many such addenda by reading *The Book Collector*, *PBSA*, and *The Library*, or more systematically by checking *NCBEL*, *LHUS*, and the annual lists of literary scholarship published by the Modern Humanities Research Association (*Annual Bibliography of English Language and Literature* [1920–], covering all literature in English) and the Modern Language Association of America

(*MLA International Bibliography of Books and Articles on the Modern Languages and Literatures* [1922–   ]). Many newsletters and journals devoted to single authors are now published, and one of their regular departments is often a section of addenda to the standard bibliographies of the authors in question; these newsletters can be located through Margaret C. Patterson's "V.I.P. Publications," mentioned earlier. One should also remember that biographies of writers frequently contain thorough accounts of the publication of their books—as do editions of their works. The recent editions of Stephen Crane, Hawthorne, and Melville, for instance, published under the auspices of the Center for Editions of American Authors, offer more detailed bibliographical information about their books than any published bibliographies do.

The production of author bibliographies that go beyond mere lists of titles began only in the late nineteenth century, in connection with the rise of interest in collecting first editions of recent or contemporary writers. Harry Buxton Forman's *The Shelley Library* (1886) was the influential pioneer, followed by such works as Thomas B. Smart's on Arnold (1892) and the long series by Thomas J. Wise covering Ruskin (1893), Browning (1897), Tennyson (1908), Coleridge (1913), Wordsworth (1916), the Brontës (1917), E. B. Browning (1918), Landor (1919), Swinburne (1919–1920), and Byron (1932–1933), among others. Wise's bibliographies are not trustworthy, because he was sometimes more interested in promoting the merits of his own copies (on which his bibliographies were largely based) than in discovering the truth; but they filled a real need in their day and firmly established the genre of the detailed single-author bibliography that informs collectors and dealers of the points for identifying particular impressions or issues. Such bibliographies, however, can also serve other functions, as certain bibliographers of the 1920s pointed out. Iolo A. Williams was ahead of his time when in 1924 (in his *Seven XVIIIth Century Bibliographies* [London: Dulau]) he recognized the importance of recording more details than are strictly necessary for purposes of identification, because they form part of the historical picture and may later be put to unexpected uses. Four years later Michael Sadleir, in his bibliography of Trollope, effectively stated the case for a bibliography as a partial history of the publishing trade; the subtitle of his bibliography is indicative of his point of view: "an analysis of the history and structure of the works of

Anthony Trollope and a general survey of the effect of original publishing conditions on a book's subsequent rarity." What is suggested by the approach of both these men is that bibliography is history and that literary scholars and collectors are mutually served by good bibliographies. The notion that these audiences must be separately addressed has been a persistent one, largely because many people have been slow to see that the study of the physical forms of books and the study of the texts they contain are inextricable.

That collectors and scholars are not distinct groups and that close attention to printing and publishing history is essential to both are points of view that have characterized the best of the author bibliographies over the years—from Henrietta C. Bartlett and A. W. Pollard's of Shakespeare (1916, 1939), through Reginald H. Griffith's Pope (1922–1927), Francis R. Johnson's Spenser (1933), William M. Sale's Richardson (1936), Hugh Macdonald's Dryden (1939), Jane Norton's Gibbon (1940), Allen Hazen's Walpole (1948), R. W. Gibson's Bacon (1950) and More (1961), Donald Gallup's T. S. Eliot (1952, 1969), L. N. Broughton, C. S. Northup, and Robert Pearsall's Browning (1953), Richard L. Purdy's Hardy (1954), Norma Russell's Cowper (1963), B. C. Bloomfield and Edward Mendelson's Auden (1964, 1972), Warner Barnes' E. B. Browning (1967), Audre Hanneman's Hemingway (1967, 1975), Edwin T. Bowden's Thurber (1968), Emily M. Wallace's William Carlos Williams (1968), Donald D. Eddy's John Brown (1973), Robert A. Wilson's Gertrude Stein (1974), and Michael Collie's Meredith (1974) and Gissing (1975). The most prolific author of distinguished bibliographies is Geoffrey Keynes, whose impressive series includes scientific as well as literary figures; he has treated Donne (1914, 1932, 1958, 1973), Blake (1921), Browne (1924, 1968), William Harvey (1928, 1953), Jane Austen (1929), Hazlitt (1931), Robert Boyle (1932), Evelyn (1937), John Ray (1951), Rupert Brooke (1954, 1959), Robert Hooke (1960), Timothie Bright (1962), Siegfried Sassoon (1962), William Petty (1971), and George Berkeley (1976). Three other notable series may be mentioned: the Indiana Historical Society's bibliographies of James Whitcomb Riley (1944), George Ade (1947), Booth Tarkington (1949), and seven authors of Crawfordsville (1952), admirably prepared by Anthony J. and Dorothy R. Russo and Thelma L. Sullivan; the Soho Bibliographies (published until recently by Rupert Hart-Davis), a series that has been influential in establishing a pattern for bibliographies of modern authors and that includes bibliographies of Yeats (by Allan Wade, 1951, 1958, 1968), Housman (John Carter and John Sparrow, 1952), Joyce (John J. Slocum and Herbert Cahoon, 1953), Norman Douglas (Cecil Woolf, 1954), Rolfe (Woolf, 1957), James (Leon Edel and Dan H. Laurence, 1957, 1961), Virginia Woolf (B. J. Kirkpatrick, 1957, 1967), the Sitwells (Richard Fifoot, 1963, 1971), D. H. Lawrence (Warren Roberts, 1963), Firbank (Miriam K. Benkovitz, 1963), Pound (Donald Gallup, 1963), Burke (William B. Todd, 1964), and Forster (B. J. Kirkpatrick, 1965, 1968); and the Pittsburgh Series in Bibliography, with bibliographies of Hart Crane (Joseph Schwartz and Robert C. Schweik, 1972), F. Scott Fitzgerald (Matthew J. Bruccoli, 1972), Wallace Stevens (J. M. Edelstein, 1973), John Berryman (Ernest C. Stefanik, Jr., 1974), Eugene O'Neill (Jennifer M. Atkinson, 1974), and Ring Lardner (Bruccoli and Richard Layman, 1976). Occasionally a single work has a complicated enough publishing history to be treated in a separate study—such as H. C. Hutchins' (1925) of *Robinson Crusoe*, Peter Oliver's (1936) of *The Compleat Angler*, Francis Falconer Madan's (1950) of the *Eikon basilike*, or Waldemar H. Fries' (1973) of *Birds of America*.

Many other worthy bibliographies could be named, but anyone who reads widely in this list of examples will have a sense of the developing traditions of descriptive bibliography (they have in fact developed chiefly in connection with author bibliographies) and of its best current practice. The best available is not always as good as one might wish, and a familiarity with Bowers' *Principles of Bibliographical Description* will help one to see ways in which many of the bibliographies mentioned here could be improved. (Some neglect publication history, for example, or fail to identify the copies examined, and many ignore later editions and impressions.) Nevertheless, they are impressive pieces of scholarship, and taken collectively they do begin, as Sadleir anticipated, to form a history of publishing practices. Brief checklists, on the other hand, cannot contribute nearly so much to the collector's or the scholar's knowledge; but it is almost always better to have a checklist with minimal information than nothing at all, and they are therefore not to be despised. For every full-dress bibliography there are dozens of checklists, and many authors have been treated in no other way. (Even the simple record of titles and dates often found in historical or literary reference books—S. A.

Allibone's *A Critical Dictionary of English Literature and British and American Authors* [Philadelphia: Lippincott, 1858–1871, 1891], *NCBEL*, *LHUS*, the *Dictionary of National Biography*, Robin Myers' *A Dictionary of Literature in the English Language* [Oxford: Pergamon, 1970], regional listings like R. E. Banta and D. E. Thompson's *Indiana Authors and Their Books* [Crawfordsville, Ind.: Wabash College, 1949, 1974], and so on—can be helpful as a starting point.)

A group of checklists is sometimes brought together in book form, with the intention of providing a convenient handbook for collectors. Several famous books of this kind have been widely used, and some of them can still be helpful for authors not otherwise covered; because the selection of authors in them is usually a reflection of current collecting fashions and literary reputations, they do often include authors who have since been given only slight attention, if any at all. Probably the best established work of this type is Merle Johnson's *American First Editions* (New York: Bowker, 1929, 1932, 1936, 1942), the last two editions of which were revised by Jacob Blanck (the authors included vary from edition to edition); like most such books it indicates "points" for identifying first impressions when they are necessary and elsewhere gives simply title, city, and year. A recent book providing this kind of treatment (but also including publishers' names) for post-1945 writers is Gary M. Lepper's *A Bibliographical Introduction to Seventy-Five Modern American Authors* (Berkeley: Serendipity Books, 1976); despite a considerable number of errors and inconsistencies, it is a start in doing for these authors what Johnson once did for an earlier group—offering preliminary guidance at a time when more detailed bibliographical work is not yet available.

The tradition began in the 1890s with such books as H. S. Stone's *First Editions of American Authors* (Cambridge: Stone & Kimball, 1893), J. H. Slater's *Early Editions . . . of Some Popular Modern Authors* (London: Kegan Paul, 1894), and P. K. Foley's still valuable *American Authors, 1795–1895* (Boston, 1897); but the chief outpouring started with the surge of collecting in the 1920s and included the three series of *Bibliographies of Modern Authors* (London: Bookman's Journal et al., 1921–1931), Gilbert Fabes' three-volume *Modern First Editions: Points and Values* (London: Foyle, 1929–1932), B. D. Cutler and Villa Stiles' *Modern British Authors: Their First Editions* (London: Allen & Unwin, 1930), Jacob Schwartz's *1100 Obscure Points* (London: Ulysses

Bookshop, 1931), which gives title-page transcriptions, Andrew Block's *The Book Collector's Vade Mecum* (London: Archer et al., 1932, 1938), on nineteenth-century English authors, and the two series of *Ten Contemporaries* by "John Gawsworth" (London: Benn et al., 1932–1933). Some of the books concentrate on selected titles by the authors in question: Merle Johnson's *High Spots of American Literature* (New York: Bennett, 1929), B. M. Fullerton's *Selective Bibliography of American Literature, 1775–1900* (New York: Payson, 1932), Leon Miller's *American First Editions: Their Points and Prices* (Kansas City: Westport Pr., 1933), William Targ's *Rare American Books* (Chicago: Black Archer Pr., 1935), and Whitman Bennett's chronologically arranged *A Practical Guide to American Book Collecting (1663–1940)* (New York: Bennett, 1941). Only two prominent works of this class include pre-nineteenth-century writers: Seymour De Ricci's *The Book Collector's Guide* (Philadelphia: Rosenbach, 1921) and Charles J. Sawyer and F. J. Harvey Darton's *English Books 1475–1900: A Signpost for Collectors* (Westminster: Sawyer, 1927); the second is presented in essay form, and both report prices (other price guides, discussed later, also serve as selective author checklists). De Ricci's description of his scope is characteristic of the point of view represented by these books in general: "two or three thousand British and American books which fashion has decided are the most desirable for the up-to-date collector."

A few multiple-author studies have been more serious than this in their aims and have incorporated solid bibliographical work, notably Michael Sadleir's *Excursions in Victorian Bibliography* (London: Chaundy & Cox, 1922), and several volumes of his "Bibliographia" series, such as P. H. Muir's two-volume *Points* (1931–1934) and I. R. Brussel's two-volume *Anglo-American First Editions* (1935–1936). But the culmination of the tradition of the multiple-author bibliography is Jacob Blanck's monumental *Bibliography of American Literature [BAL]* (New Haven, Conn.: Yale Univ. Pr., 1955–   ). It is like no other work, for it takes up nearly 300 writers (who died before 1930) and yet treats each one in considerable detail, recording signature collations, pagination, contents, points (of binding, type, or paper) identifying issues or states, publication data (drawn from copyright records and contemporary advertisements), and the specific copies examined; Blanck recognizes the importance of reporting later editions, not just firsts, and anthology appearances. If his work is less detailed than a full-scale single-author bibliography and sometimes inconsistent in its methods, it is nevertheless far more detailed than any undertaking of comparable scope and marks a significant advance over previous treatments of nearly all the authors included. Although it naturally does not obviate the need for separate bibliographies of the major figures, it may well do so for a host of lesser writers. (Collectors of French, Italian, or Spanish authors will wish to know the multiple-author bibliographies by A. Tchemerzine, Léopold Carteret, Marino Parenti, Antonio Palau y Dulcet, and F. Vindel.)

ARRANGEMENT BY PRINTER OR PUBLISHER

A fourth category consists of the bibliographies or checklists of individual printers or publishers. (In some respects this category is a subdivision of the geographical approach; but printers and publishers can of course move around, and the bibliography of a printer or publisher is not necessarily subsumed in the bibliography of a particular locality.) Although a number of excellent imprint bibliographies have appeared, their number is small compared to that of author bibliographies. Books of a few famous presses, and private press books in general, have long been collected, but for the most part the collecting and recording of the output of printers and, especially, commercial publishers have been neglected fields, despite the fact that a knowledge of printers' and publishers' practices is central to nearly any bibliographical or bibliophilic pursuit. A number of histories of, and reminiscences by, printers and publishers exist, however, and information about particular books or policies can sometimes be found in them. Material on American printers (including private presses) and publishers is listed in Tanselle; some of the work on English firms can be found in Howard-Hill and also in the selective list in Robin Myers' *The British Book Trade*. For private press books themselves, there are several composite checklists recording the items produced by numerous presses: Will Ransom's *Private Presses and Their Books* (New York: Bowker, 1929) and *Selective Check Lists of Press Books* (New York: Duschnes, 1945–1950) can be supplemented by G. S. Tompkinson's *A Select Bibliography of the Principal Modern Presses, Public and Private, in Great Britain and Ireland* (London: First Edition Club, 1928), Irvin Haas' *Bibliography of Modern American Presses* (Chicago: Black Cat Pr., 1935), and William Ridler's *British Modern Press Books* (London: Covent

248 The Literature of Book Collecting

Garden Pr., 1971), as well as the Private Libraries Association's admirable annual listing, *Private Press Books* (beginning coverage in 1959).

Among the most elaborate bibliographies of individual presses, now eagerly sought collector's items in their own right, are C. H. St. John Hornby's bibliography of the Ashendene Press (1935) and David Magee's two bibliographies of the Grabhorn Press (1940, 1957). Several of the most outstanding bibliographies of presses deal with the eighteenth century: Allen T. Hazen and J. P. Kirby's of Walpole's Strawberry Hill Press (1942, 1973), Philip Gaskell's of John Baskerville (1959) and the Foulis Press (Soho, 1964), D. F. McKenzie's of the Cambridge University Press between 1698 and 1712 (1966), and C. William Miller's of Benjamin Franklin (1974). Other noteworthy bibliographies include Falconer Madan's of the Daniel Press (1921), Julian Pearce Smith's of the Merrymount Press (1934), Melbert B. Cary's of the Village Press (1938), Dorothy Blakey's of the Minerva Press (1939), Herbert Cahoon's of the Overbrook Press (1963), Benton L. Hatch's of Thomas Bird Mosher (1966), and the four volumes on the Golden Cockerel Press (1936–1976). Few commercial publishers have been similarly treated, but two well-known instances are Geoffrey Keynes' work on William Pickering (1924, 1969) and Sidney Kramer's on Stone & Kimball (1940). These books, and those named for the other classes of bibliography as well, are merely examples—but they are prominent or meritorious examples that are often cited (in abbreviated fashion) in dealers' (and other) catalogues. Some knowledge of them not only enables collectors to read those catalogues more intelligently; it also acquaints them with the range of approaches and practices that have characterized responsible bibliography.

Catalogues

Catalogues differ from bibliographies in that they are based on particular assemblages of books, such as those in a dealer's stock or in a collector's library. But a record of the contents of an outstanding collection may often be the most comprehensive or useful listing available of the books in a particular field, and many catalogues are therefore important reference works. Naturally catalogues can range from sparse lists, with practically no bibliographical detail, to elaborate records, with full bibliographical description and historical annotation, and they can take the form of mimeographed leaves or of handsomely printed and illustrated volumes. Whatever the quality of a catalogue, it at least represents books that were in existence at the time of its compilation; catalogues are thus an invaluable source of information about individual copies of books, calling attention to presentation inscriptions or marginalia and reporting editions, impressions, issues, or states not mentioned in standard bibliographies. (The presence of such information was attested to by the "Glossary of 'Points' Gleaned from the Auctioneers' Sale Catalogues," which appeared in *Book-Auction Records* during the 1940s.) Even the catalogue of a miscellaneous group of books may contain entries for several important or unusual copies, and scarcely any catalogue can be regarded as entirely worthless. Catalogues—especially dealers' and auction catalogues, of the past as well as of the present—constitute the favorite reading matter of many collectors, and a principal source of their continuing education; but they are also valuable as reference works and should occupy a substantial place in any collector's reference library. The great mass of excellent bibliographical work that has appeared in thousands of catalogues over the years—and continues to appear daily—is difficult to get at because there is no comprehensive index to it; however, the records of auction prices (taken up below) do serve as an index to auction catalogues, and the entries in many catalogues contain references to entries for the same books in other well-known catalogues. The best introduction to the scholarly value of catalogues is Archer Taylor's *Book Catalogues: Their Varieties and Uses* (Chicago: Newberry Library, 1957), which cites many early catalogues as illustrations. Generally speaking, catalogues fall into four classes—auction, dealer, exhibition, and library (private and institutional)—and only a few examples of each can be mentioned here, as a way of suggesting the riches of this field as a whole. (Further examples can be found in Howard-Hill and in Tanselle, cited earlier.)

Auction Catalogues

Auction catalogues serve as permanent printed records of collections now usually dispersed, collections that may be of interest either because of the persons who formed them or because of the quality of their contents. A generous selection of eighteenth- and nineteenth-century catalogues of the former kind has recently been reprinted in the 12-volume series of *Sale Catalogues of Libraries of Eminent Persons* (London: Mansell, 1971–1975), under the general editorship of A. N. L. Munby (much of whose own celebrated collection of early catalogues has now passed to the Cambridge University Library). The latter category can be represented by the seven-volume catalogue of Thomas W. Streeter's collection of Americana (1966–1969); with its detailed annotations, citations of references, and numerous illustrations, it is one of the greatest auction catalogues ever produced and is understandably now a standard reference in its field. The previous great sale catalogue of Americana was that of George Brinley's collection (1879–1893); but most of the major sales of nineteenth-century collectors concentrated on English literature or early printing—such as the London sales of Richard Heber (1834–1837), the Sunderland library (1881–1883), the Earl of Ashburnham (1897–1899), W. H. Miller's Britwell Court Library (1900–1927), and Henry Huth (1911–1922), and the New York sale of Robert Hoe (1911–1912). Early important sales of American literature are those of J. Chester Chamberlain (1909) and Stephen H. Wakeman (1924), and other spectacular New York auctions of the 1920s are those of John Quinn's collection of modern literature (1923–1924)—the catalogue of which contains biographies of the authors prepared by Charles Vale—and Jerome Kern's collection of English literature (1929), which marked the peak of the upward market of the 1920s. Famous auction catalogues of the next decades include those of the collections of Marsden J. Perry (1936), Cortlandt F. Bishop (1938), A. Edward Newton (1941), Frank J. Hogan (1945–1946), Viscount Esher (1946), and Lucius Wilmerding (1950–1951). Great sales, accompanied by outstanding catalogues, continue to occur, as the Streeter sale suggests, and the present generation has had its share: In recent years Sotheby's has been issuing handsome catalogues for the J. R. Abbey and the seemingly endless Sir Thomas Phillipps sales; Sotheby's extensively illustrated catalogues of the Harrison D. Horblit collection of scientific books (A–G, 1974) and Arpad Plesch's Stiftung für Botanik library (1975–1976) are destined to become often-cited reference works; and the New York sale (1974) of William E. Stockhausen's collection of English and American literature takes its place as one of the landmark auctions. For comprehensive lists of auction catalogues, one can consult the annual volumes of auction records; and for earlier catalogues there are George L.

McKay's *American Book Auction Catalogues, 1713–1934* (New York Public Library, 1937) and the *List of Catalogues of English Book Sales, 1676–1900, Now in the British Museum* (1915), superseded in part by A. N. L. Munby and Lenore Coral's *British Book Sale Catalogues, 1676–1800: A Union List* (London: Mansell, 1977).

DEALERS' CATALOGUES

Dealers' catalogues are similarly useful as records of distinguished collections: Examples are the Holmes Book Company's handsome catalogue of Thomas Wayne Norris' Californiana (Oakland, 1948) and Peter Decker's catalogue of George W. Soliday's Americana (New York, 1940–1945). More often, of course, the dealer assembles the books to be listed, and the resulting catalogues, when well conceived and carefully prepared, can be equally important for reference. Maggs Brothers of London are known for their long series of impressive catalogues in all fields (recorded in No. 918, *A Catalogue of Maggs Catalogues, 1918–1968* [1969]); a recent outstanding example is No. 966, *Bookbinding in Great Britain: Sixteenth to Twentieth Century* (1975). The permanent reference value of certain dealers' catalogues is underscored by the decision to reprint them: Long runs of Edward Eberstadt's catalogues (1935–1956) and A. S. W. Rosenbach's (1904–1951) have been reprinted, with introductions and indexes (the former by Argosy-Antiquarian in 1966, the latter by McGraw-Hill in 1967). Sometimes catalogues are important because of their imaginative approach, which may give them a place in book-collecting history. For example, Scribner's famous series of catalogues in the 1930s, when John Carter and David Randall were responsible for the rare book department, included a pioneering catalogue of detective fiction (1934) and equally revolutionary catalogues on *Science and Thought in the 19th Century* (1938) and *Science, Medicine, Economics, Etc., in First Editions* (1940). During the same years the firm of Elkin Mathews Ltd. was issuing catalogues that were interesting not only for the books offered in them but for the introductions they contained—in one (No. 48, September 1932) John Carter wrote on "Publishing History and the Collector (with Special Reference to Binding Variants)," in another (No. 45, May 1932) Greville Worthington made additions to his bibliography of the Waverley novels, and in others there were comments by Edmund Blunden (No. 32) and Holbrook Jackson (No.

42). A few further examples of catalogues showing originality would include the first one devoted to American first editions, that of Leon & Brother in 1885; Graham Pollard's catalogue of typefounders' specimens for Birrell & Garnett (London, 1928); the series Goodspeed's put out as a periodical, *The Month at Goodspeed's* (Boston, 1929–1969); John S. Van E. Kohn's six catalogues of authors' first books (New York, 1936–1972), issued from the Collectors' Bookshop and the Seven Gables Bookshop; the Gotham Book Mart's *We Moderns* (New York, 1940); Kenneth Nebenzahl's series for map collectors, *The Compass* (Chicago, 1961–), and Justin G. Schiller's for collectors of children's books, *Chapbook Miscellany* (New York, 1970–); David Magee's *Victoria, R.I.* (San Francisco, 1969–1970); Peggy Christian's *Childhood and Youth* (Los Angeles, 1970); Bertram Rota Ltd.'s *The Printer and the Artist* (London, 1974); and K. D. Duval's *British Bookbinding Today* (Frenich, 1975).

A number of dealers have published lavish catalogues, well printed and illustrated, such as No. 40 (San Francisco, 1970) of John Howell—Books, No. 64 (Paris, 1971) of Pierre Berès, No. 39 (London, 1971) of Martin Breslauer, No. 131 (New York, 1971) of H. P. Kraus (the first item of which is a Gutenberg Bible), No. 237 (Los Angeles, 1974) of Zeitlin & Ver Brugge, the fortieth anniversary catalogue (New York, 1975) of Lew David Feldman (House of El Dieff), and No. 17 (London, 1976) of Weinreb & Douwma, to name only a few from the 1970s. There are many important nineteenth-century catalogues worth having, including such landmarks as Lackington & Allen's *General Catalogue* (1815) of some 28,000 entries, the Longmans *Bibliotheca Anglo-Poetica* (1815), based on Thomas Park's collection, Thomas Rodd's catalogue of 19,000 tracts (1819–1822), Henry G. Bohn's famous "guinea catalogue" (1841) and later catalogues (1847–1867), and the great *General Catalogue* (1887–1897) of the leading nineteenth-century firm, Bernard Quaritch—as well as the large catalogues of the prominent Americana dealers, including Robert Clarke, Obadiah Rich, Joseph Sabin, John Russell Smith, and Henry Stevens. Two of the most impressive twentieth-century catalogues are Sotheran's *Bibliotheca Chemico-Mathematica* (London, 1921, 1932–1941) and Gumuchian's *Les Livres de l'enfance du XVe au XIXe siècle* (Paris, 1931). Solid catalogues are still issued from such well-established firms as Quaritch, Francis Edwards, E. P. Goldschmidt, Dawsons of Pall Mall, Lathrop C. Harper, and many others; but there are also

scholarly and extremely appealing catalogues from newer dealers, such as Colin and Charlotte Franklin (Oxford) and Jeremy
Norman (San Francisco), both of whom issued their first catalogues in 1971. Such a sampling can be no more than suggestive, of course, and leaves out dozens of worthy names; for
more detailed information about dealers' specialties and catalogues, one should consult the various directories of dealers
(see below) and the comments on, or lists of, current catalogues
in the book-collecting periodicals.

EXHIBITION CATALOGUES

Exhibition catalogues also give the permanence of print to
assemblages of books not destined to remain together. Frequently exhibitions draw materials from a variety of sources,
sometimes bringing to public attention little-known copies that
are privately held and placing side by side related items that
may never come together again; but even when the books on
view are taken from the holdings of a single library, they can
suggest connections not so easily discernible when the books
are in their usual places in the stacks. Good exhibitions entail
considerable research, and published records of them can make
real contributions to knowledge and can be influential in pointing directions for future collecting. Although some exhibitions
include large numbers of items—as did the great 1877 Caxton
exhibition in London with over 4,600 pieces (its 472-page catalogue was edited by George Bullen)—most exhibitions concentrate on a relatively small number of displays, allowing the
persons responsible to investigate and annotate individual entries more fully. One of the greatest exhibitions of books in the
twentieth century was that entitled "Printing and the Mind of
Man," held at the 1963 International Printing Machinery and
Allied Trades Exhibition in London; a useful catalogue was issued at the time, but the exhibition received its proper monu-
ment in 1967 in the majestic volume edited by John Carter and
Percy H. Muir and published by Cassell. Similarly imposing
volumes, now standard reference works, have been published
in connection with several impressive exhibitions at the Pierpont Morgan Library: Joseph Blumenthal's *The Art of the Printed
Book, 1455–1955* (1973), Gerald Gottlieb's *Early Children's Books
and Their Illustration* (1975), and Gordon N. Ray's *The Illustrator
and the Book in England, 1790–1914* (1976). Another catalogue in

the same tradition is Dorothy Miner's *The History of Bookbinding, 525–1950 A.D.* for the Walters Art Gallery (Baltimore, 1957); and a related example of a catalogue that pushes forward the boundaries of knowledge is Michael Papantonio's *Early American Bookbindings* (New York, 1972), describing items from his collection exhibited at the Morgan and four other libraries.

Some exhibition catalogues have been widely used as basic lists of the high spots in various fields: Among the most famous are three Grolier Club catalogues, *One Hundred Books Famous in English Literature* (1902), *One Hundred Influential American Books Printed before 1900* (1947), and Harrison D. Horblit's *One Hundred Books Famous in Science* (1964); John Hayward's *English Poetry* (London: National Book League, 1947); and Cyril Connolly's *One Hundred Modern Books* (Austin, Texas: Humanities Research Center, 1971), based on his 1965 book *The Modern Movement*. Bern Dibner's selection of 200 books from his library, *Heralds of Science* (Norwalk: Burndy Library, 1955), occupies a similar position, though it is not, strictly speaking, an exhibition catalogue. The Grolier Club has published other important catalogues over the years, the most elaborate perhaps being the four-volume *Catalogue of Original and Early Editions* of English writers from Langland to Prior, prepared by Edward Hale Bierstadt et al. (1893–1905). Other unusually interesting runs of catalogues have come from the Berg Collection of the New York Public Library (in a series begun in 1940 by John Gordan and now continued by Lola L. Szladits), the Library of Congress (especially the series on the anniversaries of various states), the Humanities Research Center of the University of Texas, and the Lilly Library of Indiana University. Many other libraries have issued handsome catalogues from time to time, such as James M. Wells' *The Circle of Knowledge: Encyclopaedias Past and Present* (Newberry Library, 1968), *A Society's Chief Joys* (American Antiquarian Society, 1969), *The Turn of a Century, 1885–1910* (Houghton Library, 1970), and Ian MacPhail's *Hortus Botanicus* (books from the Sterling Morton Library exhibited at The Newberry Library, 1972). Sometimes exhibition catalogues are printed as part of the journals of individual libraries, and current ones are regularly referred to in the bibliographical periodicals.

LIBRARY CATALOGUES

Private library catalogues are valuable not only as memorials to collectors but as records of copies that—while they remain in private hands—are inevitably less accessible than copies in public institutions. Some collectors have prepared, or had prepared for them, magnificent catalogues that have become bibliographical monuments, which are consulted frequently by other bibliographers and collectors. In the front rank of such catalogues is the three-volume *Carl H. Pforzheimer Library: English Literature, 1475–1700* (New York, 1940), now an expensive collector's item itself; for the eighteenth century, the corresponding catalogue is *The Rothschild Library* (Cambridge, 1954). Two distinguished bibliographers were associated with these catalogues, William A. Jackson with the first and John Hayward with the second, and the tradition of eminent bibliographers working on library catalogues can be represented by a number of prominent instances: A. W. Pollard's editorship of the catalogue of Frederick Locker-Lampson's Rowfant Library (London: Quaritch, 1886) and the four-volume Pierpont Morgan catalogue (London, 1906–1907); George Watson Cole's great five-volume catalogue of E. D. Church's Americana collection (New York: Dodd, Mead, 1907; also English literature, 2 vols., 1909); A. S. W. Rosenbach's two-volume catalogue of Harry Elkins Widener's collection (Philadelphia, 1918); Robert Ernest Cowan's eighteen volumes on the library of William Andrews Clark, Jr. (San Francisco, 1920–1931); T. J. Wise's eleven-volume catalogue of his own collection, *The Ashley Library* (London, 1922–1936); Wilberforce Eames' catalogues of Herschel V. Jones' Americana collection (New York: Rudge, 1928, 1938); two volumes describing selected bindings from the library of J. R. Abbey, G. D. Hobson's *English Bindings 1490–1940* (London: Chiswick Pr., 1940) and A. R. A. Hobson's *French and Italian Collectors and Their Bindings* (Oxford: Roxburghe Club, 1953); Michael Sadleir's bibliographically important two-volume description of his collection, *XIX Century Fiction* (London: Constable, 1951); Howard M. Nixon's discussions of selected bindings (not intended as a full catalogue) in the *Broxbourne Library* (London: Maggs, 1956); Robert F. Metzdorf's careful record of Chauncey Brewster Tinker's library (New Haven, Conn.: Yale Univ. Library, 1959); Allan Stevenson's work on (and contribution of an important introduction on descriptive bibliography to) the second volume of the *Catalogue of Botanical Books in the Collection of Rachel McMasters Miller Hunt* (Pittsburgh, 1961); and Sir Geoffrey Keynes' catalogue of his own library, *Bibliotheca Bibliographici* (London: Trianon Pr., 1964). Other examples of well-known private library catalogues are Thomas Corser's *Collectanea Anglo-*

Poetica (Manchester: Chetham Society, 1860–1883); the sixteen-volume catalogue of Robert Hoe's English and foreign literature (New York, 1903–1909); the *Bibliotheca Lindesiana* (Aberdeen Univ. Pr. et al., 1910–1913), with its strong holdings of broadsides and proclamations; Morris L. Parrish's catalogues of his Victorian literature at Dormy House (New York [later London: Constable], 1928–1940); the *Britwell Handlist* (London: Quaritch, 1933), compiled from the auction catalogues of the Britwell Court Library; Dennis I. Duveen's *Bibliotheca Alchemica et Chemica* (London: Weil, 1949); and J. R. Abbey's four volumes on depictions (1770–1860) of Britain and foreign places in aquatint and lithography (London, 1952–1957). Retrospective lists of now dispersed collections constitute another type of private library catalogue—represented by Gabriel Austin's "Preliminary Catalogue" of *The Library of Jean Grolier* (New York: Grolier Club, 1971), which traces the history of the ownership of each of the presently known volumes from that great sixteenth-century bibliophile's collection, and by the catalogue section of Anthony Hobson's *Apollo and Pegasus* (mentioned earlier).

The borderline between private and institutional library catalogues is not distinct, because many private collections move into institutions, and some collections are given catalogues only after an institutional association has been made. For example, the *Bibliotheca Osleriana* (Oxford: Clarendon, 1929), the catalogue of Sir William Osler's distinguished medical collection, announces on its title page that the library has been bequeathed to McGill University; the handsome five-volume catalogue of George Arents' collection of tobacco literature (New York: Rosenbach, 1937–1952) has been continued since the collection became part of the New York Public Library; E. Millicent Sowerby's magisterial five-volume *Catalogue of the Library of Thomas Jefferson* (Washington: Library of Congress, 1952–1959) is a scholarly reconstruction based on books now in the Library of Congress and on contemporary lists of the books he sold to Congress in 1815; *The Rosenwald Collection* (1954) catalogues Lessing J. Rosenwald's illustrated books, housed at Jenkintown, Pennsylvania, but presented to the Library of Congress; *The Sterling Library* (1954) enumerates the books presented to the University of London by Sir Louis Sterling; Sinclair Hamilton's *Early American Book Illustrators and Wood Engravers, 1670–1870* (1950, 1958, 1969) describes his collection in the Princeton University Library; *The Osborne Collection of*

Early Children's Books, 1566–1910 (1958; supplemented in 1975) records a collection in the Toronto Public Library; Colton Storm's *A Catalogue of the Everett D. Graff Collection of Western Americana* (1968) provides meticulous detail about a collection in The Newberry Library; and Edwin Wolf 2nd's *The Library of James Logan of Philadelphia, 1674–1751* (1974), with its excellent annotation, serves handsomely to document this great colonial collection in the Library Company of Philadelphia. Several exemplary catalogues—like Joan St. C. Crane's *Robert Frost* (1974)—have been based on the contents of the Clifton Waller Barrett Library at the University of Virginia; similarly, the Humanities Research Center at the University of Texas has published what amount to bibliographies of several authors based on the holdings of its library (for example, Manfred Triesch on Lillian Hellman, 1966; Laurence G. Avery on Maxwell Anderson, 1968; A. H. Goldstone and J. R. Payne on John Steinbeck, 1974).

In the nineteenth century many institutional libraries published complete catalogues of their holdings; among twentieth-century catalogues, the following are some that come readily to mind as important references: J. R. Bartlett's catalogue of the John Carter Brown Library (Providence, 1901–1931; supplemented in 1973); T. H. Darlow and H. F. Moule's *Historical Catalogue of the Printed Editions of Holy Scripture in the Library of the British and Foreign Bible Society* (London, 1903–1911; the English part was expanded beyond the one library in 1968 by A. S. Herbert); the British Museum (Natural History) catalogue (London, 1903–1940); the *Catalogue of Books Printed in the XVth Century Now in the British Museum* (1908–); P. Lee Phillips' *A List of Geographical Atlases in the Library of Congress* (1909–1920; supplement by Clara E. Le Gear, 1958–); Frances M. Staton and Marie Tremaine's *Bibliography of Canadiana* (Toronto Public Library, 1934, 1959); the Kress Library of Business and Economics *Catalogue* (Boston: Baker Library, Harvard, 1940, 1956, 1957); F. N. L. Poynter's *Catalogue of Printed Books* in the Wellcome Historical Medical Library (London, 1962–); Ruth Mortimer's catalogues of French and Italian sixteenth-century books collected by Philip Hofer in the Department of Printing and Graphic Arts at Harvard (Cambridge, Mass.: Belknap, Harvard Univ. Pr., 1964, 1974); and P. J. W. Kilpatrick's *Catalogue of the Edward Clark Library* on typography, illustration, and binding (Edinburgh: Napier College, 1976), with its extensive annotation by Harry

Carter. When one thinks of published library catalogues, of course, the primary examples are those of the great national libraries: the catalogues of the British Museum, now the British Library (1965–), the Library of Congress (1942–1948; now superseded by the *National Union Catalog*), and the Bibliothèque Nationale (1897–). The technique of reproducing the actual catalogue cards has made possible in recent years the rapid publication of many important library catalogues. The G. K. Hall Co. (Boston) has been most active in this field and has published (among others) the catalogues of the Wing Foundation (printing) and the Edward E. Ayer Collection (Americana and American Indians) of The Newberry Library (both 1961, 1970), the Bancroft Library (1964, 1969, 1974), the theater and drama collections of the New York Public Library (1967, 1973, 1976), Dr. Williams' Library on nonconformity (1968), the Berg Collection of English and American literature (1969, 1975), the William L. Clements Library of Americana (1970), the Folger Shakespeare Library (1970, 1976), the Harris Collection of American Poetry at Brown (1972), the University of Illinois Rare Book Room (1972), and the William Andrews Clark Memorial Library (1974).

Published card catalogues are easily accessible, but many other card catalogues also constitute valuable reference tools in various fields. To become acquainted with the libraries that maintain special collections in one's areas of interest, one can turn to several guides such as Brian J. Wilson's *Aslib Directory* (of British libraries), 3rd ed. (London: Aslib, 1968–1970), Lee Ash's *Subject Collections . . . in the United States and Canada*, 4th ed. (New York: Bowker, 1975), and Richard C. Lewanski's *Subject Collections in European Libraries* (1965); or to Robert B. Downs' lists of published catalogues and discussions of libraries, *American Library Resources* (Chicago: American Library Assn., 1951, 1962, 1972) and *British Library Resources* (1973); or to Anthony T. Kruzas' *Directory of Special Libraries and Information Centers*, 3rd ed. (Detroit: Gale, 1974), and the *Subject Directory* based on it; or to A. R. A. Hobson's *Great Libraries* (London: Weidenfeld & Nicolson, 1970), the *World Guide to Libraries*, 4th ed. (New York: Bowker, 1974), and Colin Steele's *Major Libraries of the World* (New York: Bowker, 1976). Information about rare book libraries' holdings also frequently appears in their annual reports, many of which are highly readable and detailed, and in volumes displaying selected highlights from their collections, for example, *The Houghton Library, 1942–1967* (1967), *Major Acquisitions of The Pierpont Morgan Library, 1924–1974* (1974), and A. G. and W. O. Hassall's *Treasures from the Bodleian Library* (London: Fraser, 1976). A list of private library catalogues, prepared by Charles van der Elst, appears in *Le Livre et l'Estampe*, Nos. 2, 4–6 (1955–1956); and further information about published catalogues can be found in Archer Taylor (see above) and in Robert Collison's *Published Library Catalogues* (London: Mansell, 1973).

Price Records and Guides

Some of the most frequently consulted of all reference books used by collectors and dealers are those that list current prices of antiquarian and secondhand books. Of course, the price of any given book varies according to its condition and the circumstances surrounding its sale, and prices named in these works must be interpreted accordingly. There are essentially two kinds of price lists (although the line between them is not always sharp): those that record the actual prices paid for books (at auction) or asked for books (by dealers) and those that attempt to provide a guide to the generally accepted prices of a representative selection of titles, without offering details of specific transactions or quotations.

In the first category, the records of auction prices are much fuller than those of dealers' catalogue prices and more established as a reference tool. Auction prices, however, are notoriously difficult to interpret, because they are influenced by such factors as the particular people who were bidding against each other at the sale and the prestige of the collection being dispersed (and thus the interest its sale generated). Furthermore, they are sometimes the prices dealers are willing to pay for stock (wholesale prices) and at other times the prices that collectors have commissioned dealers to pay. For these reasons, one cannot simply accept the latest reported auction price of a book as the current standard but instead should check for other appearances in order to establish a range of prices; if the book has not turned up at auction for a considerable number of years, that fact in itself is of significance. Therefore, not merely the recent volumes of records but earlier ones as well must constantly be used. The runs of these volumes constitute a valuable historical resource, helping one, for instance, to trace the history of particular copies of books or the reputation of writers as reflected in the market. When searching the records, one should remember that generally books making less than a specified minimum price (recently about $20 or £8) are not listed, and this minimum has naturally risen over the years.

Fortunately, for auctions in the English-speaking world there is thorough coverage extending back into the nineteenth century; there are in fact three sets of records with long runs, and two of them are still being published, covering much of the same ground and wastefully duplicating one another. One of them, *American Book Prices Current* (edited by a succession of skilled bookmen, including Luther S. Livingston, Colton Storm, Edward Lazare, and Katharine Leab; New York: Dodd, Mead et al., 1895–), begins with the season of 1894–1895, and the other, *Book-Auction Records* (London: Frank Karslake [later Henry Stevens, Son & Stiles, then Dawson], 1903–), begins with 1902. In the early years there was less duplication, but the two series have gradually become more alike. At the beginning *ABPC* covered only American sales, but Sotheby sales were added in 1958 and other London and occasional foreign sales in 1961; *BAR* started out covering only English sales, then expanded to include all the British Isles, then took in the United States (between 1914 and 1921, and from 1939–1940 onward), and now also reports sales from several other European countries. *BAR* from its inception has given the names of buyers as well as the prices, and *ABPC* began giving some buyers' names in 1959. In one respect, however, the series have moved farther apart: *ABPC* has always reported manuscripts as well as printed items, whereas *BAR*, having a small section on early manuscripts through the 1952–1953 volume, then dropped its coverage of manuscripts entirely. (English sales of manuscripts during 1914–1922 were also reported in *Autograph Prices Current* [London: Courville].) *BAR* in the recent past has had the reputation of being somewhat more prompt in its coverage, but somewhat less accurate, than *ABPC*; a comparison of two recent volumes (those for 1973–1974) shows that *BAR* covers a larger total number of sales than *ABPC* because of greater attention to English provincial and foreign sales. In view of these shifting relationships, one must consult both *BAR* and *ABPC* when making a thorough search. This work is facilitated by the cumulative indexes that both series have issued, reducing considerably the number of alphabets to be checked: *BAR* now has eight indexes covering 1902–1968, and *ABPC* has ten cov-

ering 1916–1975. Prices have been included in the *ABPC* indexes since 1923, but this practice did not begin in *BAR* until
1948; even when the prices are furnished in the indexes, it is
still advantageous to look up the original entry for the additional information that may be found there. As of 1976 *BAR* began
publishing its records periodically as *BAR Quarterly* (which also
contains articles and auction news at the front), before gathering them together into annual volumes.

The other long-running English series extends the coverage
of English auctions back even farther: *Book-Prices Current*, edited by J. Herbert Slater and others (London: Stock et al., 1888–
1957), covers the years 1887–1956 in 64 volumes (with three cumulative indexes for 1887–1916), providing buyers' names and
including some American sales (especially after 1915) and some
manuscripts (especially after 1920). In using this set, one should
be aware of the fact that before 1914 the entries in each volume
are arranged by sale, with an alphabetical index at the end (as is
true of the first 38 volumes of *BAR* also). Additional information
about English sales of 1895–1898 can be found in Temple Scott's
Book Sales of 1895 [–1898] (London: Cockram [later Bell], 1896–
1899), which includes introductions and annotations. Another
impressive work of these years enables one to locate some still
earlier prices: Luther S. Livingston's four-volume *Auction Prices
of Books* (New York: Dodd, Mead, 1905) contains not only the
data from the early volumes of *BPC* and *ABPC* but also "some
thousands of important quotations of earlier date." For the
years 1940–1951 the American records are further duplicated in
S. R. Shapiro's three-volume *United States Cumulative Book Auction Records* (New York: Want List, 1946–1951). Separate coverage of Australia and Canada has recently begun, with Bernard
Amtmann's *Montreal Book Auction Records, 1967–1971* (Montreal:
Amtmann, 1972) and Margaret Woodhouse's *Australian Book
Auction Records* [1969–] (Sydney: Woodhouse Bookshop, 1971–).
Collectors of continental books (and even of English ones)
should not overlook the records that concentrate on continental
sales, especially the *Jahrbuch der Bücherpreise* [1906–1939] (Leipzig: Harrassowitz, 1907–1940) and the *Jahrbuch der Auktionspreise
für Bücher und Autographen* (Hamburg: Hauswedell, 1950–). The
current French series *Catalogue bibliographique des ventes publiques
(livres et manuscrits)* [1964–] (Paris: Publisol [later Editions May-
er], 1966–), was preceded by a succession of relatively short-
lived records: Gustave Brunet's for 1866–1889, *Livres payés en*

vente publique (Bordeaux: Lefebvre, 1877), and *La Bibliomanie en 1878* [–1889] (Brussels: Gay & Douce et al., 1878–1889); the *Index bibliographique* for 1895–1901, cumulating the weekly *Repertoire des ventes publiques; Annuaire des ventes de livres, manuscrits, reliures armoriées* [1918–1931] (Paris: L'Agence générale, 1921–1932); and *Le Guide du bibliophile et du libraire* [1942–1956] (Paris: Rombaldi, 1945–1959).

In contrast to the thorough indexing of auction prices over nearly a century, there has been very little systematic effort to index dealers' catalogues. Completeness in this area would be virtually impossible to achieve, but dealers' catalogues contain so much important information that it is frustrating not to have an efficient means of access to at least a large selection of them. A valuable start in this direction has been made by Daniel F. McGrath's *Bookman's Price Index* (Detroit: Gale, 1964–); although it does not make clear how the catalogues are selected for inclusion, at least we now have current coverage of a sizable group of English and American (and a few foreign) catalogues (the total number of entries, by the twelfth volume, amounting to about half a million). Prices in such a listing, as in the auction records, require interpretation, because pricing policies and assessments of condition vary among dealers; one should also keep in mind that these are prices asked, not necessarily received, because a book may find no buyer at its catalogued price. It is essential, therefore, that the dealers be cited and their descriptions of books quoted—a fact recognized in *BPI* but not in its predecessor, *Trade Prices Current of American First Editions* [1937–1940] (New York: Bowker, 1938–1940), along with *Trade Prices Current: Press Books* (1938). A work similar to *BPI*, Mildred S. Mandeville's *The Used Book Price Guide* (Kenmore, Wash.: Price Guide Publishers, 1962–1964, 1972–1973), contains in its second edition 74,000 entries based on dealers' catalogues from 1967 through 1973, each entry reporting condition and identifying dealer and catalogue. The Canadian service, *Canadian Book-Prices Current* [1950–] (Toronto: McClelland & Stewart, 1957–), includes citations from some non-Canadian dealers' catalogues if they contain items of Canadian interest.

The Mandeville book is on the borderline between two kinds of work, for its aim, if not its methods, conforms to a second large category—price guides that intend not so much to preserve a historical record of the prices of a given season as to offer current estimates of value for the guidance of dealers and collectors. The entries in such a guide need not be limited to the books offered for sale during a particular period, and the assigned prices may reflect the compiler's own judgment as well as reference to auction records and certain retail catalogues. These guides are put together in a variety of ways, but generally the sources of individual prices are not specified. A well-known work of this kind is Philip M. Roskie's *The Bookman's Bible* (Oakland: Roskie & Wallace, 1956–1963), which presents, in a highly compressed and coded form, a chronological listing of books published between 1850 and 1949, with prices obtained by averaging dealers' or auction prices. More recently, Van Allen Bradley's *The Book Collector's Handbook of Values* (New York: Putnam, 1972, 1975) has achieved an extremely wide circulation, both because it has been effectively marketed by its publisher and because it is the most comprehensive one-volume price guide now available (with about 16,000 entries valued at $25 and over). It does not record the specific sources of prices (except that auction prices are labeled "A" and dated by year), although the introduction states that dealers' catalogues and stocks have been extensively used (the reliance on particular catalogues is suggested by the variability of the treatment among the entries—for example, some books are priced lacking jackets, others with jackets; some in ordinary issues as well as limited issues, others only in limited issues). Bradley had earlier published two popular price guides for American books, *Gold in Your Attic* (New York: Fleet, 1958; revised in 1968 as *The New Gold in Your Attic*) and *More Gold in Your Attic* (1961), each of which contains discussions of several dozen "fabulous" American books, followed by listings of about 2,000 titles and prices. (William Targ, Bradley's editor at Putnam's, was also his predecessor in this field, publishing through his Black Archer Press in Chicago several guides, such as *American First Editions and Their Prices* [1930, 1931, 1941], *Modern English First Editions and Their Prices* [1932], and his and Harry F. Marks' *Ten Thousand Rare Books and Their Prices* [1936].)

A number of other guides to more specialized fields have appeared over the years, particularly some substantial listings of Americana: Stanley Wemyss, *The General Guide to Rare Americana* (Philadelphia, 1944, 1950), with dated auction prices; J. Norman Heard et al., *Bookman's Guide to Americana* (Washington, D.C. [later Metuchen, N.J.]: Scarecrow, 1953, 1960, 1964, 1967, 1969, 1971, 1977), with prices from a selected list of dealers; and

Howes' *U.S.-iana* (mentioned under "Bibliographies" above), with its lettered categories indicating price ranges. Examples of other recent lists, covering smaller fields, are Louis Ginsberg's *Methodist Book Prices, 1955–1965* (Petersburg, Va., 1965), William M. Morrison's *Texas Book Prices* (Waco, 1963, 1972), William Thomas' *Pennsy-iana: A Price Guide to Pennsylvania Books* (Harrisburg, 1972), Richard Clear's *Old Magazines: Collectors Price Guide* (Gas City, Ind.: L-W Promotions, 1974), and Allen Ahearn's *The Book of First Books* (Rockville, Md.: Quill & Brush Pr., 1975). Many other lists exist, and even those that are obsolete are of historical interest and worth preserving (for instance, the American Book Mart's lists of the prices it would pay for books [Chicago, 1935–1938] or Alexander C. Wirth's *First Editions with a Future* [Baltimore: Proof Pr., 1935], both of which name identifying points, are characteristic of their period). But it is clear that most of these price guides (with a few exceptions, such as De Ricci and Sawyer-Darton—mentioned under "Bibliographies" above—and the Targ and Marks work) are limited to nineteenth- and twentieth-century books; information on earlier books must be looked for in the auction and dealer records. And of course those records remain fundamental for the later books as well; the main value of a compendium like Bradley's is the convenience of having a consciously selected group of titles reported in a single volume that is less expensive to buy and less time-consuming to consult than *ABPC* or *BPI*. Such volumes serve a real function, but they are not substitutes for the basic documented records. In the end, one must recognize that all these printed records and guides are retrospective in nature and cannot reveal what will happen in future transactions.

Directories of Dealers and Collectors

Directories of book dealers are obviously useful to collectors who wish to learn the names of those dealers specializing in a particular field or located in a particular area, especially lesser-known dealers whom one might not be as likely to hear about in other ways. Such guides are especially helpful to a collector who is traveling, for they generally provide more information than local classified telephone directories and are more convenient for planning an itinerary in advance. The most thorough directory—though hardly one to be carried along on a trip—is the *American Book Trade Directory* (New York: Bowker, 1915–), which was in its twenty-second edition in 1975. Arranged geographically (by state and then by city), it is a remarkable listing of all dealers in new and old books, classified by type and with their specialties named. It contains an alphabetical index of the firms' names, but no index of specialties; and it now includes, despite its title, information on booksellers in Britain, Ireland, and Canada, as well as miscellaneous book-trade information, such as the names of appraisers, auctioneers, and book clubs. Another large work, listing geographically some of the new and antiquarian shops in many countries, is the *World Directory of Booksellers* (London: Wales, 1970–). Also on an international scale, but much more portable, is the excellent *International Directory of Antiquarian Booksellers* (in its fifth edition in 1972), the official directory of the International League of Antiquarian Booksellers, listing (by location, specialty, and name) the members of the constituent national organizations. Another convenient listing is B. Donald Grose's *The Antiquarian Booktrade: An International Directory of Subject Specialists* (Metuchen, N.J.: Scarecrow, 1972), arranged by subject and by name. (An earlier standard work that can still be consulted with profit for its lists of bibliographical material is James Clegg's *International Directory of Booksellers and Bibliophile's Manual* [Rochdale, England: Clegg, 1886–1914].)

For directories of lesser scope, there is the outstanding series published by the Sheppard Press of London: *A Directory of Dealers in Secondhand and Antiquarian Books in the British Isles* (1951–), *Book Dealers in North America* (1954–), *European Bookdealers* (1967–), and *Bookdealers in India, Pakistan and Sri Lanka* (1977–). These volumes (with geographical, name, and subject alphabets) indicate for most dealers the size of the stock, the fields of interest, the hours of business, and the availability of catalogues, and they contain introductory sections of miscellaneous book-trade information. Two other British directories are the *Annual Directory of Booksellers in the British Isles Specialising in Antiquarian and Out-of-Print Books* (Wembley [later Birmingham]: The Clique, 1970–) and *The Complete Booksellers Directory* (formerly *Small Booksellers Directory*; Wilbarston: Gerald Coe, 1966–). The second includes some American dealers, and both place their primary entries in an alphabetical section of names, which is followed by geographical and subject lists. American dealers can also be located through R. H. Patterson's *Directory of American Book Specialists* (New York: Continental, 1972–), ar-

ranged only by subjects, and through the directory and advertising sections of the *AB Bookman's Yearbook*. Examples for other
countries are Maria Szivos Szalay's *Canadian Antiquarian Booksellers Directory* (Brandon: Brandon Univ. Library, 1965–), *La
empresa del libro en America latina*, 2nd ed. (Buenos Aires: Bowker, 1974), and the *Répertoire officiel des membres* of the Syndicat
de la librairie ancienne et moderne (Paris, 1973–).

Directories of collectors also facilitate communication in
the book world: They not only constitute a source of names for
dealers' mailing lists but also provide a means for collectors to
learn of others with similar interests. The most extensive
(though no longer current) listing of American and Canadian
collectors is the series that began in the *American Library Annual*
for 1912–1913, was expanded in the *American Book Trade Manual*
for 1915, and was then published separately by Bowker as *A List
of Private Book Collectors* (or, later, simply *Private Book Collectors*)
from 1919 through 1953 (eight volumes with geographical,
name, and subject alphabets, edited by John Allan Holden et
al.). Other early efforts are *Book Collectors and Their Hobbies*
(Washington: Rare Book Shop, 1913) and *A Record of British and
American Private Collectors and Lovers of Books, Prints, Mss., Etc.*
(London: Bookman's Journal, 1927). In recent years there has
been no comparable service, although attempts have been
made by R. J. Hussey (editor of a short-lived periodical, *The
Book Lover's Answer*) in the *TBA Directory of Book Collectors and
Rare Book Dealers* (Webster, N.Y., 1966) and by Gerald Coe in *The
Book Collectors Directory* (earlier *Small Booksellers and Collectors Di-
rectory*; Wilbarston, 1967–). A promising new venture is Roger
and Judith Sheppard's *International Directory of Book Collectors*
(Beckenham, Kent: Trigon Pr., 1976–), although it unfortunately does not index the names according to collecting interests.
(The Sheppards have also announced a more specialized guide,
*Crime & Detective Fiction: A Handbook of Dealers & Collectors in Brit-
ain & America*.) The *American Book Collector* runs a column ("Private Collectors Directory") in each number, listing the names
and interests of subscribers who choose to purchase an entry,
and a somewhat more comprehensive "Directory of Private
Book Collectors and Their Subjects Collected" (containing free
listings for subscribers) is printed in the magazine at intervals of
roughly a year; in England *The Book Exchange* similarly contains
supplements listing collectors. Of course, the printed yearbooks

or membership lists of book clubs (such as those of the Grolier Club, Caxton Club, Rowfant Club, and Association internationale de bibliophilie) and bibliographical societies also serve as directories of collectors, and a few of them record members' interests (for example, those of the Private Libraries Association and the American Printing History Association). In using all these directories, one should remember that the information they contain is generally supplied by the dealers and collectors listed and has not been independently verified.

Three Related Fields: Conservation, Bookplates, Manuscripts

Collectors of books generally find that their activity leads them, sooner or later, into several related areas. Conservation, bookplates, and manuscripts are three such fields, each with a large literature of its own—from which only a few basic titles can be selected here. All collectors should know something about the proper conditions for housing their books and the latest methods of conservation. Much has been learned since the days of William Blades' *The Enemies of Books* (London: Trübner, 1880), or even of H. M. Lydenberg and John Archer's *The Care and Repair of Books* (1931; 4th ed., revised by John Alden, New York: Bowker, 1960), as one can tell by reading the W. J. Barrow Research Laboratory's series of booklets on the *Permanence/Durability of the Book* (Richmond, 1964–), or the January 1970 number of *Library Quarterly* on "Deterioration and Preservation of Library Materials," or the Boston Athenaeum's 1971 seminar papers on *Library and Archives Conservation*. An older standard work is Douglas Cockerell's *Bookbinding, and the Care of Books* (1901; 5th ed., rev., London: Pitman, 1962), and a useful newer one is Bernard C. Middleton's *The Restoration of Leather Bindings* (Chicago: American Library Assn., 1972). But although one should not overlook material in these books and in H. J. Plenderleith's *The Conservation of Antiquities and Works of Art* (1956; 2nd ed., with A. E. A. Werner, London: Oxford Univ. Pr., 1971), the best places to begin are Carolyn Horton's *Cleaning and Preserving Bindings and Related Materials* (Chicago: American Library Assn., 1967, 1969, revision in progress) and Willman Spawn's chapter on conservation in this book, which contains a checklist for further reading. A more elaborate listing of references is G. D. M. Cunha's *Conservation of Library Materials: A Manual and Bibliography*, 2nd ed. (Metuchen, N.J.: Scarecrow, 1971–1972).

Bookplates are of interest to book collectors as objects associated with books and as valuable evidence for reconstructing the history of particular copies of books; bookplates are also collected, by book collectors and others, for their own sake, because they constitute a challenging and appealing art form. The collecting of bookplates, and the study of their long history, flourished in the 1890s, with the founding of the Ex Libris Society in England (its elegant *Journal* ran from 1891 to 1908) and the production of important books on both sides of the Atlantic—Egerton Castle's *English Book-Plates* (London: Bell, 1892) and Charles Dexter Allen's *American Book-Plates* (New York: Macmillan, 1894). Basic references, dating from this period, are Henry W. Fincham's *Artists and Engravers of British and American Book Plates* (London: Kegan Paul, 1897) and E. R. J. Gambier Howe's *Franks Bequest: Catalogue of British and American Bookplates* (British Museum, 1903–1904). At present the Bookplate Society in England and the American Society of Bookplate Collectors and Designers issue informative newsletters (the American society also puts out an attractive *Year Book*); and the Private Libraries Association has recently published several handsome books on the subject, including Mark Severin and Anthony Reid's *Engraved Bookplates: European Ex Libris, 1950–70* (1972) and Brian North Lee's *Early Printed Booklabels* (1976). The first of these can serve as a brief modern introduction, for it contains preliminary chapters on such subjects as "Commissioning a Bookplate" and "Collecting Bookplates." The periodical literature is well under control, as a result of Audrey Spencer Arellanes' *Bookplates* (Detroit: Gale, 1971), with its 5,445 annotated entries; books can be located through George W. Fuller and Verna B. Grimm's *A Bibliography of Bookplate Literature* (Spokane Public Library, 1926).

All book collectors are to some extent manuscript collectors as well, because they invariably consider books with authorial presentation inscriptions, or marginalia by important figures, to be more desirable than copies without those manuscript additions; and most book collectors are always eager to locate other manuscript material relevant to their interests. Many introductory guides have been published, but the one that has remained standard for several decades is Mary Benjamin's *Auto-*

graphs: A Key to Collecting (1946; rev. ed., New York: Benjamin, 1966), which supplanted the still respectable volume by Henry T. Scott, *Autograph Collecting* (London: Gill, 1894), the best of the earlier books. Among the more recent works Charles Hamilton's *Collecting Autographs and Manuscripts* (Norman: Univ. of Oklahoma Pr., 1961) and Jerry E. Patterson's *Autographs: A Collector's Guide* (New York: Crown, 1973) stand out; both contain annotated book lists and numerous reproductions of signatures. Volumes of facsimiles are of course indispensable, and there have been a considerable number, of which Charles Geigy's *Handbook of Facsimiles of Famous Personages* (Basle: Geering, 1925), W. W. Greg's *English Literary Autographs, 1550–1650* (London: Oxford Univ. Pr., 1925–1932), and P. J. Croft's *Autograph Poetry in the English Language* (London: Cassell, 1973) are famous examples. One can ascertain the locations in American institutions of manuscript collections of particular figures by consulting the *National Union Catalog of Manuscript Collections* [1959–] (Ann Arbor et al.: Edwards et al., 1962–). Another basic kind of work, as the titles suggest, is represented by Albert S. Osborn's *Questioned Documents* (1910; 2nd ed., Albany: Byrd, 1929) and Wilson R. Harrison's *Suspect Documents* (London: Sweet & Maxwell, 1958, 1966). The principal organization for collectors at present is the Manuscript Society, which publishes a quarterly journal, *Manuscripts*. Another well-known periodical, *The Collector* (1887–), is actually a catalogue of the Walter R. Benjamin firm of New York, but it has contained some useful articles over the course of its long existence. Reminiscences by dealers include Thomas F. Madigan's *Word Shadows of the Great* (New York: Stokes, 1930) and Charles Hamilton's *Scribblers & Scoundrels* (New York: Eriksson, 1968). Some of A. N. L. Munby's historical studies have already been mentioned; for America, see Lester J. Cappon, "Walter R. Benjamin and the Autograph Trade at the Turn of the Century," *Proceedings of the Massachusetts Historical Society* 78 (1966): 20–37. Many other comments on manuscripts occur in the memoirs and studies of book collectors and dealers.

Guides to Further Reading

The books and essays that have been mentioned here are intended simply as examples to characterize the diversity of materials available; most collectors will find that they wish to go beyond these basic references in reading about the subjects that interest them. Many of the works, of course, contain reading lists, and a few special guides have already been referred to. But checklists of writings about books constitute an important category of reference works in their own right, and there are several that all collectors should be aware of. Three books, previously cited, record a considerable number of the books (and many of the articles) that a collector of British and American materials needs to know: Robin Myers' *The British Book Trade* (which is broader in coverage than its title suggests), T. H. Howard-Hill's *Bibliography of British Literary Bibliographies*, and G. T. Tanselle's *Guide to the Study of United States Imprints*. On British books and collecting these should be supplemented by the extremely thorough lists in the *New Cambridge Bibliography of English Literature* on "Book Production and Distribution" (containing sections specifically on collecting), prepared by Nicolas Barker (for the period before 1660), Terry Belanger and Graham Pollard (1660–1800), James Mosley (1800–1900), and Peter Davison (1900–1950). Still more encompassing, and the basic work to consult for references on any aspect of the production and collecting of books, is the *Dictionary Catalogue of the History of Printing from the John M. Wing Foundation in The Newberry Library* (Boston: Hall, 1961, 1970). Less up-to-date library catalogues in this field are the *Catalogue* of the St. Bride Foundation (London, 1919) and *Books about Books* (1933; 5th ed., Cambridge Univ. Pr., 1955), the catalogue of the National Book League. Also outdated, but still of use for their annotations, are Horace Hart's *Bibliotheca Typographica* (Rochester: Leo Hart, 1933), R. W. G. Vail's pamphlet on *The Literature of Book Collecting* (New York Univ. Book Club, 1936), and Winslow L. Webber's *Books about Books* (Boston: Hale, Cushman & Flint, 1937), which includes magazine articles as well as books.

To keep up with current books and articles from many countries, the best source is H. D. L. Vervliet's *ABHB: Annual Bibliography of the History of the Printed Book and Libraries* (Hague: Nijhoff, 1973–), which begins its coverage with 1970 (and has a section on bibliophily). For the years from 1949 through 1972 (American participation in *ABHB* starts with 1973), *Studies in Bibliography* provides good lists of British and American bibliographical scholarship prepared by Howell J. Heaney and others; for 1926 through 1940 the *Internationale Bibliographie des Buch- und Bibliothekswesens* includes a number of important English language journals; and from 1920 to the present the *Annual Bibliography* of the Modern Humanities Research Association has offered a section on "Bibliography" (including collecting), which has been expanded and improved in recent years. The Bibliographical Society's forthcoming *Bodleian Index to Certain Bibliographical Journals* will provide more convenient access to many English and American articles after 1932 (extending G. W. Cole's *Index* [Univ. of Chicago Pr., 1933] to *The Library* and a few other English journals, which covers 1877–1932).

George Parker Winship, after looking over the titles in Horace Hart's *Bibliotheca Typographica*, wrote in his introduction, "All of the books that I have examined are of uneven merit, and I do not know of any—including those that carry my own name—that are not misleading to uninformed readers." Probably the same can be said of the selection offered in the foregoing pages. But the best way for readers to become less uninformed is to read widely enough that they begin to recognize discrepancies between books and relative strengths and weaknesses in them. The education of collectors—or of anyone else—cannot consist of the reading of one or two prescribed books; it must involve the building up of a body of facts and attitudes. The books named here cannot be guaranteed never to lead one astray; but they all contribute to the process by which collectors come to understand their field and to make their own contributions to it.

Notes on Contributors

FREDERICK B. ADAMS entered the world of rare books as a private collector and an editor of the *Colophon* (1936–1940, 1948–1950). Turning his avocation into his vocation, he left industry to become Director of The Pierpont Morgan Library from 1948 to 1969. He has also served his turn as president of various organizations: the Grolier Club (1947–1951), the Bibliographical Society of America (1960–1962), the New-York Historical Society (1963–1971), the Yale University Press (1959–1971), and the Association Internationale de Bibliophilie (since 1974).

TERRY BELANGER is a professor at the School of Library Service, Columbia University, where he teaches descriptive bibliography and is the proprietor of the Library School's bibliographical teaching laboratory, the Book Arts Press. He collects books on the history of printing, publishing, and the allied arts, subjects on which he writes frequently in his monthly *Bibliography Newsletter*. He is Chairman of the Rare Books and Manuscripts Section of the Association of College and Research Libraries.

JOAN M. FRIEDMAN is Curator of Rare Books at the Yale Center for British Art, an art gallery and research center at Yale University. There she is responsible for acquisitions to one of the most important collections of English illustrated books and books about the practice of the visual arts in England from the fifteenth through nineteenth centuries, which includes the famous J. R. Abbey collection of color-plate books. Her personal collecting interests include books about the processes of illustration.

ROBIN G. HALWAS is with the firm of E. P. Goldschmidt, & Co. Ltd., rare booksellers, London. He collects books in the field of English historical scholarship, especially of the eighteenth century.

DANIEL J. LEAB, historian, and former Assistant Dean of Faculties at Columbia University, is Editor of *Labor History*, and co-editor of *American Book Prices Current*. His books include a study of the formation of the American Newspaper Guild entitled *A Union of Individuals* and a social history of the cinema image of black people, *From Sambo to Superspade*. He has accumulated some 15,000 books, several thousand of which constitute what is probably the largest collection of books on film in private hands.

KATHARINE KYES LEAB, co-editor of *American Book Prices Current*, finds her collecting activities somewhat limited by the 15,000 books that her husband has accumulated. Accordingly she limits herself to books illustrated by or written about Paul Klee and Yeats books that she is unable to resist.

WILLIAM MATHESON has been chief of the Rare Book and Special Collections Division of the Library of Congress since 1972. On completion of a one-year fellowship in rare books at Indiana University's Lilly Library in 1962, he organized the newly formed Rare Book Department at Washington University in St. Louis, heading it for nine years. His personal collecting interests include novels by poets, fashions in collecting, discographies, and twentieth-century handprinted books using the Arrighi italic.

JEAN PETERS is librarian of the R. R. Bowker Company's Frederic G. Melcher Library of Books about Books. Her personal collecting interests include certain twentieth-century English and American authors, among them Virginia Woolf and Kay Boyle, and books published by the Hogarth Press.

ROBERT ROSENTHAL, Curator of Special Collections at the University of Chicago, foregoes the pleasures of personal book collecting by doing it for an institution. In lighter moments, however, he collects books with the names of his wife and children in the titles and books published in the year 1900, that year being as good as any. He is also known to collect books with unintended *double-entendre* titles, all of which make the reading of catalogues and booksellers' shelves that much more fascinating.

WILLMAN SPAWN has been conservator of books and manuscripts at the American Philosophical Society Library, Philadelphia, since 1948. He planned the first library conservation shop in Canada for the Toronto Public Library in the late 1950s and has acted as consultant on conservation and water damage to many American libraries. He lectures on conservation and on his research into eighteenth-century American bookbinding, and with his wife, Carol, a librarian, has published a number of articles on these topics.

LOLA L. SZLADITS is Curator of The New York Public Library's Berg Collection of English and American Literature, a celebrated collection of first editions, autograph letters, and manuscripts. She is the author of numerous articles and exhibition catalogues and is a Fellow of The Pierpont Morgan Library and a member of the Council of the Bibliographical Society of America. Her personal collecting interests include seventeenth- and eighteenth-century Dutch and Italian drawings.

G. THOMAS TANSELLE, professor of English at the University of Wisconsin, has published a *Guide to the Study of United States Imprints* (1971), recording bibliographical studies of books printed in America or by American writers. The author of several articles on editing and descriptive bibliography, he is Bibliographical Editor of the Northwestern-Newberry Edition of *The Writings of Herman Melville* (1968–) and is working on a descriptive bibliography of Melville. His own collecting has emphasized certain American publishers between 1890 and 1930, and he has written about this aspect of his collection in the summer 1970 number of *The Book Collector*.

SUSAN O. THOMPSON is a professor at the School of Library Service, Columbia University, where she teaches the history of the book. Her publications include the section on books in *The Arts and Crafts Movement in America 1876–1916* (1972); *Caxton: An American Contribution to the Quincentenary Celebration* (1976); and *American Book Design and William Morris* (1977). Her own collection consists of books about books and exemplars of bookmaking, especially from the turn of the century.

ROBERT A. WILSON has been the proprietor of the Phoenix Book Shop in New York City since 1964 and is the compiler of bibliographies of Gregory Corso, Denise Levertov, and Gertrude Stein, the latter of which, published in her centennial year of 1974, was based on his own collection of her work, one of the most extensive in existence. Other collecting interests are the plays of Edward Albee as well as twentieth-century poetry. He is a regular contributor to *Book Collector's Market*, for which he writes the auction column as well as occasional articles and book reviews.

Appendix:
Some Useful Addresses

AB Bookman's Weekly. Box AB, Clifton, N.J. 07015.

Alcuin Society. Box 94108, Richmond, B.C., Canada.

American Antiquarian Society. 185 Salsbury St., Worcester, Mass. 01609.

American Book Collector. 1434 S. Yale Ave., Arlington Heights, Ill. 60005.

American Book Prices Current. 121 E. 78 St., New York, N.Y. 10021.

American Institute of Graphic Arts. 1059 Third Ave., New York, N.Y. 10021.

American Library Association. 50 E. Huron St., Chicago, Ill. 60611.

American Printing History Association. Box 4922, Grand Central Sta., New York, N.Y. 10017.

American Society of Appraisers. Dulles International Airport, Box 17265, Washington, D.C. 20041.

American Society of Bookplate Collectors and Designers. 429 N. Daisy Ave., Pasadena, Calif. 91107.

Antiquarian Book Monthly Review. 30 Cornmarket St., Oxford OX1 3EY, England.

Antiquarian Booksellers Association. 9 Stanton Rd., London SW20, England.

Antiquarian Booksellers Association of America. Concourse Shop 2, 630 Fifth Ave., New York, N.Y. 10020.

Antiquarian Booksellers Association of Canada. 1022 Sherbrooke St. W. (Rm. 6), Montreal 110, P.Q. Canada.

Antiquarian Booksellers Center. Concourse Shop 2, 630 Fifth Ave., New York, N.Y. 10020.

Aslib. 3 Belgrave Square, London SW1X 8PL, England.

Association Internationale de Bibliophilie. 1 rue de Sully, 75004 Paris.

Bancroft Library. University of California, Berkeley, Calif. 94720.

Beinecke Library. Yale University, New Haven, Conn. 06520.

Bibliographical Society. Bodleian Library, Oxford OX1 3BG, England; William H. Bond, American Membership Secretary, Houghton Library, Harvard University, Cambridge, Mass. 02138.

Bibliographical Society of America. Box 397, Grand Central Sta., New York, N.Y. 10017.

Bibliographical Society of Australia and New Zealand. Box 1278, Canberra City, A.C.T. 2601.

Bibliographical Society of Canada. 32 Lowther Ave., Toronto, Ont. M5R 1C6, Canada.

Bibliographical Society of Northern Illinois. Dept. of English, Northern Illinois University, DeKalb, Ill. 60115.

Bibliographical Society of the University of Virginia. Alderman Library, Charlottesville, Va. 22901.

Bibliography Newsletter. Terry Belanger, ed., 21 Claremont Ave., New York, N.Y. 10027.

Bodleian Library. Oxford OX1 3BG, England.

Book Arts Press. Columbia University School of Library Service, New York, N.Y. 10027.

Book Club of California. 545 Sutter St., San Francisco, Calif. 94102.

Book Collector. 3 Bloomsbury Pl., London WC1A 2QA, England.

Book Collector's Market. Box 50, Cooper Sta., New York, N.Y. 10003. (Ceased publication with V. 3, no. 2/3, 1977.)

Bookdealer and *Book Exchange*. Fudge & Co., Sardinia House, London WC2A 3NW, England.

Bookplate Society. 32 Barrowgate Rd., London W4 4QY, England.

Bowker (R. R.) Company, 1180 Avenue of the Americas, New York, N.Y. 10036.

British Library. Great Russell St., London WC1B 3DG, England.

Bro-Dart (Library Supplies, Equipment and Services). 1609 Memorial Avenue, Williamsport, Pa. 17701.

California Book Auction Galleries. 270 McAllister St., San Francisco, Calif. 94102.

Cambridge Bibliographical Society. University Library, West Rd., Cambridge CB3 9DR, England.

Center for Book Arts. 15 Bleeker St., New York, N.Y. 10012.

Chicago, University of, Library. Chicago, Ill. 60637.

Christie's. 502 Park Ave., New York, N.Y. 10022.

Clark (William Andrews) Memorial Library. 2520 Cimarron St., Los Angeles, Calif. 90018.

Clements Library. University of Michigan, Ann Arbor, Mich. 48109.

The Clique. 109 Wembley Park Dr., Wembley, Middlesex, England.

Columbia University Libraries. New York, N.Y. 10027.

Demco Educational Corp. (Library Supplies and Equipment). Box 7488, Madison, Wis. 53707.

Edinburgh Bibliographical Society. National Library of Scotland, Edinburgh EH1 1EW, Scotland.

Fine Print. Box 7741, San Francisco, Calif. 94120.

Folger Shakespeare Library. 201 E. Capitol St., Washington, D.C. 20003.

Gaylord Bros., Inc. (Library Systems, Supplies, Equipment and Publications). Syracuse, N.Y. 13201.

Grolier Club. 47 E. 60 St., New York, N.Y. 10022.

Guild of Book Workers. 1059 Third Ave., New York, N.Y. 10021.

Gutenberg Gesellschaft. 65 Mainz, Liebfrauenplatz 5, Germany.

The Hollinger Corp. Box 6185, 3810 S. Four Mile Run Dr., Arlington, Va. 22206.

Houghton Library. Harvard University, Cambridge, Mass. 02138.

Humanities Research Center. University of Texas, Austin, Tex. 78712.

Huntington Library. 1151 Oxford Rd., San Marino, Calif. 91108.

International League of Antiquarian Booksellers. Stanley Crowe, President, 5 Bloomsbury St., London WC1B 3QE, England.

Library Company of Philadelphia. 1314 Locust St., Philadelphia, Pa. 19107.

Library of Congress. Washington, D.C. 20540.

Lilly Library. Indiana University, Bloomington, Ind. 47401.

Manuscript Society. 429 N. Daisy Ave., Pasadena, Calif. 91107.

Montreal Book Auctions Ltd. 1529 Sherbrooke St. W., Montreal 109, Canada.

Morgan (Pierpont) Library. 29 E. 36 St., New York, N.Y. 10016.

National Book League. 7 Albemarle St., London W1, England.
New York Public Library. Fifth Ave. and 42 St., New York, N.Y. 10018.
Newberry Library. 60 W. Walton St., Chicago, Ill. 60610.
Oxford Bibliographical Society. Bodleian Library, Oxford OX1 3BG, England.
Princeton University Library. Princeton, N.J. 08540.
Printing Historical Society. St. Bride Institute, Bride Lane, Fleet St., London EC4, England; Terry Belanger, American Membership Secretary, 21 Claremont Ave., New York, N.Y. 10027.
Private Libraries Association. 3B Hurlingham Court, Ranelagh Gardens, London SW6 3UN, England; Harold Berliner, American Membership Secretary, Box 6, Nevada City, Calif. 95959.
Rare Books and Manuscripts Section of the Association of College and Research Libraries. American Library Association, 50 E. Huron St., Chicago, Ill. 60611.
St. Bride Library. Bride Lane, Fleet St., London EC4, England.
Sheppard Press. Box 42, 15 James St., London WC2E 8BX, England. North American distributor: Standing Orders, Inc., Box 183, Patterson, N.Y. 12563.
Society for Italic Handwriting. 59a Arlington Rd., London NW1, England.
Society for the Bibliography of Natural History. British Museum (Natural History), Cromwell Rd., London SW7 5BD, England.
Society of American Archivists. The Library, Box 8198, University of Illinois, Chicago Circle, Chicago, Ill. 60680.
Society of Scribes. Box 933, New York, N.Y. 10022.
Society of Scribes and Illuminators. 6 Queen St., London WC 1, England.
Sotheby Parke Bernet & Co., 34 & 35 New Bond St., London W1A 2AA, England.
Sotheby Parke Bernet, Inc., 980 Madison Ave., New York, N.Y. 10021.
Stanford University Library. Stanford, Calif. 94305.
Swann Galleries. 104 E. 25 St., New York, N.Y. 10010.
TALAS. Technical Library Service. 104 Fifth Ave., New York, N.Y. 10011.
The Typophiles. 140 Lincoln Rd., Brooklyn, N.Y. 11225.
University of Chicago Library. *See* Chicago, University of, Library.
Welsh Bibliographical Society. National Library of Wales, Aberystwyth SY23 3BU, Wales.

Index

Note: Many of the works mentioned in Chapter 12, "The Literature of Book Collecting," are not referred to in this Index under author or title, but all of them can be located by means of class entries.